WOMEN TALKING

Mary Stott, who comes from a family of journalists, is best known for her 15 years' editorship of the Women's Pages of the *Manchester Guardian* and *Guardian*, especially because of her close relationship with the contributors and readers. But in fact she had spent more than 30 years editing Women's Pages in Leicester and Bolton (Lancs) and the women's and children's journals of the Consumer Co-operative movement (published in Manchester) before joining the *Guardian* in 1957.

Since her retirement Mary Stott has written four books, *Forgetting's No Excuse*, *Organization Woman* (a history of the National Union of Townswomen's Guilds), *Ageing for Beginners* and *Before I Go . . .* (which she sub-titled 'Reflections on My Life and Times'). Beginning with the formation of Women in Media and its strikingly effective campaign for a Sex Discrimination Act, she has devoted much of her time to many aspects of the women's movement, notably the campaign for more women in public life.

WOMEN TALKING

AN ANTHOLOGY FROM

THE GUARDIAN
WOMEN'S PAGE

1922-35 · 1957-71

EDITED BY
MARY STOTT

PANDORA
London

First published in 1987 by Pandora Press
(Routledge & Kegan Paul Ltd)
11 New Fetter Lane, London EC4P 4EE

Set in Times 10 on 11pt
by Columns of Reading
and printed in Great Britain
by the Guernsey Press Co Ltd
Guernsey, Channel Islands

British Library Cataloguing in Publication Data
Women talking: an anthology from the
  Guardian women's page, 1922–35 and 1957–71.
  1. Women – Social conditions
  I. Stott, Mary   II. The Guardian
  305.4'2   HQ1121

ISBN 0-86358-087-4

For *Guardian* readers,
past, present, and future
with gratitude

Contents

Contents

Contents

Acknowledgments

This book is offered in gratitude to all those people, known and unknown, alive and dead, who made it possible . . . the *Manchester Guardian* and *Guardian* contributors and readers. I wish to thank particularly the authors – and their executors – who have given permission for the publication of their work in this volume. Every effort has been made to trace them all.

Special thanks are also due to the *Guardian*'s library staff, most particularly to Kenneth Murphy who humped heavy bound files off and on the shelves for me, set up the micro-film screen and even did much photocopying for me until a cricket anthology understandably took precedence with this cricket fanatic!

When I pursued my researches at the splendid British Newspaper Library at Colindale, North London, I found the staff unfailingly courteous and helpful and began to have a hankering to spend the rest of my life poring over old newspapers there.

Thanks also are owed to my one-time secretary, Sonia Erstling. Soon after I moved from Manchester to London she took up a post in Tel Aviv, but we have kept in touch and she generously typed a number of articles in this book for me.

The Vera Brittain articles 'Standing Up for Ourselves' and 'Open Letter to My Son', and the extract from 'Canonising the Heretic' are included with the permission of her literary executors.

'Ladies in Restaurants' and 'The Personal Pronoun' by Winifred Holtby appeared in *Testament of a Generation: The Journalism of Vera Brittian and Winifred Holtby*, published by the Virago Press Ltd and are reprinted by permission of

Virago. 'Fashions and Feminism' and the extract from the Ethel Smythe article by Winifred Holtby are included with the permission of her literary executor.

Introduction

Fashion, food, family, furnishing – these were the main props
of most national newspaper Women's Pages between the two
world wars. So it was no wonder that I, an undomesticated,
un-fashion-conscious young Lefty, a bookworm, daughter of
journalists, reared in a family very involved in local affairs,
mad about the theatre and about music, never regarded the
Women's Page as a worthy target of ambition. When in 1926,
at the age of 19, I was told to take charge of the *Leicester
Mail*'s Women's Page, I put my head on a file table and wept.
I believed that this had finished any chance I had of becoming
'a proper journalist', covering inquests and magistrates courts
and the city council meetings. In fact I did only escape from
some form of women's journalism for the five heady years I
was a news sub-editor on the *Manchester Evening News*.

But as 'Lestrienne', contributing a regular comment column
on women's activities in Leicester, and on the *Bolton Evening
News* I was learning a great deal about what women, especially
organised women, like the Women's Institutes, the National
Council of Women, Women Citizens and the political and
religious groups were doing and thinking. I learned to
communicate with them. From my Manchester-based office of
the Co-operative Press, where I was in charge of women's and
children's publications, I not only wrote editorials for
'Woman's Outlook', through which I learned the importance
of writing to be understood, but reported in full many
conferences of the Women's Co-operative Guild, a political
education for which I shall always be grateful.

It took me a very long time to realise the value of what I
had been learning in those years, but when the chance came,
at the end of 1956, to edit the Women's Page of the
Manchester Guardian I was not intimidated by its world-wide

prestige. But I must make it clear that though by this time I had mournfully accepted that I was never going to get the sort of 'straight news' job that I coveted, there was no Women's Page job, absolutely not one, for which I would have applied other than the *Manchester Guardian*'s. I had been a devoted reader ever since I grew up; it had educated me as a feminist, and indeed, a pacifist. This was a job any feminist might be glad to do. And the idea of this book stems, in fact, from my desire to make a collection of articles that influenced my generation, long before many of today's readers were born, in the page edited by my great predecessor Madeline Linford.

It was only on reflection that I realised that many faithful *Guardian* readers today are too young even to have read the page during my own editorship, which was from 1957 to the beginning of 1972. And that the two periods make a most interesting comparison, being both similar and dissimilar. Until the late 1920s we were still battling for the vote at the age of 21; we were agitating ourselves about the nationality of married women, the custody of children, the marriage bar, equal pay and the possibility of another world war. Not so very different from the 1950s and 60s, if you substitute the Sex Discrimination Bill for the Representation of the People (Equal Franchise) Bill of 1928?

The differences between Madeline Linford's page and mine were 'social' rather than 'political'. It surprises and often displeases young readers to discover how preoccupied their foremothers were with the shortcomings of their domestic helpers ('maids' and 'chars'). And it was not just women like the Hon. Mrs Dowdall (see p. 51) – who, as the daughter of a peer might have been expected to have a houseful of servants – who wrote on this theme, but, among others, women like Margaret Cole, lifelong Fabian socialist. Leonora Eyles must sound patronising in the example we print of her series on the life of working-class wives and mothers – but she was quite unaware of any condescension. Right up to World War II it was much more a 'them and us' society than it is now.

In those far-off days the *Manchester Guardian* was a committed supporter of the Liberal Party and this allegiance was accepted even in the Women's Page. In the first few years it always contained a forecast of what women's issues were likely to come up in the next session of Parliament, and what happened at Liberal women's conferences. Alas, to quote too many out-of-date political articles might easily become boring. Perhaps some day a 'women's studies' book will take a profitable look at all this?

I have thought a great deal, naturally, about Madeline Linford herself while compiling this book. I am certain she was a true feminist, probably a pacifist also. But was it *her* decision to stop running so much 'political' stuff? Was it her decision to run for some months in 1936 regular articles on 'Beauty for the Busy Woman'? Did she have a huge file of useful little items to plug the gaps at the foot of an article which did not quite fill the allotted space . . . items like 'in defence of antimacassar', 'fixing a broomhead', 'the history of the nail', 'how to choose a teapot', 'the life of the greenfly', 'the best way to deal with the eelworm' and 'brighter cabbage'? So many things I would like to ask her now!

I came to know Madeline Linford around 1940 when a group of Manchester women journalists got together to meet monthly and asked Miss Linford, as the most prestigious among us, to take the chair. She agreed rather reluctantly for she was a shy and very private person, but she and I conversed as we walked back to our office after lunch – 'Miss Linford' and 'Miss Waddington', of course; no first names then. I learned that she had very little personal contact with her contributors, whether distinguished or not. (I confess to being rather huffed when I read in Vera Brittain's diaries that she only once called upon Miss Linford in the *Manchester Guardian* office and didn't much like her!)

In 1963 Madeline Linford told the story, in an article on my page, of how she – for very many years the only woman on the staff – was instructed by C.P. Scott, at rather short notice, to start a women's feature, three columns long, on six days a week. 'My briefing was lucid and firm. The page must be readable, varied and aimed always at the intelligent woman. . . . I saw her as an aloof, rigid and highly critical figure, a kind of Big Sister, vigilant for lapses of taste, dignity and literary English.'

A quarter of a century later I envisaged my typical readers as being either teachers or clergymen's wives, very remote and academic. We both had a most pleasing surprise. The 'intelligent woman' of Madeline's day and my own day was keen not only to read our pages but 'anxious to maintain its standards by her own efforts'. Many of Madeline's writers were illustrious; so were mine. Vera Brittain and Winifred Holtby virtually started their journalistic careers on the *Manchester Guardian*'s Women's Page. Shirley Williams, Vera Brittain's daughter, was a regular contributor to the 'Women Talking' feature which gives this book its name.

The greatest satisfaction I found in editing the *Guardian* Women's Page was that I was able to draw so much of its contents from the readers themselves, even though they were in no way professional journalists. It all felt rather like a club, as many a 1960s reader has told me. It was in this kind of atmosphere that the 'Do-it-Yourself' organisations were sparked off (see p. 225).

There are large areas of the *Guardian* Women's Page that are not covered in this anthology: cookery, though Ambrose Heath, one of the best-known cookery writers of his time, wrote for both of us; not much fashion, though we had two of the most distinguished and enjoyable fashion writers who ever wrote for newspapers – Alison Adburgham in London and Phyllis Heathcote in Paris; no consumer guidance and no 'design', though the 1960s were the age of consumerism. We had top-class specialists in assessing 'good buys', like Elizabeth Gundry and Peta Fordham, and busy beavers like colleagues Shirley Lewis and Elizabeth Dunn. The Scandinavian design wave changed the way many of us (including my husband and I) looked at home furnishings, and Fiona MacCarthy, my assistant for several years, was and is, an expert in the design field.

But the choices for the book had to be made according to a certain pattern from two periods, echoing and contrasting with each other. The choice had to be mine . . . when during my Women's Page editorship I was asked, 'But how on earth do you choose what to print?' I always said, 'I choose what *I* like. I have been a devoted *Guardian* reader nearly all my adult life. I think I am fairly typical and the odds are that if I like it a substantial percentage of the readers will.' I hope that holds good for this book.

1 Independence for What?

Change in society's manners and mores comes even more slowly in custom and practice, it seems, than in law. Are not many young men still embarrassed if a female companion offers to share the bill, even to foot it? Are not unaccompanied women still regarded with suspicion late at night in bars and restaurants?

Yet attitudes to sexual behaviour and morality changed noticeably in the years between 1922 when this anthology opens and 1972 when it closes, and in the decade since then they changed even more radically. What would Mary Stocks be writing now?

BRIEF ENCOUNTER (1925)

Ray Strachey

Ray Strachey was the wife of Oliver Strachey, who was the brother of Lytton Strachey and also of Philippa Strachey, honorary secretary for something like half a century of the Fawcett Society. Ray Strachey's immensely readable and influential history of the women's movement, The Cause *was first published in 1928.*

May 1925: The modern middle-class girl has many careers open to her in the pursuit of which her ambition may be satisfied; but there is a rather vague but attractive line of life about which many girls are thinking, but which they find it a little difficult to enter, and that is public work – the political and semi-political jobs which can be carried out by women now that they are part of the voting community. There are openings for women agents and sub-agents, lecturers, ward or county organisers, appeal organisers, propaganda speakers and political investigators. But these professions are not standardised as others are: there are no qualifying examinations or written texts and I do not think there ever can be. The thing that makes for success in such work is ability to deal with people as well as with ideas. And how can an examination test that? . . . Let no one go into this work from ambition alone or for the desire for an amusing life. Let no girl think that the intention to make a mark and 'be somebody' is motive enough. In public work, even more than in other things, character counts and the girl who cares more for herself than for her cause will never get on at all.

LADIES IN RESTAURANTS (1930)

Winifred Holtby

Winifred Holtby was one of the outstanding novelists of the 1930s; a director of the feminist/literary journal Time and Tide *as well as a regular contributor to it – and, of course, to the* Manchester Guardian. *She died, aged only 37, in 1935 and her best-known novel,* South Riding *was not published until 1936. She was a close friend of Vera Brittain from their Oxford days onwards.*

I shall certainly attend if I can a meeting in Kensington Town Hall on 4 April, 1930 to protest against 'the refusal of certain restaurants, cafés and other places of refreshment to admit women unaccompanied by men after certain hours'. The reason is not so much because I see that Lord Balfour of Burleigh is to be in the chair and that Mrs Cecil Chesterton, Mrs Abbott of the Open Door Council and Miss Alison Neilans are among the speakers, nor even because the meeting is organised by the St Joan's Social and Political Alliance, the Roman Catholic feminist organisation. It is for a personal and particular reason of my own.

One night four or five years ago, I went to the theatre in a big North-Country town with an old friend of the family, a middle-aged woman who was then matron of one of the houses of an old and famous boys' public school. I doubt if there is among my whole acquaintance a more admirable and respectable person or one whose looks inspire more confidence in her tact, wisdom, moderation and morality. Her face, her bearing, even her hats emphasise the strong sense of responsibility towards the young which has developed during her life's work. She has also, mercifully, a sense of humour, a knowledge of human nature, and many other pleasant qualities.

The play was a long one and kept us until the usual theatre train had gone. There was one other, but it was not due to leave until nearly midnight. It was a cold evening. It was raining. The fire in the ladies room had gone out. The refreshment room was closed, but I remembered that the Station Hotel, an old-established and respectable institution opened right on to the platform. I restored the drooping spirits of my companion with promises of a seat, a fire and coffee and went boldly through the revolving doors. On we went to the quite familiar lounge with its deep pleasant sofas, its huge fire and waiters moving about with trays of light refreshments.

We sat down. I beckoned a waiter, gave my order and did not notice at the moment his puzzled look. It was my friend who said 'I think there's something wrong'. And she was right. The waiter went off and fetched a fussy little man whose face was quite familiar to me.

'I'm sorry,' he said, 'but are you residents?'

'No,' said I. 'We're waiting for the 11.45 train and just want some tea.'

'I'm sorry,' he said. 'I'm afraid you can't stop here. We can't serve you. You must go.'

'But it's not after hours,' I protested. 'We only want some tea. I've often been here before.' I told him my name, which he knew. He was regretful, but rules were rules. We were females entering the hotel without a man after a certain hour – I forget what it was – and we were not going to stay the night. Out we must go.

And out we went. We walked up and down the bleak, chill, damp, draughty platform until the train arrived – twenty minutes late. Next day my companion was in bed with a bad cold and acute rheumatism. When I made enquiries about the hotel regulations I was told that it was a pity but nothing could be done. The rule had been made to safeguard public morality and no exceptions could be allowed.

3

Of course, I was an idiot. I should have taken the course of a more courageous woman whom I know in London. She is a political organiser and a person of great experience and initiative. She had been to the House of Commons to follow the fortunes of a Bill in which she was greatly interested, and having sat in the House, as one does, until late at night, she came out and walked with one or two friends to Piccadilly Circus. They too were tired, they too were thirsty, they too saw an open cafe and longing for tea or coffee, they went in. They too were refused admission because they were unaccompanied by a man. 'Well,' said their leader, 'that's easily remedied.' It was. In two minutes they found their man and brought him in triumph to the cafe door. Nothing is easier to find than an accommodating man in Piccadilly Circus. This time they were admitted. The man was fortunately both sporting and sympathetic. He appreciated their plight and played his part perfectly. They had their refreshments and went on their way rejoicing.

Another woman whom I know, once prominent in the suffrage movement, told me that she actually broke down the rule herself by threatening to go out and collect a sandwich-man drearily promenading the street outside a restaurant which forbade her to enter. But best of all I think, is the public protest to be made now, which asks for the abolition of the rule itself.

For what sort of protection does such a regulation offer to the public? It is already possible, without it, for an innkeeper or a restaurant proprietor to order out customers who behave improperly. Are women unaccompanied by men the only people to menace public propriety? Does the refusal to serve women really protect male customers from temptation? And is it not rather insulting to presume that every unaccompanied woman who enters a cafe after 10 o'clock does so for purposes of prostitution?

For that is clearly the purpose of the rule. Women are dangerous. Especially women after 10 o'clock at night. All women who go about the streets alone at this hour may be suspected, in spite of the growing army of women doctors, political secretaries, programme sellers, office cleaners, actresses, midwives, members of Parliament, rescue workers, night-school teachers, journalists, hospital nurses and all those other workers whose lawful pursuits may keep them up late at night – to say nothing of the millions of ordinary people who sometimes stay up late to see a play or go to a dance or visit a friend.

Is it not time we insisted on the removal of a regulation which really offers a considerable insult to our sex? If women want to behave badly they can do so at any time of the day. Temptation cannot be confined within hours like the sale of alcoholic liquor. Bad behaviour is not limited to women who go about without the restraining companionship of a man. On the contrary, women alone, or in twos and threes, are on the whole rather more likely to behave in a decent, orderly manner, perhaps, than women with men. There is no rule, so far as I know, that men unaccompanied by women should not be served.

Indeed, the longer I think of it the more furious I am with myself for not going on the platform, that night four or five years ago, finding a nice friendly porter and bringing him back to the hotel. That would larn 'em!

GREENGATE CLINIC (1962)

Mary Stocks

Mary Stocks, constitutional suffragist and lifelong feminist, helped to found the National Union of Townswomen's Guilds in 1928, and was one of the small band of women who set up one of the first family planning clinics outside London (in Salford, 1926). She was an educationalist and for some years was principal of Westfield College, London, but achieved her greatest fame as a broadcaster, especially on the radio programme 'Any Questions'. She became a member of the House of Lords in 1966.

It was, I think, as far back as 1925 that a small group of Manchester women conceived the idea of starting what was then called a birth control clinic and is now more discreetly referred to as a family planning clinic. This change is not due

5

merely to discretion, but also to an expansion of function; the new name emphasises the fact that such clinics aim at helping those who want babies to have them, as well as helping those who don't want babies not to have them. But in 1925 the latter object was uppermost in the minds of those Manchester women, for Lancashire was running into the great depression and one was more conscious of the hard conditions of over-burdened, poverty-stricken mothers than of the no less real unhappiness of childless couples in need of helpful medical advice.

I was one of that small group for when I came to Manchester in the preceding year I found a long-lost schoolfriend, Mrs Frankenburg, who had since trained as a midwife and become a devotee of causes relating to maternal welfare. There was also of the same mind Mrs Burrows, whose husband was a leading colliery owner. And then came Mrs Blumberg. The first three of us have since decamped from Manchester, but Mrs Blumberg has remained at the post from that day to this – and the expansion of the first clinic's work owes more than can be measured to her persistence and initiative. There were, of course, other participants, but not many.

My own inspiration had come from a visit to the Walworth clinic in London, but I think I had been led to that visit by reading a wartime publication of the Women's Co-operative Guild, describing contemporary conditions of working-class childbirth – and later by reading the works of Dr Marie Stopes.

And so we set to work. We collected some money – I can't remember who from – got some helpful hints from Walworth as to how to run the show, and acquired two small rooms over a cooked-meat shop in Greengate, Salford. We acquired the part-time services of Dr Olive Gimson, who was not afraid of anyone, and of two experienced, practising midwives, Sister Pulford and Sister Lloyd.

The climate of opinion generally was cold towards birth control. In Salford it was, to say the least of it, frigid. We had to face intense opposition from the Roman Catholic clergy. Mrs Frankenburg and I were singled out for special obloquy. We were 'the kind of women who visited matinees and sat with cigarettes between their painted lips'. The image was in one respect comforting, for we had envisaged ourselves as rather dowdy social workers. And our clinic was described as being reached through a 'stinking entry'. This was a little hard for the stink was in fact merely the homely smell of good hot meat pies. But the location of the clinic through the shop made attendance easy for shy mothers – and they came, the shy and the not so shy.

But it was not only the Roman Catholic clergy who regarded us as less than respectable. The Church of England stood aloof. The medical profession, with one or two shining exceptions, was to say the least of it, unhelpful. By many people 'birth control' seemed to be regarded as a dirty word. Moreover, strange misconceptions were afoot. We were abortionists. We helped unmarried women to evade the consequences of their sins. We recommended practices which caused cancer. In fact, of course, we did none of these things: but it took quite a lot of public speaking to explain that we didn't. And that perhaps was the most inspiriting part of the work.

It is a lovely experience to address an audience when you have something to say that your hearers don't already know and which you are certain will interest them. The women's organisations heard us gladly – Co-operative Guilds and Women Citizens Associations. They were the people who knew at first or second hand the stresses and strains of uncontrolled pregnancies. I remember one particularly inspiriting meeting organised by the Bolton Women Citizens' Association. An organised gang came over from Salford and shouted us down. That roused the sympathy of Bolton for the speakers and the local press did us proud.

What made those early days a joy was the feeling that the tide of public opinion was flowing – sluggishly at first but then in spate. And now we have become so respectable we scarcely know ourselves. Local authorities grant-aid us. Bishops commend us. The medical profession directs our technique. Today the Manchester clinic has no need of a 'stinking entry'. It has fine premises of its own and two branch clinics. It trains doctors for family planning work; it deals in sub-fertility; it conducts cytological tests. Next week it begins, in collaboration with Manchester University's Extra-Mural Department, a series of fortnightly lectures on family planning.

When I go to Manchester and observe these things going on, I feel like a really hoary pioneer. I feel as though the time has come for me to sit back and 'visit matinees with a cigarette between my painted lips'.

'Talkback'

In November 1965, Mary Stocks, soon to be Baroness Stocks of the Royal Borough of Kensington and Chelsea, wrote again on contraception, expressing a conviction that it should not be offered to young unmarried women. The Talkback was swift and mainly in disagreement with her. As in this letter:

I am sorry that Mrs Stocks would deny the liberating possibility of obtaining contraceptives to single women.

Not all are immature or teenagers. There are some who believe that they need to try themselves and discover themselves sexually, as in other ways, in order to develop and achieve control over their own personality, if only in getting a sense of proportion about sexual experience. The resultant confidence helps in dealing with the situation referred to where women become more involved than men. And it is all too easy to marry mainly to satisfy sexual curiosity.

My own most bewildering problem in growing up was in reconciling the excellent reasoning of the seducers with the ineffective arguments of the protectors. The removal of a taboo that we all know is not unanimous would have been no devil's advocate, but would have allowed me to talk to a Mrs Stocks.

To Mrs Stocks's 'self-restraint' I would oppose 'self-knowledge'. I am sure that will lead to a happier world for women.

Spinster
London SW15

LONE WOMAN (1964)

Fiona MacCarthy

Fiona MacCarthy was the assistant to the Guardian's *Woman's Page editor for several years, contributing many 'Women Talking' articles and highly regarded features on design. She is now a literary critic and the author of books on famous designers.*

Single women are all right in grand hotels: as anonymous when they go as when they come. And anonymity, I know, is what I want when I go away on business alone. An hotel isn't anything like home, and it's no good pretending it is. I don't feel like making friends. I'd rather have a quick, impersonal check-in, a quiet room, an unobtrusive table with an unobstrusive waiter than any amount of welcomes on the mat. In most of the big hotels in Britain businesswomen can stay as comfortably (and as uncompanionably) as businessmen: so long as their firms will face the bill.

But firms don't always think their women worth three or four pounds a night. And even if they did, grand hotels aren't everywhere. Smaller towns may have only one hotel with 20 to 30 rooms, and 20s. to 40s. charges. At that level, all equality ends: women have a much worse time than men.

'No, we don't have a sex bar here,' you'd be told if you thought of asking. But they have to admit that not very many women come. It's not surprising. We all know how Southern Europeans assume that lone women are loose: the British are not really much more civilised. When I've booked in in the Midlands and north as far as Scotland, hoteliers have often looked surprised to see someone as respectable and solitary as me. The manager hands his attitude down to his staff. I had the rudest awakening of my life in a Lancashire hotel. I wanted a long sleep, and I certainly left my name off the early morning call list. But at 7.45, the maid decided I ought to get up. She almost banged down my firmly locked door. Then enlightened – so she thought – by my silence, she shouted right along the corridor: 'That young girl must have stayed out all night.'

This maid was particularly officious. But no noisier than the rest. In small hotels, commotion starts at about half-past six: tea-making, vacuum cleaning, muddling up and sorting out shoes outside the doors, stamping, clattering, shrieking. You can't be late for breakfast however hard you try to sleep on. I know because I have tried quite hard quite often. But I have failed about forty times in my life and sat down to breakfast in a dining-room of men. Most of them stare and wonder. Early in the week when they're sitting at separate tables, roughly half of them leer: a sad little private leer, a sort of businessman's tradition. Later in the week when they've ganged up and packed in, six to a four-place table, they urge each other on to greater devilry. 'What are you doing tonight,' I'm sometimes asked.

What am I doing, in fact? I'd be rash to admit it in the dining room: I'm frequently lying on my bed in the dark. Alternatives are terribly few. There's the hotel sitting room, of course. But whether it's a blatantly shabby Jubilee lounge or a slicker-sounding Madison bar, the scene is the same: a mass of men drinking around the television set. Drinking seems to be competitive. I hear them adding up their scores in the morning. There isn't always a cinema in the town. There isn't often a reading lamp in the bedroom, or even an easy chair. Ease is not what businesswomen get.

Hoteliers could certainly help. I'm only asking for a light and a chair and a table and six hangers and some cheerful curtains and a few coats of paint and some peace.

Businessman, especially salesmen, could help more. Not only in hotels, but at trade fairs and press receptions and wherever they get together. They could stop their tedious nudge and wink routine. They could try to talk to a woman without a double entendre. Innuendo seems to be a point of honour: by themselves they may forget it but in a crowd of colleagues they don't dare. This makes communication very complex. One's simplest comment is seized upon with roars of ribald laughter, as if every second word you'd said was bed.

We can educate our women for all we're worth, give them good jobs and maybe, eventually, feminise hotels. But some of our sons, our fathers and our grandfathers will always, I'm afraid, fight back: their sexual bravado, like Falstaff's, outlives the performance and lasts well into the grave.

'Talkback'

A few months after my husband died my doctor suggested that I should have a holiday so I naively drove off to a three-star hotel alone. I felt strange at first but supposed it was my first time driving out alone after ten years of marriage. Gradually I realised what everyone thought I was up to until finally a man stole my room key. I vowed I would not go away again without my two little boys – even if I did not get a rest at least I could look respectable. So I have just returned from another holiday at a famous camp. That was even worse. It took a lot of nerve to go out alone after I had put the children to bed, but after being stared at in the bar and whistled at all round the camp I felt like someone off Piccadilly. After that I kept the children up until 9.30 p.m. and then sat on my bed in the dark. At other times the people there were more outspoken and left me in no doubt what they thought about me. How can people be so cruel? Six months ago I was amused, but now I am angry.

I do not know when I shall dare to go away again.

Mary E. Goulding
Lichfield

HITCH-HIKING (1967)

Phyllis Heathcote

Phyllis Heathcote was the Guardian *fashion correspondent for many years, also fashion correspondent of the* Glasgow Herald *as Phyllis Jenkins. Her husband Dudley Heathcote was an avid collector of Napoleonic memorabilia. Mrs Heathcote returned to England after her retirement and at the age of 90 is still enjoying life in Kent.*

I hate to be a spoil-sport, but with the holiday season already upon us it seems to me that a word in edgeways on the subject of hitch-hiking on the Continent will not come amiss to young hikers themselves and to their parents.

All right, hitch-hiking saves fares, gets you farther, and no doubt because uncertainties and hazards are all part of the game, it is generally thought to be 'fun' by those who go in for it. Looked at objectively, however, and leaving aside the doubtful ethics of using other people's petrol and involving them in the possibility of risk with no gain whatsoever to themselves, are the *very real* hazards involved, really worth the taking? No, they are not. Certainly not when you are alone; even two does not necessarily guarantee immunity from misadventure.

To begin with, there is the question of language. To talk oneself out of an awkward situation demands a better knowledge of a foreign tongue than the average run of British hitch-hikers can lay claim to. More important still is a knowledge of the habits and mentality of the people in whose country you are travelling. If a girl thumbs a Latin driver, can he be blamed for putting his own interpretation on an advance which a decently intentioned girl in his own country would never dream of making? You mean one thing, he understands another. His morals may be as basically sound as the next Englishman's – he interprets things differently, that's all.

At the only bullfight I ever attended I was on the side of the bulls from the word go; in the same way, all my sympathies were with the lorry driver who some years back got himself into a serious scrape for having drawn his own conclusions (and acted accordingly) when thumbed by two shorts-clad English girls in the south of France. That man went to prison for attempting rape when the real culprits, in my view, were the girls themselves; and still more culpable the parents who had allowed them to go footloose on the Continent with casual hitch-hiking in view.

In these fuddy-duddy views I am confirmed by the findings of an association known by the rather forbidding name of 'Equipes d'Action contre la Traite de Femmes et des Enfants'. The Equipes d'Action with a great deal of experience behind them, have come out strongly against the growing practice of 'L'Auto-Stop'. They see in it not only the risk of immediate misadventure and imbroglios but far more serious dangers. Thousands of girls disappear every year in France, and according to the findings of Equipes d'Action hitch-hiking is a recognised method of 'recruitment' for the white slave traffic.

They give chapter and verse of hair-raising cases of all kinds that have occurrred over the past few years: murder, rape, theft, fatal accidents, disappearances.

On the lighter side of the story – that concerning theft – there are two stories that I particularly like. The first concerns four students – two English, one American, one French, who thumbed a lift between Beauville and Abbeville. During a halt in Abbeville and on the pretext of a fill-up, the driver of the *camionette* suggested that the young people waited for him at a café. Two hours later they were at the police station lodging a complaint about loss of luggage.

The other concerns two Swiss girls whose 'obliging' chauffeur suggested they take a swim in an inviting river on the way. This they joyfully did, for the day was warm. They lost not only their luggage, money and papers, but their clothes as well. Cold and dripping they turned up at the nearest gendarmerie in their swim suits. Serve them jolly well right.

I am fully aware of the counter-arguments – the point of view of the hikers themselves. Without thumbing how can he/she get around? That, I fear, is his/her problem, not mine. My advice is to go as far as you can afford and no further. Or as the Equipe d'Action poster has it, 'Voyager normalement'.

FRIGHTENED ONES (1969)

Claire Rayner

Claire Rayner is very widely known now as a television 'agony aunt'. She was formerly a nurse, and first became known for her advice columns as a contributor to The Sun *and the* Sunday Mirror. *She is the author of many books.*

It was during the fifth session of a series of talks I'd been giving at a North-east London youth club that one of the girls asked about queers. So I talked about homosexuality, both male and female, and told them it was so common that it was normal for people to go through developing crushes on members of their own sex, but that some people didn't leave

13

the phase behind. Simple and straighforward.

At the end of the evening one of the girls asked to talk to me privately. She was a pretty child of sixteen, with an air of innocence that didn't match her well-documented record of being the club's 'easy girl', ready to huddle into the bushes with any and every boy who beckoned. She wanted to know what to do about herself; she didn't enjoy being promiscuous one bit, she said; it was a drag. The thing was, in her first job at a hairdresser's she had fallen head over heels for the receptionist, an elegant woman in her thirties. 'And I went wild with the boys to show I was all right.' And now, what should she do, she wanted to know; now she knew she wasn't the queer she thought she was. Was it too late to start being a nice girl again?

At a teenage magazine for which I write, a frantic letter arrived which made us feel pretty frantic, too. A girl who had been in love with boys in the past had now developed a violent attachment to the girl next door, and was so sick of herself, and so frightened, that she couldn't cope any longer. She'd taken half a bottle of aspirin, and was going to take the rest as soon as she'd posted the letter. We alerted the mental welfare officer for her area, hoping desperately that someone would have got to the child in time, and that she had survived her panic and could be helped to accept the probably temporary stage of emotional development through which she was passing.

A Roman Catholic boy wrote to the same magazine pleading for help. He couldn't possibly talk to anyone, not even his priest in confession. 'If I'd been having it away with a girl, well, that's easy to confess. I think the priest expects that. But how could I tell him the way I feel about my boy friend? It's a terrible sin, and I can't escape because suicide is almost as bad a one.' Almost as bad!

It seems to me that in all the hoo-hah about sex education, all the adult breast-beating about helping the young to handle their boy-girl relationships far too little thought has been given to helping them to handle their girl-girl, boy-boy relationships. In the days when one-sex schools were far more common than they are now, the fact that one got pashes – as we called them back in the 1940s was common knowledge among the young.

14

Even boys and girls at mixed schools knew people at the other kind of school, and found out how common a phenomenon it was. We didn't talk to adults about it, but we talked to one another.

But not any more. Now girls, like boys, talk about their sexual conquests – real and fantasy – with the other sex. But how many trendy dollies of today could talk about the frisson of pleasure they get from the company of their best girl friends?

Very few. Some boys seem to be aware of it, though. A sixteen-year old girl I know asked her mother in some trepidation if she was normal; a boy she had refused to sleep with because she just didn't want to had accused her of being a bit 'les-be-friends'. I wonder how many virgins have been tumbled into bed with the same ploy?

Of course, sex education is high fashion as the moment. All over the country, in schools and youth clubs, people are sitting round mopping up the biological facts of reproduction and talking endlessly about the rights and wrongs of pre-marital chastity. But I wonder how many of the teachers running these classes create opportunities for their pupils to talk about the difference between adult homosexuality and the normal teenage crush. Together with masturbation (another experience that seems to terrify uninformed children) I believe this to be the area in which many young people need most solid information and reassurance.

I haven't yet heard what happened to the girl who turned to the aspirin bottle because she was frightened of her own normality. I don't know how many other children have been pushed to the stage of desperation that makes suicide seem a possible solution to an intolerable dilemma. But isn't it time that we made sure that sex education included the whole body of information about human love in all its manifestations?

COPING WITH THE LONE FEMALE (1971)

Jill Tweedie

Jill Tweedie is one of the Guardian's *outstanding columnists. Her 'Letters from Mary to Martha' made a*

15

delightful television series. She has worked for other newspapers and also taken time off to write books but returned to the Guardian *Woman's Page in 1986.*

A short while ago two perfectly respectable young women were refused coffees at the Churchill Hotel in London because the rules do not allow unaccompanied women to be served in the evenings. The same treatment is meted out to women alone at Wimpy Bars after midnight and, in fact, almost all large hotels follow the Churchill practice – though, to give them credit, most apply the segregation in rather subtler ways.

And though the Hilton, for instance, makes a special point of looking after single women in restaurants (a recent survey gave them top marks for single-woman cherishing) most hotels will admit that what they call 'the unwanted female guest' is a major and constant problem to security staff. One large West End Hotel predicts that if one night manager was lax in his duties for a month they would be entirely overrun with prostitutes. On the other hand, hotel staff say that their biggest problem today is not the professional (usually known by sight) but the amateur lady on the now-and-then game. As one security officer puts it: 'Twenty years ago you could tell who was who by their clothes. Nowadays this criterion has vanished and we are left with a dreadful problem. Only last month one of our men told a woman he called "obviously a tart" to leave the premises, only to find out that she was an ambassador's wife. In fact the muddle gets so bad sometimes that we've had a man going up to a blonde waiting around in the lobby, to put a word in her ear, and got a straight left to the jaw. She turned out to be a man.'

Most hotels stoutly maintain they are not in the business of guarding the public morals, only in protecting their guests from unpleasantness. Any professional lady who manages to be both well-dressed and discreet may well encounter no opposition because she is not likely to come to the attention of other guests. Discretion, as in so many other things, is the better part and it is more for this reason than for the rules themselves that the Churchill stands condemned. As others in the hotel business point out, rules are unnecessary if the security staff are sufficiently sophisticated.

2 Education for What?

Quite a high proportion of contributors to the *Manchester Guardian*'s Women's Page from its earliest days must have been graduates, well aware of the fierce struggle their foremothers had had to get higher education for women, but they seldom went on about this. Nor did their successors, though in the early 1960s the popular myth about the nature of the *Guardian* woman reader was that she was a 'whining graduate housewife'. The one real outburst of feeling came when Lois Mitchison ventured some rather startling views.

'BRIEF ENCOUNTER'

Jacky Gillott

Jacky Gillott, novelist, journalist, and broadcaster, sadly took her own life after a long period of depression.

December 1971: Looked at with an ecological eye many sacred cows seem to have been worshipped the wrong side of idolatry. Take education. Dutifully we train people to leap the hurdles between themselves and the high material expectations we have taught them to hold until they are fully equipped to take their place within the polluting production/consumption cycle of industrial society. When a man is measured by his material possessions, he has the greed motive built into him.

Growth is honorably presented as the one means of giving all the people the things they lack. But 'lack', like 'growth' is one of those words with a new contemporary ambiguity. It can mean a lack of things people *want*, rather than need. For need, substitute greed.

NEWNHAM REVISITED (1932)

Francesca M. Wilson

Francesca M. Wilson was well-known for her post-war relief work in various countries after World War I especially during the famine in Russia; also for refugees in Spain and France during the Spanish Civil War. She was principal welfare officer for UNRRA for the Dachau concentration camp victims.

In externals Newnham has changed little since Edwardian days. The same tall redbrick halls – are they ugly? I never thought of them in aesthetic terms – the same delicious garden shimmering with orchard and wild flowers, the same birds drunk with the damp warmth of Cambridge, the same bells calling for meals at the same times. Yet how different it seemed to me as I strayed about it for the first time since the war.

It seemed to have become much younger. How grown up we looked in those days when we came up at eighteen with our long skirts and blouses that had collars propped with whalebone, our hair stuffed out with pads or twisted into sausages on top of our heads. It never occurred to me that I or anyone around me was young. I felt half-baked, it is true, inadequate, uncertain. I didn't know what I believed or what I thought and my hair which had just been put up was always coming down, but I didn't know that I was young, and as for the people round me, they looked incredibly grown up – so poised, so finished and accomplished.

The beginnings of friendship were an excitement, milder than but not unlike the first stages of falling in love. Getting to know the people you admired, endlessly talking, games if you liked them, in summer the river – that was college life, with lectures and study as an interruption you had to put up with. One liked learning in a general way, only in Cambridge there were ever so many things to be interested in. What were they, I wonder now? Men we came across to some extent, but there were chaperones and rules. It was all made rather difficult and our contact with the other sex wasn't enough to deflect our

18

interest from each other. That was all right, no doubt for those who were to emerge into a larger world, as so many of us did when we left college, but how confining for those who were to go from one convent life to another.

It changed soon after we left. I remember with what envy we heard of the tea parties and picnics without chaperones, the university societies you could belong to, of the free, frank days that had come.

Freer and franker – that is why these girls look so much younger than we did. Their dress is more natural and becoming, and their dress is something more than itself – it is symbolic of a fresher and more natural attitude to life. It was beginning in our day. Frankness was coming in, campaigns were made against sentimentality, and there was an effort towards a more direct contact with things. But we had been born in the nineteenth century; illusionism dies hard; sentimentality is like creeping elder, a difficult weed to eradicate. But a fresher air was blowing. Shaw had already laughed some hypocrisies away. H.G. Wells's earlier novels had a refreshing candour, folk songs were driving off the ditties of Victorian drawing rooms. It was a jumble, of course; every age is. The aesthetes of my day, with their cult of beauty and of subtle speech, wore the air of Meredithian heroines and we could all recite yards of 'Modern Love'. As for the crème de la crème, their talk was all of Henry James. The age was turning its mind to the subtleties of psychology; atmosphere was in vogue. I remember how dashing I felt when I got hold of a complete Ibsen and plunged into the interiors he has made so heavy with gloom and the cries of imprisoned women. Our cult of the stark and violent seems feeble now that the stark and violent have become a religion, and sweep through art and music and poetry. Masefield's 'Everlasting Mercy' seemed daring to us then. It must seem deplorably lucid, restrained and decorous, the stuff we read and the things we talked of, to the generation that loves the obscurities of T.S. Eliot, Gerard Hopkins and James Joyce.

I respect but do not envy them their literature. I envy them the fact that they are less inhibited than we were and that the world of men is open to them, more than it was to us. In one respect, however, we were better off than they. Though it is scarcely more than twenty years ago, we lived on a much less crowded earth. How little we worried about our futures – how lightly we took our careers. We knew we could get jobs if we wanted them. There was no hurry. Fathers in the safe Edwardian days, unoppressed by income tax, unthreatened by falling dividends, made their daughters feel they were behind them if they wanted to go abroad for a year or two, or do unpaid political work (the suffrage campaign was all the go at that time) or train at a school of drama just for fun.

All this is changed now. These young things who look so alert and bright and trim, are at heart less carefree than we who, with all our gaiety, were so serious, with our belief in progress and the suffrage, our sense that somehow or other we must reform the world. But responsibilities towards the universe are, after all, lighter than those towards oneself, and nowadays the third-year feels the burden of her own future, though she may not worry about the world's. What shall she be? She knows that Cambridge has, with Oxford, an advantage over most places. Still, every profession is crowded and there seem to be so few for women, when one gets down to it. Most of them don't want to teach but suppose they'll have to – a grudging attitude. Social work requires further training and they have been at great expense already. As for politics, they are anathema to the majority. Only the League of Nations is in favour, for these girls, more forward-looking than our statesmen, look to something bigger than nationalism to salvage the world. But Geneva can't absorb them all. What is left? Marriage? You can't count on that in the present state. Business? There is the present crisis.

There are so many things for which I envy the modern Newnhamite that it is something of a relief to feel that we had some advantages in those old Edwardian days, and that in this matter of careers we were better off than our descendants.

THE PRICE OF EDUCATING WOMEN (1960)

Lois Mitchison

Lois Mitchison, one of the Guardian's *most stimulating contributors, was on the reporting staff of the* Manchester

Guardian *for a while. She is the daughter of Naomi Mitchison and sister of Val Arnold Forster,* Guardian *radio critic.*

In a 'Panorama' television programme some little time ago a group of Girton undergraduates were almost unanimous in asserting that politics was not a good career for women. It was unfeminine, and difficult to combine with marriage, they said. Many of their mothers must have been horrified at the rejection of sex equality they had struggled for . . . as horrified as a grandmother I met a few weeks ago. Her daughter, a don's wife, and herself a science graduate, had said she would send her own daughter to a university only if the family found they could afford it after her two brothers had been educated. The small girl is at present at a state-maintained school, her two brothers at expensive boarding schools. The don's wife argues that education is a necessity for boys but a frill for a girl who is likely to marry in her early twenties.

If higher education really is a frill for a girl who gets married immediately she leaves university, society, as well as her family, is spending unnecessarily. Schools, universities and graduate training in most professions are directly or indirectly state subsidised. (It costs about £10,000 of state and family money to produce a doctor, about £5,000 to produce an arts graduate). It is not only money, either. At universities, time taken teaching undergraduates is often time taken from research. At grammar schools, universities and some professional schools each student admitted means that another has to be kept out. An arts teacher at Edinburgh University told me that she thought girls should be legally or morally bound to do a socially useful job for a period of years after they graduate. But it would be a difficult law to apply.

I have been told that an educated girl makes a better companion to her husband, a better mother and a better housekeeper. I suppose it is true that educated women are more stimulating and amusing companions. (But surely some over-amused and over-stimulated husbands must long for restful stupidity?) Educated women can read books on child welfare, follow a cookery recipe and the directions on the backs of packets. But to justify higher education for women on

21

these sorts of terms is surely like using a steam hammer on a drawing pin.

I have been told by an Oxford woman graduate that she thought her university training had definitely hindered her in working in her house and looking after her two small children. She says that at Somerville she was taught to concentrate on a particular problem, excluding all irrelevances from her mind. What she has to do as a wife and mother, she says, is never to concentrate so that she excludes the irrelevant. Otherwise she finds that while she is concentrating on the pudding for lunch, her two-year-old has poured her milk over her brother and the baker's van has passed without her catching it.

A more obviously disastrous consequence of a university education is that women become discontented and guilty about their work in their home. Here in Oxford I have met women at parties who introduce themselves blightingly as 'just a wife', and apparently see themselves as exiles from a glamorous outside world. Other women worry as to whether they are letting their 'minds get rusty' or whether it is a sign of mental degeneracy that they like looking after their homes and children. The most socially embarrassing women are the ones who nag publicly at their husbands about the careers they have ruined.

One of the difficulties, I think, is that some schools and colleges lay the foundation of later guilt by assuming that careers and celibacy are the highest aims for women, or even the normal aims. I suppose that in the generation that grew up after the 1914 War particularly, a professional woman was not very likely to get married. There were not enough men to go round and educated girls were not socially acceptable every-where. Those university women graduates who did marry sometimes managed to combine full-time careers with their family life, and this, at any rate in intellectual quarters, was socially approved.

Today there are more young men than young women and no woman under 25 is likely to have to remain single. After marriage only the very exceptional woman is going to go on working full-time outside her home. Middle-class families are larger than they were in the 1920s, servants are difficult to get and expensive; modern psychologists stress the importance to

22

young children of the mother's continuous presence and fashions about what is socially approved in the home and in a wife have changed over the last 30 years. A career woman in the 1920s could pride herself on the plain living and high thinking in her household: her counterpart today spends hours grating, mixing, beating and mincing to keep up with the rising middle-class standards of cooking.

What I wonder is whether schools have accepted this changed social situation? It is surely a mistake to make girls feel guilty about abandoning their careers for marriage if that is what the majority of them are going to do anyway. If careers are not going to be given up completely, some combine more easily with marriage than others. A niece tells me that her school still encourages girls without a strong sense of vocation to become doctors. But at present it seems particularly difficult for women doctors to get part-time jobs unless they have specialist qualifications and it is even difficult for women doctors to get full-time jobs (particularly if they want free evenings) if they have stopped working for a time while they looked after their small children. The Civil Service was my college's favourite career for undecided graduates, a career that is particularly difficult to work at part-time or to take up again after a gap of years spent raising a family.

For a woman who is not going to work outside the home after marriage there is surely much to be said for for short-term excitement and interest: work in some types of business, a job involving travel, or perhaps badly paid social work (so badly paid that the man or woman who wants a life-long career cannot afford to take it up). For the woman who wants to work part-time all through her married life, or full time only after her children grow up, the most suitable jobs at present seem to be teaching, particularly science teaching, journalism, shorthand and typing (although top secretarial jobs, like top teaching and top newspaper jobs will go to full-timers), nursing, commercial art work, and crafts like dressmaking and housework.

In spite of the ivy growing on so many middle-class sitting room wallpapers and the return to many Victorian ideals of family life I suppose we are unlikely to return to early Victorian ideas of women's education and accomplishments.

But I think it is time we asked ourselves again whether we have gone too far in giving women the same education as men on the same terms. Girls' schools behave like boys' schools when they encourage girls to go to universities because they are cleverer than the rest of their class. Perhaps other qualifications, like exceptional energy (apparently needed to combine a job and a family) or a very strong sense of vocation are better guides as to which girls will make best use of their university and professional qualifications. At present many girls know by the time they reach university that they want to marry as soon as possible and devote most of their time and energy to running a home.

Or could the clever girl, determined on a fashionable Victorian marriage, be discouraged from going to a university at all? An alternative might be superior finishing schools set up in the main university towns so that girls will still have wide social contacts and a choice of husbands. These finishing schools, with courses in subjects like current affairs, art, literature, languages and cooking could specifically aim to produce the woman who would stimulate her husband and her children by the breadth of her interests, while discouraging the misplaced concentration and guilt of the present academically trained wives and mothers.

'Talkback'

The plaintive wailings of the graduate wife and her wasted life fill me with disgust. Any woman who has had the privilege of a university education and who does not thereafter find life twice as exciting and who cannot find at least a dozen interesting things to do – full-time, part-time, unpaid or underpaid – ought to be ashamed. The fault, dear graduates, lies in your own inertia, not in the universities, the state, your demanding husbands, your toddling children or your kitchen stove. If you could drag yourselves out of that sea of self-pity you would see that your chip is showing.

Nancy Wynne
Blackpool

I have always understood that the object of an academic education at university level was to produce a trained mind and a sense of judgment, a necessary bulwark against the sentimentalism and hysteria of the twentieth century. Society needs its quota of such minds in both men and women. If this is so, why in the name of society should we grudge a share of graduates to marriage and motherhood, which is generally supposed to be an important job for women? It is comforting to think that at least one section of the community, the young university woman, is pursuing learning without an immediate eye on the pay packet.

Beatrice Moorcroft
Worcester

Even if ended in the sixth form, no education is wasted. My headmistress once said 'If you educate a boy, you educate a man. If you educate a girl you educate a family.' The half-alive conversation I have met among former neighbours and 'born mothers' makes me shudder at the thought of 'restful simplicity' whether produced by 'superior finishing schools' or by watching television.

Olga Evans
London N2

I think the trouble with graduate wives is that intellectuality has blinded them to the sensuous pleasure of many unintellectual activities – the smell of cakes baking, the colour of damson jam when you are stirring it, the lovely polish on well-kept furniture, the smell of tomato plants in the greenhouse, the endearing antics of the family dog, the pure, almost shockingly bold happiness of a chortling baby, the song of a thrush in the garden, the sound of the woman next door singing. I think this sensuousness is as important as intellectuality. Anxious to be equal with men, women have seen equality only as the opportunity to do the same things as men and to excel in the same way. One should be equal – but different.

Mary McLean
Billinge, Wigan

25

Education for What?

In one library where I worked I had to spend weeks cleaning parcels of documents with a vacuum cleaner and in another I polished books for some hours each week. Anyone who thinks dish-washing boring had better try that. Yet in each case I was appointed for my high academic qualifications.

Dr Gwenda W. Thompson
London NW7

And Mother spoke too:
At the risk of a family row I am sticking my big nose into the controversy on educating women, and let me say at once I shall sit back and laugh if, after my university educated daughters have turned their faces away from all that useless nonsense, my granddaughters come to me for help in getting a university education. . . .

It is all nonsense about concentration being bad for housework or looking after babies. In my day certainly one had nurses and all that but I did my share of pram-pushing (in those days we were told to push prams, not leave them in front gardens as people do now) and while I did this I wrote my books, concentrating extremely hard with part of my mind. . . . When I was writing *The Corn King and the Spring Queen* I was concentrating like mad and wondering with another bit of my attention whether the tower that was being built by Lois, her brother and 'an Oxford woman graduate' would come down before the last sentence was on paper: I just beat it. . . . A final word: the present fashion that forces mothers to be with their children all the time and to feel guilty if they are not, is something that will pass. Nor is there virtue in personally washing nappies, or even blocking up drains with disposables.

Naomi Mitchison
Carradale, Campbelltown

Daughter's Postscript:
Of course my mother should have taken a university degree and of course she would have managed to combine an outside career and a family. Even with the drains blocked by disposable napkins over Christmas, and my father, eleven grandchildren, ten sons and sons-in-law, daughters and

daughters-in-law and a number of other friends in the house, my mother wrote half a book over the holiday, did much of the household cooking and organised a dance . . . but not all of us have the capacity or the energy.

Lois Mitchison

BACK TO SCHOOL (1968)

Nesta Roberts

Nesta Roberts started her newspaper career in South Wales, moved to North Lincolnshire (where she now lives in retirement) and then to Nottingham before joining the Manchester Guardian. *She moved to the London office as news editor when the* Guardian *started printing in London in 1960. Later she was health and welfare correspondent, and then ran the Paris office and wrote a much-enjoyed 'Letter from Paris' on Saturdays.*

'One of those seaside places where you are continually driven off the pavement by a school crocodile,' the woman was saying. Automatically, almost before the words were out of her mouth you had come back with a horrified: 'But the croc gets off the pavement for other people. Which school was it? Oh *them*!' As if it were not 40 and 60 and 80 years on.

Because our girls were taught to get off the pavement for absolutely everybody. Our girls answered invitations promptly and never went out in town without gloves and wrote their Collinses practically in the train going home and did their little bobs as for royalty when they went up to the platform on Speech Day and must have been dreadfully handicapped in all those fish queues that were waiting for them not so far ahead, since they were conditioned to go through life saying 'After you!' Our girls didn't push.

We were not pushed, either; the climate was all against it. At that time the school motto, instead of crying 'Faster', or 'Beyond' or something equally stimulating, just said 'As poor, but making many rich'. Nobody ever told us there was room at the top; nobody talked about success. Apart from obviously desirable objectives like becoming a concert pianist or making

27

good as a novelist we would have found success difficult to define. Certainly it wasn't money. Money was nice to have some of, but too much hovered on the brink of vulgarity. Anybody who seemed rather rich, and heaven knows, there were few among us, might have people who, unthinkably, were in trade. Also, money counted as advantages, which had accompanying obligations. If something happened to make you a millionaire, the obligations would be so crushing that the moral income tax would act as a disincentive.

It was long before the elbowing for university places started, so even for those who wanted to go, there wasn't really all that need for pushing. The rest, if they had their five wits, were cantered gently through what was still known as School Cert, then settled down to working for something like a music scholarship or just having a civilised year in the sixth where you could wangle seven hot baths a week instead of two, and go into the village on Saturday mornings to drink coffee and eat vanilla slices, and get yourself into three separate English sets just for fun.

Learning things for fun was perfectly OK, and being clever was OK, but a reputation for earnest toil did you no particular good with what was not then called your peer group. Status in the seeking sense of it just wasn't on, and a league table of careers specially approved by authority was upside down. The absolute tops would have been to become a teaching or nursing nun married to a missionary doctor in charge of a leper hospital in darkest Africa, with three daughters to follow in your footsteps and three sons to go to one of our brother schools.

Since, on several counts, that was recognised to be difficult, the 'News of Old Girls' section in the school magazine was nicely impartial between Helen, who was studying something terrifying to do with engineering, and Monica who was presented this year (which made her at least an osprey, if not a roc, in our flock), and Rosemary, who was helping her father in the parish and had started a Brownie pack.

What it amounted to was that little rats hardly had to run, let alone race. Looking back, one regrets the absence of the prophetic vision which would have made one know one's luck. It would have been something to set against the penitential

winter cold and the raging boredom of compulsory dancing in
the hall on Saturday evenings, when you wanted to do
something else, and the ghastliness of the food and the
peculiar awfulness of Tuesday. Tuesday meant an endless,
windswept walk for those non-joiners who were not in the
Guide company, and mince and mud (chocolate mould that
hadn't moulded) for dinner, so that you contemplated two
successive cow pats, and a double period of science in the
afternoon. That meant nearly an hour and a half of the ignoble
smells of the lab, and you could not often count on diversions
like somebody boiling the turps instead of the water when we
were doing specific gravities. (Dear Porky! O where are you
now?)

As it was, we took for granted all that luxury of leisure, all
that time for drunken reading, on and off the Index. *Plays
Pleasant* and *Plays Unpleasant* and *St Joan* all in three days,
tonsillitis helping, and *The French Revolution* mostly in bed by
an illicit candle after lights out. The Index was a bit dodgy.
The English mistress invited my views on *Point Counterpoint*,
but one of her colleagues nearly had a stroke about *All Quiet
on the Western Front*. Quite needlessly, since at 16 I had no
idea what a brothel was, though I did think the bit about
latrines rather outspoken.

The beauty of the place was a bonus. There were jade and
cobalt seas below and a flowing line of hills behind; layered
cedars in the Long Drive and white roses on the terrace. The
walls of the chapel were white too, and the voices roses true
between them to the joyful roof paintings that illustrated like a
page out of a missal, the hymn about the heavenly Jerusalem
they were singing about in procession.

Eighty years on things must have got rather more strenuous,
because eight of the eight candidates they put up for university
were accepted. But they can't have changed radically because
the one who made Oxford went off to spend the interim
teaching small Pakistanis in Bradford.

'The land of spices'. Eighty-one years on they closed it.
Wrong ethos for the *Zeitgeist*, I suppose. *Lux perpetua. . . .*

3 Marriage and Money

The urge to secure the legal right of married women to have money of their own has been a spur to the women's movement for at least a century and a half. The financial dependence of the married woman was not infrequently discussed in the *Manchester Guardian* in the 1920s and 1930s – but one of the most extraordinary explosions of letters in the *Guardian*'s 'Mainly for Women' in the 1960s was on this theme, following an article by the page's editor headed 'Women Talking to Men' in 1964.

HUSBANDS AND WIVES (1923)

Helen Fraser

An assertion that husbands and wives should each legally have a right to a certain proportion of the other's income is one that calls forth lively arguments against it – and sometimes. I find, even shocked invective. But nothing is clearer than the fact that the position of women in marriage in relation to money must be radically changed from the legal point of view if we are going to express our changed attitudes and our growing sense of justice and get our legislation in line with common sense. We have given women the right to vote, to enter the professions and to participate in the administration of the law. We extend the boundaries of women's rights all the time in these days and it is essential that we should not only continue to recognise and extend their rights but it is equally essential that we shall see to it that women shoulder their responsibilities as well as get their rights.

The House of Lords has just passed a measure removing 'presumption of coercion' on the part of a married woman and making her responsible for crimes committed with her connivance or in her presence, as any other citizen is. It is also time that a married woman should be made responsible for her own personally contracted debts and that we stopped having cases brought into our courts because women possessing large incomes of their own, after having ruined their husbands, refuse to pay the debts they have contracted. A married woman must be made personally responsible for the debts she contracts and she must also, if there is any sanity and common sense in the marriage contract, be required, if she has means of her own, to contribute to the joint expenses of the household a certain proportion of her income.

Some years ago a husband used to take on marriage the control of the whole of his wife's income, a state of affairs that every person today would agree to be unjust. We changed that position into one giving the wife the entire control of her own income. Now we ask that the marriage contract shall legally recognise the partnership implied in marriage, and that men and women shall be treated alike on the question of the right to a proportion of the other's income.

Now we come to the contention that the legal right of a wife to a certain proportion of her husband's income should be embodied in our lives, so that all married women may be made responsible persons in regards to contracts and debts. This can only be done if they are ensured the right to some proportion of the husband's income. I do not think that anyone will be found to deny that a wife 'who is doing her duty in that relationship' has a moral right to the use of a proportion of her husband's income, and that it is desirable she should have such a share and the responsibility accruing to the spending of it, as most wives have.

As a matter of fact we do recognise the right of a wife to a share now, by custom and by law. The marriage settlement is simply the recognition of this claim. In our law we lay down that a wife is entitled to food, clothing and shelter; that she can pledge her husband's credit for necessities (necessities to be interpreted according to his position). The husband now, if he has a wife who is not content with spending a proportion of his income, can announce that he will not be responsible for debts contracted by her. He can also announce this for no just reason at all.

31

Let us remember that such legislation will affect only those husbands and wives who do not act fairly by each other. The majority of married people do act fairly and reasonably, but the wife who cannot get the use of any fair share of her husband's income – and there are such wives – is in a position that is unjust and intolerable. Only too often we find that deep in human nature there are people who like to make others feel always that they are dependent on the giver's bounty, that there seems to be a subtle joy for some people in making others feel their complete and absolute dependence. There are men who feel that it is a grace on their part and a rather noble thing to hand over the housekeeping money, who like to make their wives ask for things that they know they should give without the asking, because it panders to their sense of power. There are women who want to be allowed to keep all their own money and to spend all they can get otherwise and more, women who are as unscrupulous and as selfish as the worst of men could ever be in this relationship and feel we might fittingly pass a law today which will show these people what really civilised people think.

Those of us who ask that our laws shall embody this definite recognition of the partnership of marriage, of the dignity and rights the marriage position should give, of the responsibility that husbands and wives take upon entering into marriage feel that such a law would not only be just and moral and in accord with all that is best in us, but that it will help to right some deep, profoundly felt indignities to women and to men.

'Talkback'

It is in accordance with justice and commonsense that men and women alike should be responsible for the debts they personally contract and also that they should contribute in proportion to their means to the expenses of the joint household and the maintenance and education of the children of the marriage. It is just and right that both the husband and the wife should be responsible for all private debts so that a careful and thrifty partner shall not be ruined by the extravagance or dishonesty of the other party to the marriage.

Such an adjustment of the present pecuniary obligations of a husband and wife would be welcome to all right-minded couples and it would enhance the dignity and stability of their sacred relationship.

(Dr) Mary Scharlieb
Harley St
London

Feminism, if it means anything at all, means recognition of women as responsible human beings. As regards the economic position of the wife in the marriage partnership, I have not the happy faith of Miss Fraser in the beneficent effects of remedies enacted in Parliament. Custom, not law, is the deciding factor in the average matrimonial partnership; and, since the passing of the Married Women's Property Act, our law is ahead of our custom in recognising the right to a separate income. I suggest that if the average British parent in the last 40 years had acted up to the spirit of the Married Women's Property Act a very large proportion of women in every rank of life would enter the holy estate of matrimony with a modest dowry. And I suggest further that it is our unthrifty national custom of regarding the dowry as superfluous that makes the Married Women's Property Act something like a deadletter in the classes that most need its benefits. A thrifty custom of securing to the bride an actual financial stake in her household would effect a greater revolution than any legislation, however well-intentioned and framed.

Cicely Hamilton
London SW3

Would Miss Fraser kindly explain the administrative machinery through which she hopes to achieve her object of giving husbands and wives a definite share in each other's income? Fancy legislation is always undesirable and it is clear that many men and women would offer strenuous resistance to this scheme. In cases of dispute a court of law alone could decide whether the statutory proportions of income are being paid by the husband or wife. Can we contemplate unmoved the vast increase of legal actions of a necessarily complicated character? Or the type of sordid domestic wrangle which

would precede any appearance in court? . . . The remedy
would appear to lie in an improvement in the general moral
consciousness, not in piling legislation on top of legislation.

Violet Markham
Bloomsbury
London

PROPERTY AND MARRIAGE (1957)

Thelma A. Hunter

In 1941 a husband and wife separated. At that date there was
standing to the credit of the wife in the book of a co-operative
society a sum of £103 10s. This amount represented savings by
the wife from her housekeeping allowance which, she claimed,
belonged to her. The court decided, however, that the money
belonged to the husband. It had been saved out of his
earnings, and by law, each individual has exclusive rights to
what he earns.

Financial disputes of this nature, some more simple, many
more complicated, occur regularly. They are dealt with under
Section 17 of the Married Women's Property Act. When
passed in 1882 this Act was heralded as a landmark in the
movement for emancipation of the married women. For the
first time it introduced into law the principle that she could
retain any property or earnings which she might possess or
acquire before or after marriage. In this way the married
woman kept her own individual legal rights, which previously
she had forfeited completely on marriage.

But as subsequent disputes and court decisions revealed,
this equality has proved to be rather formal than actual.
Section 17 has been described as the *bête noire* of the law
courts; and a growing volume of criticism has brought the
property relations of man and wife under review by the Royal
Commission on Marriage and Divorce which sat between 1951
and 1955.

Most critics now stress the injustice to the married woman
of a law which attributes no economic value to her work in the
home. In our society the majority of married woman neither

own property nor do they, for much if not all of their married lives, earn an income. The family income is usually a single income earned by the husband and therefore, in law, owned by the husband. It follows that any property accumulated by the couple during their marriage, including house, furniture and savings, also belongs to him. A wife, in law, has no specific rights to a share of the family income nor to the family home and its contents. (On the other hand, she has a common law right to be maintained by her husband 'in keeping with his means' and may apply for a maintenance order if he fails to perform his duty.)

Many witnesses before the Royal Commission claimed that the effect of the law was to place the wife, in spite of her strict legal equality, in a position of economic servitude. This seems an extreme view of the position. However, it is significant that the courts themselves have often been reluctant to enforce a rigid interpretation of the law. In cases, for example, where property has been bought by the contributions of both partners and subsequently sold the courts may rule that the proceeds of the sale be divided equally rather than in strict accordance with individual contributions. Similarly, they have often protected the wife's interest in the family home. A deserted wife, for example, would not readily be ejected unless her husband could provide suitable alternative accommodation. Nor could her husband, contrary to her wishes, arbitrarily give up the tenancy of the home, if he is a tenant under the Rent Restrictions Act.

On the other hand, in order to qualify for such protection the wife must have been left in possession of the home; that is, the husband must have moved out, not she. The woman who leaves her husband, even if she is subsequently awarded a legal separation or a divorce against him is not thus favoured. The onus is entirely on her to find another home, furnish it and with her maintenance allowance tend to herself and perhaps her family.

The women's situation is often aggravated if the husband's payments of maintenance allowance have in the meantime fallen into arrears – by no means a rare occurrence. In 1956, for example, the Married Women's Association estimated that there were in England and Wales 100,000 deserted wives whose allowances were in arrears. Moreover, when this happens, the wife herself must ensure regular payments and this often means tracing her husband if he chooses to vanish. And she cannot enlist the support of the police or of any Government body, such as the Inland Revenue or the Ministry of Pensions. When found, the defaulting husband often chooses prison rather than pay up: for if he does so he is automatically absolved of his liability to pay arrears. In 1955 alone, no fewer than 3,400 men chose this way out of their obligations. At the moment a Private Member's Bill for the attachment of wages in England and Wales is before Parliament.

Although the Royal Commission admitted that some amendment in the law is desirable to give more effective recognition to 'the wife's contribution to the marriage' its ultimate recommendations in this respect were half-hearted. It rejected, for example even a limited version (applying only to the home and contents) of the Scandinavian system of community of property which provides, broadly, for joint ownership of all property and income acquired at the time of marriage and after. Instead it recommended only that family savings should be owned in common unless specific arrangements were made to the contrary. It did little to alleviate the pressure which the law puts on the wife who, other things being equal, would leave her husband were it not for the practical difficulties of finding another home. It rejected the most popular proposal to alter this situation, that the court be empowered to allocate as it saw fit the family home and its contents as soon as a separation order had been made. Finally, it rejected the principle of arrestment of wages and suggested merely that a man whose maintenance allowance falls into arrears should continue to be liable even if he went to prison.

It is difficult to avoid the conclusion that the Royal Commission's recommendations constitute but a feeble conservative effort to remedy serious anachronisms in our law.

JUST A KEPT WOMAN (1957)

Anne Bradley

The other day I said, quite casually to a young friend who is getting married next month, 'Will you take a job when you are settled in London?' She looked at me with raised eyebrows. 'Of course. What else would I be likely to do?' 'Well,' I said almost apologeticaly, 'you seem to take it for granted, but women who married before the war, like me, didn't go on working.' 'And do you mean to tell me,' said Jean sternly, 'that you expected your poor husbands to provide you with everything?'

The condemnation in her voice was like a slap in the face. I felt a worm . . . a parasite . . . a kept woman.

But the young wives of my generation didn't go out to work, as a rule. The majority of Englishwomen triumphantly handed in their notices when the wedding day was fixed and never anticipated working for a salary again. A woman who deliberately kept on a job was inviting suspicion that her husband couldn't keep her in the style to which she was accustomed or she would be criticised for taking the bread out of an unmarried woman's mouth.

Jean was shaking her head over the unaccountable habits of an older generation. 'I can't imagine how you filled your time,' she remarked. 'Of course, if all the wives had nothing to do you'd be able to have lots of tea-parties and golf and bridge, I suppose.'

That same suggestion, that if you haven't a paid job you have nothing with which to occupy your time was voiced again by two girls sitting behind me on the bus the other day.

'You're keeping on your job after the wedding, aren't you? That's right. I didn't, and it was a big mistake. You think it will be marvellous to go round Woolworth's and Marks' every day, but you'd be surprised how soon it palls.'

Were we really as aimless as that? I know we were very proud of our status as married women; we waved our husbands off in the morning and looked forward to their return to a well-kept house and an appetising meal as the highlight of the day. There were tea-parties, certainly, but once the bride had been welcomed and hospitality returned they didn't occur often. Most of us preferred to do our entertaining when our husbands were free.

Golf and bridge? Not much among the young wives of my acquaintance. For one thing, we were poor, to a degree that few young couples of today can realise. Our husbands, struggling to believe the old lie that two can live as cheaply as one, did their best with the one income and assured us that we must have our share of personal money, though the pocket-money of both was swallowed up in the unexpected expenses of a home. We weren't all born good managers and had to learn the hard way. But we had no time to be bored. For one thing, practically every couple started out with a whole house to themselves and there weren't all the labour-saving devices that are taken for granted now. Housework took up a great deal of time and was more tiring that it is now.

I won't pretend that I disliked the knowledge that I hadn't to turn out in the morning; that I could arrange the day's programme to suit myself. There was opportunity to do things I'd never had time for before – as long as they didn't cost too much. I joined a class at the School of Art. I helped with a newly established baby clinic and I extended my work in the Girl Guide movement.

There was no lack of interesting work, and play too, available for women with free afternoons. None of it was paid, of course, but the advantage of that came to light when the first baby arrived. We had no major financial adjustments to make; we had done that when we first got married.

Don't think for a minute that I am decrying the hard-working wife of today. She has a heavy task, carrying on a profession by day and doing housekeeping at night and at the weekends. Even with every labour-saving device under the sun it can't be easy. It isn't surprising if she has little time and energy left for outside interests.

And for that very reason, it's the old brigade of kept women who are the backbone of the WVS, the Hospital Reserve, the Citizens Advice Bureau and a score of other unpaid social services. Perhaps, after all those of us who were able to concentrate on the exacting profession of home-making in the early years of married are not to be scorned, but rather envied.

WOMAN TALKING TO MEN (1964)

Mary Stott

In the sad, bad days before the war, when the Jews were fleeing from Nazi persecution, I helped a gentle and timid young woman named Charlotte to find a home with an English family. I explained to them that it was not possible legally to pay her a salary for her help with their children, but that I hoped they would give her 'presents'. A few weeks later Charlotte wrote to me and asked if I would make her a loan against the security of her watch. The only present she had been given was a pair of bedsocks – not a penny for toilet needs, stamps, bus fares, stockings, or anything else – and she could not bear to ask for cash. I had Charlotte out of that house within days and I have never forgotten or forgiven.

It was this story of total lack of imagination and respect for human dignity that came at once to my mind when a reader told me the other day that after 30 years of married life she had persuaded her husband to give her a personal allowance. The sum was five shillings a week. When I said I was astounded and that he must be a rare relic of a dying breed, she promptly replied with a list of 19 of her friends and acquaintances in all parts of England only five of whom had any personal spending money. And they included two teachers who turned over the whole of their salary to 'the head of the house'.

I am not a warped spinster waving the feminist flag. I am a rather amiable married woman whose domestic arrangements are perfectly harmonious and who all her life has enjoyed the fun and stimulus of working with men, talking to them, being teased by them. But it makes me hopping mad when I hear of any man who regards a woman, especially his wife, as less than an adult human being.

Can any man who reads this column help me to understand? Do men regard women as human beings? A human being is not an animal on two legs who has learned certain tricks necessary to exist in a civilised society, but a creature different from the animals in being able to think, plan, and make a reasoned choice. And in a civilised society choice is dependent over and over again on the expenditure of money. Deprive a person of money of his own and you deprive him of the right of choice in a very large part of everyday life. And to deny a human being the right of choice is to humiliate and degrade him.

I know perfectly well that there are a great many men – I used to think happily that they were a majority; now I am not so sure – who regard their wives as equal partners, equal contributors to the wellbeing of the joint home. (My reader told me of a husband who refused to put their home in their joint names on the ground that *she had contributed nothing to it*.) But even they may be able to help me to see into the mind of the others – who, I fear, are not the sort of men to read a column written by a woman.

To try to get at what goes on in a household where the wife has no separate allowance, I picture the day when she thinks she needs a new coat.

Husband A may say: 'Any time you like. Have the bill sent to me.' (But suppose when she starts shopping around she finds that she would gladly make her coat do for another season if she could spend the money on an album of records, a pear tree, a couple of important books, and a dangling bauble for her little black dress. If it is his money she is spending she has, in all honesty, to ask her husband if he minds. Some would not. Some would.)

Husband B may say: 'I can't afford it.' (Often true; sometimes not. Not many wives who are kept informed of the state of the family finances would ask for a new coat unless there was money in the kitty, where every penny has to be used just for paying the rent, fuel, food, and clothes, and if the wife has a personal allowance it is a token payment only, for she will certainly spend most of it on the children. But that is her choice.)

Husband C may say: 'How much do you think you will need?' (It will depend on the relationship between them whether she puts the figure too high, too low, or just about right for her husband's means. But whatever sum he gives her the chances are that it will not be exactly right for the coat she finally wants to buy. If it is too much, does she return the balance or buy a new hat? If it is too little, does she borrow the balance from the housekeeping and ask later for a refund; cut down on the food shopping for a week or two to make up the difference; or defer the purchase until she can ask her husband if he is willing to spend more?)

I just cannot think myself into the skin of a man in circumstances like this and I need help to understand. I suppose there is many a man who thinks quite simply that as he alone brings money into the home he alone has the right to dispose of it, and that his wife is only his agent in doing the shopping, even for her own clothes. This seems to me to reduce the wife to the level of an unpaid employee (or slave, some would say), but I think that such a man tells himself that it is just because he does not regard the wife of his bosom as an employee that he does not want to have any kind of financial contract with her; that petty bookkeeping would make the whole relationship sordid and loveless.

But really, I think, these husbands subconsciously apprehend the truth that money means independence and that the wife with pennies in her pocket can cock a snook at him and go off on a bus to visit mamma, buy a highbrow magazine or a pop record, have a drink in a pub, or whatever she fancies. And this they cannot bear.

Why not? This is what absolutely baffles me. How can a man endure to share his home with someone who is of adult years but only of semi-adult status? I should loathe to be tied to someone whom I did not expect to spend time and money rationally and considerately. Some unfortunate people have to and manage heroically to carry the millstone around. But who in his right mind would choose to if he did not need to? In fact would insist on doing it?

And I certainly cannot imagine what it would be like to be the wife of a man who doled out money as to a backward child. But I could quite well imagine what it was like to be Charlotte . . . and I got her out of her cage within days.

'Talkback'

I receive no personal allowance from my husband and feel no need of one. We both work out a household budget which includes a certain sum for each of us, in my case to cover housekeeping expenses, in his case lunches and travelling expenses. When it comes to buying items of clothing or furniture we discuss it and budget together, agree priorities and decide what we can afford, and then go ahead. My husband would no more think of buying a new suit without consulting me than I would go out and buy a new coat without discussing it with him first.

Mrs J.A. Stuart
Pontyclon
Glamorgan

I think that if I were a woman I would not like to have an allowance 'given' to me by my husband, with all that this implies. I find the whole concept of this problem being posed in terms of giver and receiver faintly amusing and decidedly quaint. . . . In my own case my wife and I have equal access at all times to all the money.

Mr P.W. Burgess
Leicester

Anonymously. . . :

Wife No. 1: A wife reported that when she gave up her job to have a baby she pointed out that she would be economically dependent on her husband to the humiliating degree of having to ask him for money with which to buy his birthday present. 'He replied seriously that he didn't expect a present from me as I didn't have the money, and quite sharply that if I'd wanted financial independence I had no right to have married but should have remained a career girl. Yet he is otherwise very kind and considerate and is very generous, finances permitting.'

Wife No. 2: Often my husband, apparently extremely generous, provides me with a blank cheque and tells me to buy 'that' dress. He forgets that he spent the night before telling me in detail that last year he spent 1s 8½d more than he actually earned. That life is hard and we cannot afford anything really. What sensitive and guilt-ridden woman will then rush off to the 'Young and Gay' department? And what about the fare up to town? And the lunch? Husbands forget that the cheque can only be spent in one shop – not possible to show it at the station barrier, in the restaurant, or in the coffee bar. How tedious to find a shop where you can have lunch, buy a dress, the needed stockings, the lipstick etc and pay with the one cheque after you have driven the staff mad with administrative work.

Wife No. 3: If I need a new coat or a new dress my husband comes into the shop with me and writes a cheque. This I find galling and as a result have very few clothes.

Wife No. 4, who married young and 'gladly gave all the financial reins to her husband': Thirteen years and two children later I never have more than £1 in my purse. Even that is searched in case I have purloined an extra 10s. and may be tempted into a wild orgy of spending. There was a look of horror when I once spent £1 on a book. Is it too much to hope that I could look after 5s. a week?

Wife No. 5 who had three children in three years: 'My planning was not made easier by the fact that I never had the ready cash for contraceptives or examinations.'

Wife No. 6, a woman with a very strong social conscience, married to a man 'kind and responsible in almost every way but with so much inborn prejudice about 'the lower class' and 'coloureds' that when she wished to help such people their disagreement brought them to the verge of separation.
'I salved my conscience by working secretly for a whole year on a home-help job, and the 24s. I earned I felt was mine to give away to a young coloured couple in need. I have now come up against it again with a young mother and baby deserted by the husband because the baby is not his. I helped her with baby milk and shillings for the gas until I could get her to the National Assistance Board, but my own children objected that I was using "Daddy's money."

43

'Happily last week I managed to get a night duty job at an old people's home for Saturday nights. I can only do Saturday nights as the hours are from 8.30 p.m. to 8.30 a.m. and on weekdays I must get my husband and five children breakfasted and out of the house by 8.30 a.m. Fortunately on night duty I am not even using my housekeeping hours to gain my weekly "charity 30s.", so now my conscience is at peace.'

Husband No.1: My wife is a very efficient housekeeper who has never asked for a personal allowance and has no desire to go out to work for one. When my wife wants anything I usually find the money for it: this can be from £1 to £50. Holidays are solely borne by myself. I think if I were to give my wife a fixed personal allowance she would spend it and there would be no reserves for the very frequent claims for furnishing, clothes etc.

Husband No. 2, a Cheshire teacher: I will agree that men do like to keep spending power out of the hands of their wives, for a reason that is more understandable than the ones you put forward. This is a basic disagreement on what money should be spent on, between men and women. Men look, above all, for endurance value, strong cars, houses, shoes, clothes that last. I know that this is very strongly so in my case. Women look for a fleeting beauty of fashion or material that comes very low down in the endurance scale. My nylon socks last three years, my wife's nylon stockings three weeks. This dichotomy is desirable – it makes for variety and balance, but it makes for man's distrust of woman as a spender. And man is responsible for keeping his family safe, warm and fed.

April 1, 1964: Sidney Rothwell, Manchester: No reference has been made to the remarkable phenomenon of the wife who does not know what the husband earns. This, I understand, is not uncommon, but to my mind is completely unforgivable and betrays a remarkable lack of affection, trust and understanding in a relationship which must, by definition, be based on these qualities.

Staffordshire reader: Women are generally irresponsible about money, mainly because they fail to get their priorities right.

In my case I pay all the large bills (mortgage, rates, electricity etc.) and I see that my wife has sufficient for day-to-day expenses, groceries, milk etc., and for herself in the form of cigarettes, cinema, make-up etc. . . . I would love a personal allowance of my own to buy records, books and theatre tickets, but I know the treasury wouldn't stand it: why then should I give my wife an extra allowance for what we both know are unnecessary extravagances? The point is, surely, that if women are given an allowance of 10s. a week they will spend it on things which are unnecessary and still ask for a new dress or coat when it is wanted. Men tend to anticipate expenses and provide accordingly; women for the day.

Sally Tomlinson: If marriage is to continue to develop as a partnership, sooner or later the wife will have to be legally entitled to a share of her husband's earnings. As Judge Sir Jocelyn Simon recently pointed out, English law is unfair in that it ignores the functional division of labour and a wife has no legal monetary reward of her own, even though she may work harder than the actual breadwinner. This makes more sense now than it would have done 50 years ago as nowadays many women are as well qualified as their husbands (or more so) to earn money outside the home, and will not take kindly to giving up potential earning capacity to receive a condescending 'allowance'.

Muriel Miller, Southsea: When I hear girls purr and preen when they are called 'chicks', 'birds', etc. I have misgivings. Why does a woman allow herself to be called 'a tasty bit of stuff', and all the other rude descriptions we hear? And why should someone who has been thought of like this suddenly rise to the status of responsible handler of money just because a wedding ring has been placed on her finger?

THE TALE OF THE FIVE-BOB-A-WEEK WIFE (1964)

E. Margaret Wheeler

Mrs E. Margaret Wheeler, wife of a local government official in Cockermouth, Cumbria, wrote many letters to the Guardian *Women's Page and to its editor. Earlier she had carried on a long correspondence with George Bernard Shaw, which started with her interest in his ideas about a new English alphabet, but became a discussion of her profound conviction that she had been given the wrong baby in the nursing home. (The families of the two babies became close friends.) In the 1970s the Wheelers travelled extensively together and took up crafts (handmade furniture and pottery). Two years ago a play based on Mrs Wheeler's pen-friendship with G.B.S. was performed at the Redgrave and other Surrey theatres.*

In order to write this, I have had to ask my husband to buy me paper, envelopes and a stamp: he brings these things quite cheerfully and sees nothing wrong in my being put into a position where I either have to ask him for them or do without.

Last year I badly wanted to join a specifically women's organisation, so I asked my husband for the subscription money and after casting his eye over a pamphlet about it he said it seemed to him to be a useless and abortive affair and refused the money. And that was that.

Farther back than this he found it necessary to have an economy drive, and books and newspapers were ruthlessly jettisoned: I was compelled with some anxiety, to plead to be able to keep the *Guardian*, which he doesn't read. Can there be any adult woman who has ever earned her own living and been independent, who would not find circumstances like this – now the commonplaces of my life – humiliating? Could anybody at all be surprised at my asking for some personal pocket-money?

My housekeeping allowance may best be described as adequate; it is neither mean nor generous, but it was never intended to cover odds and ends of a personal nature or clothes. Major items of clothing like suits and coats and Sunday-go-to-meeting dresses my husband pays for by cheque; for smaller items I am once again compelled – whenever it is absolutely impossible to fiddle any more out of the housekeeping – to ask him for the money. There is always the risk, if he is frustrated, or worried, or feeling hard-up, of being refused, in the time-honoured words, 'Do you think I'm made of money?' or 'I gave you some the other day – what have you done with it?'

Then there may come a time when I haven't got something I ought to have because I've been afraid to ask for the money and an exasperated husband will turn on me and say 'Why on earth didn't you ask me for it? You know you've only got to *ask*.' He has no idea how utterly humiliating I find this eternal 'asking'.

How does such a state of affairs arise with any couple? From my own experience, I would say there are three stages at least in the turning of a self-supporting working-girl into a dependent and financially subordinated wife. Our courtship days didn't count in this, of course; we both had money to spend on our much-planned, much-considered and much-desired future home. Happy days! The solid and durable things we bought then with *my* money we are still using, regarded as 'ours' and part of 'our' home; but whatever was bought by either of us was talked over and chosen by both of us together, in a happy and carefree unison. Which, of course, is how it should be.

After marriage (my job relinquished and nest-egg well and truly spent) we had to get down to the business of adjusting ourselves to a totally new situation: my husband earned our living, and I managed our household affairs: had housekeeping money, it is true, but all the money that came in was regarded as 'ours' and expended that way. No girl, surely, could be blamed in these circumstances for not perceiving that the first stage of her financial dependence had begun; for legally and actually all the money that came in belonged to my husband, though neither of us behaved as though that were the case. It seems incredible to think of it now, but in those days having money and spending it was fun.

The second stage began with the arrival of the children and

47

lasted until they were grown up and had left home. During this stage both of us were, in many ways, enslaved. My husband took his responsibilities to his family very seriously and conscientiously; he worked very hard and gave of his utmost; it could perfectly well be said at that time that neither of us had any real freedom. It took all we both had to bring up our family. Nevertheless it was at this time that I slipped gradually and almost imperceptibly into the position of unpaid domestic servant, and it was taken for granted by all concerned even me, that it was my lot, day in, day out, to cope with the endless dusting, scrubbing, bed-making, cooking and washing involved in the bringing up of a family. It *had* to be done and there was no-one to do it but Mum, so Mum got on with it, for the sake of the children.

Now they have gone (and with them a great deal of the housework) and the third stage, of complete financial subjugation is upon me. My unpaid domestic service after more than 30 years of it, is now absolutely taken for granted as well as my willingness to spend the rest of my life doing it.

Whether I like it or loathe it; whether I could do something more socially useful or not, just doesn't count; because my husband controls the purse-strings and wants things that way. I am stuck with the job just as surely as any slave of ancient Rome.

4   Married to a House

One outstanding difference between the *Manchester Guardian* women readers between the two World Wars and the *Guardian* readers of today is that in the 1920s and 1930s contributors discussed domesticity on the assumption that in homes like theirs there would be living-in domestic help. From 1945 onwards the living-in maid disappeared from all but the wealthiest homes. Today's homemakers have far more labour-saving equipment than their mothers and grandmothers – but keeping the home clean and decent is a job many, perhaps most, do without any help at all.

THE REBEL ON THE HEARTH (1924)

Evelyn Sharp

Evelyn Sharp, first regular columnist of the page, was a prolific novelist and journalist. She was a pacifist and a feminist (she referred from time to time to her knowledge of Holloway prison!) In 1933 she married the well-known foreign correspondent Henry Nevinson, who was for some time on the Guardian *staff.*

Spring-cleaning always seems to me a confession of failure. Obviously, if the house is dirty enough to require special cleaning in the spring, the implication is that it has not been kept clean in the preceding summer, autumn and winter, and to clean it with a flourish of dusters at one season is not to guarantee it will not need cleaning again during the other three. Indeed, spring-cleaning acts rather as a deterrent than otherwise. For weeks beforehand it seems hardly worth while to clean the house since it is going to be turned upside down shortly; and after the dreadful event is over to start cleaning it again is like going to church on Easter Monday or making a speech the day after the poll.

There are so many rebels on the hearth in these emancipated days that an organised revolt against spring-cleaning ought to be easy to provoke. It should certainly be one of those so-called women's movements that should have the hearty co-operation of all the men of the household, for the wail of the husband, father or brother is the recognised accompaniment to this yearly disaster. Spring-cleaning is quite an important part of the traditional jest about women, but there is no reason why it should be an essential part, and if there still remain some mockers who would sooner suffer the inconvenience of spring-cleaning than lose one chance of laughing at the absurdities of women, they would be largely outnumbered by those in favour of abolition, and as everybody knows, the next best thing to defeating the enemy is to divide the enemy's ranks.

But many will still be found to defend this ancient custom. Chimneys have to be swept, they will say, and the sweep alone entails a spring-cleaning. But does he? At this one season of the year he may, with truth be said to 'come to dust'. But where there is a kitchen chimney the sweep comes at other seasons of the year, too, and except at springtime does not disorganise the whole household. In the case of all other chimneys, the sweep is even an active argument against spring-cleaning – for there are still archaic housewives who permit no fire to be lighted after the chimney has been swept at spring time; and if the sweep could come and go unobtrusively at other times of the year, as the window-cleaner does, whole families would not shiver before a fireless grate in the bitter winds of an English summer.

If spring-cleaning is to be abolished the psychological motives underlying it cannot be ignored. One must allow for the sense of novelty and excitement that seems to be satisfied by this yearly outbreak of cleanliness. Nothing is duller than to keep a house clean by removing a little dirt every day; it is as wearing to the spirit as it would be to sew one stitch – an impossible feat in any case – in order to save problematic nine. The house may be no cleaner after a week's onslaught upon 51 weeks of accumulated dirt, than if the dirt had never been allowed to accumulate, but the difference between making a house clean and keeping it clean is the difference between having loved and lost and never having loved at all. Clearly, if the spring-cleaner is ever to be converted from this annual orgy of domesticity, domesticity must be itself rendered more exciting and adventurous from day to day.

The elemental desire to wallow in dirt in order fully to enjoy converting it into driven snow is not, however, the only motive underlying the universal love of spring-cleaning. Equally universal, though a little more subtle, is the feeling in the early part of the year – long before the weather justifies it – that 'summer is i'comen in'. It makes us do all sorts of mad and delightful and pleasant and poetic things; but unfortunately the means for satisfying it in poetic and pleasant ways are not so universal as the feeling. The housewife in the straitened city dwelling, the charwoman who comes in by the day, the domestic servant with her Sunday and her evening out, are all victims of the age-long desire to do something new in the spring-time, something to celebrate the renewal of life after death. To make the house smell of furniture polish and soap from top to bottom, to put up clean curtains on the assumption that the sun is waiting to come in, to make the place temporarily unlivable in, and to try to wipe out in a week the neglect of a year, is merely the spring-cleaners' way of welcoming the eternal miracle of Mother Earth. And that was never done in olden times without a human sacrifice. But if spring-cleaning seems rather inadequate as the charwoman's Saturnalia, the only cure for her and for all spring-cleaners is to provide other ways of celebrating the return of spring. Until we do that she will continue to worship the fetish of spring-cleaning, and the house will be more or less dirty for eleven and a half months a year.

THE INCOMPETENT DOMESTIC (1927)

The Hon. Mrs Dowdall

The Hon. Mrs Dowdall (1876–1927) was the daughter of Lord Borthwick. She wrote many novels and also books like Manners and Tone of Good Society.

'Don't take her if you can possibly get anyone else,' said the friend whom I had asked for a 'character' for a (domestic) 'wench'. I couldn't, so I did. I shall use this 'wench' whom I shall call Gladys, to illustrate why I am pessimistic about the training, either by the state or by mistresses, of those young women who say that they would be prepared to enter domestic service if they had shorter hours and could receive instruction. The elect few are found in towns or in houses where a large staff is kept. I am only speaking of the average beginners who are scrambled for by the perspiring housewives of the middle classes in their desperate fight against waste and squalor.

Gladys has explained to me that she is 'the baby of the family', and 'Dad's pet' and has never had much to do in the house, though mother is ever so particular. Dad didn't want her to work and she would never have gone into service but that she didn't get on at school.

As a friend she has all the virtues – honesty, fidelity, generosity. She 'loves washing greasy pans', she tells me, and I think she adds to her labours for the sheer enjoyment she gets from the mess she makes. Her sink is a trough of horrors in which she wallows by the hour, carolling with joy. Floating fat, tea leaves, skins, rags, a stray knife or two with the handles soaking rapidly adrift, bits of bread, hairpins, vegetables and a pudding dish which the cat has not been able to lick quite presentably enough to pass my eagle eye. Into all this Gladys, in radiant spirits, dishevelled, smutty-faced, her collar fastened with a pin, her shoes a shapeless, damp squadge, and an apron that makes me sick proceeds to plunge the breakfast dishes.

She knocks them rhythmically against the taps while she carries on an animated conversation with Edith, her understudy. There is no hurry.

Edith has laid her dustpan on the stove while she hunts through the oily waste paper, crumbs, derelict boxes, plate powder, burned ironing blankets, and broken jars for her tin of metal polish. It is discovered, after a nice chat and a cup of tea, between an open jam pot with a fly in it and a plate of leathery biscuits put on the shelf with the old bits of cheese.

If I spend my whole day at it I can get things done, more or less; a few hours absence means a total relapse. Gladys and Edith are delighted to oblige me, but neither tears nor prayers nor anger will convince them that it is not just faddiness and a waste of time to fuss so long as there is any kind of mess to eat (something tinned, preferably), chairs to sit on and, above all, a door to get out by. You see Gladys can sleep soundly and dream of blissful Bank Holidays in a room that smells like a fox's den, dressed in a flannelette nightgown which she leaves all day under the bed in two inches of dust and stands on while she does her hair with a brush that is never washed. She prepares herself for a party with a piece of livid flannel and a sponge like a dried jelly fish. So of course she thinks it unaccountable that I mind sitting among furniture that looks as if it had been out in the fog all night, when there isn't even any company coming. Not all the lectures in the world, by the state or by thoughtful mistresses, will persuade her that her leisurely smearing and messing and perpetual clearing up are not inevitable, but also more English and respectable and politically sound than labour-saving of any kind.

Good housework is largely automatic, a matter of observation and accurate movements, which is perhaps the reason why a man when he does it well, does it so much better and in less time than a correspondingly intelligent woman. He uses habit to give greater freedom to his thoughts. Only fear or pride could induce Gladys to acquire habits, for she is one of the most feminine things left on earth. Education has only scratched the surface of her mind, giving her a taste for 'getting a notion of the piano' without love of art – any art – for art's sake. A love of efficiency apart from the admiration of beholders is not yet constitutionally feminine.

The wench would not weep if I gave her notice because there are a dozen women waiting to pounce on her if she chooses to go. In earlier times fear and pride would have done something for her. Fear of disapproval and scolding, even of a good slapping, not to speak of the horrors of being sent back to her parents' wrath and the difficulty of ever earning any more wages with such a character for dirt and untidiness as she would have been given. There used to be pride, too, pride in the beauty of a house by those who helped to make it. I do not want to discourage anybody but it amuses me to think of a Board of Admirals, proposing to train a sailor who wanted no better ship than Noah's Ark, whom it was forbidden to punish,

53

who had a hundred other ships clamouring for his incompetence, and who would be well paid whatever he did, and still better if he did nothing.

'Talkback'

I am constantly receiving reminders from disgruntled mistresses that no good purpose is served by constantly harping on the delinquencies of bad employers. With my personal limitations I endeavour to follow the advice they give me, even when I have facts and figures to prove every charge I make. Recrimination gets us nowhere, however greatly we feel disposed to air our grievance. Recognising this, I have attempted to use my influence towards an amicable settlement of the points in dispute between mistress and maid.

The whole tone of Mrs Dowdall's article, on the contrary, is unfair and one-sided. It attacks one of the finest bodies of women workers in the country. Sarcasm, irony, humour, wit – call it what you like – may titillate the ears of women who take a similar short-sighted view of their responsibilities, but in the long run it simply serves as a lash to reopen old sores and prevent an even temper being displayed in a discussion of this problem.

No one will deny that there are inefficient maids, although it would seem from Mrs Dowdall's article that all modern domestics fall within this description. She cites the case of a girl who she admits is a willing worker, and from that example lays down a rule. Were I in Mrs Dowdall's place I would attempt to teach my maid better ways. Surely such a willing worker could be persuaded.

Of course this brings us to a point I have often discussed – namely the need of raising the status of the occupation so that only the best type of woman shall be attracted to it. How is this to be done? The experiments carried on in the training centres up and down the country supply the answer. Despite the criticisms of these centres undoubted success has attended the venture.

It is my great desire to see permanent training centres established, on which the Domestic Workers Union should have representation. Girls entering these centres should have six months' general training. Those desiring to specialise should serve at least another six months in the kitchen, the house, or at the table, according to their choice. During the training they could be sent out daily to gain experience. When their period of training was finished they would sit for an examination in practical and theoretical domestic science. To those who passed this successfully a certificate of proficiency would be awarded. The cost of the training centres might be largely met by making them also hostels for professional and businesswomen.

Naturally girls trained in this way would require the wages of efficiency. Surely no broadminded mistress would object to this? A trained worker could get through her work in half the time taken by the inefficient, and the loss involved in broken crockery and burnt meals would be almost entirely eliminated.

At the same time I suggest there are quite a few mistresses who themselves require training, not only in the best methods of running a home, but also in the proper way to treat maids when they get them. For instance, proper bedroom accommodation should be provided. My experience over the last two years shows me that a considerable amount of persuasion is required on this point alone.

The other day I walked into a grocer's shop in the West End of London just in time to hear a lady ask for half a pound of 'servants' butter'. She was not honest enough to ask for margarine outright. This question of the provision of good wholesome food equal in quality to that provided in the dining room is a sore point with hundreds of my members. Further, there must be some limitation of the hours of duty. Fourteen to sixteen really are too many. Maids tend to become 'slaveys'. Meal hours should not be interrupted. It is neither fair nor just. A mistress really desiring to keep her maid must consider all these points but reduced to a single sentence this means: 'She must look upon her maid as an intelligent human being, with aspirations and desires even as she has.'

The fact that a girl comes of the working class is no criterion of her ability or inability to be the mental equal of her employer. Very often, as I could prove by chapter and verse, she is the superior, yet there are still those who pine for the old bad days when employers could treat girls as they pleased and the maids dared not complain openly.

We are through with that. Today girls want to know exactly under what conditions they are required to work. They are suspicious of the attack on them in the press, because they feel something must be wrong with an occupation which requires the principle of conscription being used to get recruits.

Although anger gains the upper hand within me at times when I read of the demands of some servantless mistresses, I still think that domestic service should be one of the most attractive occupations for women. Moreover I think it is destined to reach that stage, but only so soon as we have a mutual understanding between the two sides.

Homemaking is one of the most important functions in any country. For that reason it should have a much higher status than it possesses at the moment. At one time a mother sent her daughter to service if she was no use for clerking or factory work. The stupid girl would cut a poor figure today, because modern days have brought modern ways and the need for the exercise of intelligence and ability.

Jessie Stephen
Hon. General Secretary
Domestic Workers' Union

Jessie Stephen tried to get domestic workers organised in a trade union, the domestic Workers Federation, as early as 1909. She was a member in 1919, and again in 1923, of a committee set up by the Ministry of Labour to 'enquire into the present conditions as to the supply of domestic servants'. At that time women trying to secure additional unemployment benefit were asked whether they had sought domestic work.

PUBLIC ENEMIES (1935)

'*C*'

An interesting book has been written lately demonstrating incontestably that the rat and the louse in history are between them responsible for more disasters than any human tyrants or policies, however cruel or mistaken. No wars have claimed so many victims as the lice have claimed, and in the American Civil War the soldiers who died of wounds were far outnumbered by those who died of infection carried by lice.

Strangely enough, the other insect, the bug, does not seem to carry any disease in its horrid train. Yet it is full of the unhealth of dirt and is a menace to peace throughout whole districts of our great cities. Steps have been taken to keep the plague down and it is now possible by notifying one's local public health authorities to have not merely a room disinfected for a moderate fee but to have all suspicious furniture put into a special disinfecting van until it is fit for removal to another house or return to the cleansed rooms. Occasionally the insect arrives concealed in the cracks of a piece of second-hand furniture into a perfectly clean house and establishes itself before making its unwelcome presence felt, by which time there is no saying in which part of the walls or wainscoting it has made its breeding place.

I have just been having a most instructive talk with a reconditioning slum builder in London. He tells me that after debugging the whole of one street in the West Central district of London he found that people from the other side of the street, which had not been so treated and belonged to another proprietor, carried bugs across when paying friendly calls, so that the good work was all undone. Again, one of the problems of the slum improver is to move from buggy houses which are being pulled down to newly built dwellings those inhabitants whose belongings have long been hopelessly infected.

DOMESTIC SERVICE (1937)

Margaret Cole

Margaret Cole and her husband G.D.H. Cole were leading Fabian Socialists and close friends of Beatrice and Sidney Webb. Margaret edited Beatrice Webb's diaries. She was deeply involved for many years in further education, under the old London County Council.

The problem of domestic service, which is believed to be

haunting the pillow of the Minister of Labour, has recently again found its way into the press, but in the form of more reasoned and serious discussion than the diatribes against 'the servant class' which one used to expect. Employers are beginning to be really worried, partly because of the shortage of supply, which statistically, I think, is more due to the decline in the young population in the countryside and the mining districts than to any other single cause, and partly because even those employers who pride themselves on being 'good', and in fact do what they can, are distressed by realising how far domestic service, despite its advantages of security and – in decent houses – fairly comfortable living, fails to compete in privacy, in free time, in the society of others, with the life of the factory or office girl.

Domestic service is, of course, an enormous industry, covering all manner of conditions of employment. It would be foolish to try to legislate for it as one can legislate, for example, for the mining industry. But it is not impossible to suggest experiments which might be fruitful, for example, in the direction of rationalisation. Every day in thousands of households quantities of work are done in a manner thoroughly wasteful of labour, often by persons who do not want to do it, hate doing it and only do it because it must be done somehow. Rooms are turned out, clothes are washed and patched, cooked meat 'used up', with inferior equipment, inconvenient arrangements, dear materials and the absence of solitude.

Women who want to do other work are the most irritated at the waste of time and labour involved in domestic jobs, but the irritation goes beyond them and translates itself to those who must do the domestic work and find it so difficult to make a satisfactory job of it. Individual employers cannot rationalise their employment more than a very little. But I can visualise a good deal of rationalisation being introduced by larger-scale organisation from outside. With all their complaints against the laundry, most middle-class households use this rationalised service and many employ window-cleaning companies. I can see a home-mending service which would darn and patch the weekly wash, a house-cleaning service which would clean round the house from time to time as required; I can even see a home meals service which would bring round containers of hot food selected from a day's menu for people who could not cook or did not want to.

I can see these as separate services or as a combined service which sent out domestic workers by the day or shift to do such tasks as were required of them. Presumably such an agency would be able to have some say in the conditions of work and refuse to send its staff to houses which it could not recommend. There would thus be some leverage other than the clumsily working law of supply and demand for improving the abominable conditions which still exist today in some areas.

Of course, such services, either specialised or general could not be monetarily very cheap. But saving of time and nerves pays in the long run, the services would cheapen as their scale became larger, and it is surprising what can be done in a short intensive day as compared with a long day in which some leisure is sandwiched unsystematically. Not all could afford the services; some would not care to make use of them. But I should say that they would be welcomed by enough women to make it worthwhile to experiment, say in some newly-developing estate or in an area where domestic help was for any reason particularly needed or particularly scarce.

SLAVE OR SLUT? (1970)

In October 1970, the Women's Page Editor posed a long list of questions to readers and invited their comments as well as their honest answers. The questions ranged from 'How often do you clean the oven/windows/bath and loo?', 'Do you order your household priorities by hygiene, by appearance, by what the book says, or by the standards your mother set?' Then, more emotive, were the questions 'Do you like housework or loathe it?' 'Do you think that as human beings' detritus causes a large part of the work of a house those who cause the mess, however young, should help to clean it up? or do you think it is less troublesome – or your duty – to do it all yourself?' Finally, 'Do you think making an elegant/charming/gracious home for your husband, presuming the children are grown up is a worthwhile as well as an enjoyable job?'

Replies poured in. First the angry comments:

I am bloody fed up with this type of article. Regular readers of this page get a constant barrage of nonsensical editorial opinion on 'The Housewife'. We are, apparently, little better than battery hens if 'Woman's Guardian' is to be believed, continually exploited and nearly driven out of our little minds with the daily task of living. . . . Both my husband and I think the housewife is one of the privileged classes.

Mrs Elizabeth Roberts
Saltash

. . . The questions are supposed to elicit lofty, intelligent answers from busy career women, whereas the home woman admits with a shock that if she actually admitted doing a 'stitch in time' she would be dismissed from the company of the female club.

Mrs Laura C. Porter
Neston
Wirral

We have endured this 'slave/slut' theme with regularity for years. Must the 'Woman's Guardian' encourage such triviality? Are the slave/sluts liberated? Liberate them! Educate them! Feed their minds with constructive ideas; encourage them to overcome their environment. Tell them to cease thinking of themselves as the wife of a house and be married women of dignity instead of snivelling slaves, organising the home efficiently; leaving time for the continued education of their lively minds, helping those in need, doing charitable work. Charity? But that is what began it all.

Mrs Ailsa C. Maude
Liverpool

Then there were the readers who admitted to guilt feelings:

'I am basically lazy and only do the work because of a guilt feeling that the place should look a great deal better than it does most of the time.'
'I would dearly love to provide my husband with a beautiful

well-run home but shed tears over my inability to do so. . . . I think if he ever noticed anything in the way of cleaning or polishing that I did and commented upon it I should be happier about doing it more often.'

The guilty were answered by other readers:

'I do wish that women would not feel so guilty about the housework they do not do or want to do and realise how short life is, and if they do not make an effort to enrich their lives no one else will.'

'Are we not utterly *mad* to spend so many hours physically exhausting ourselves? Life is so short, so precious, and there is so much music to listen to, so many books to read, so much conversation to enjoy.'

One of the 'surprise' responses was from the head of a college of education who had to leave her job, on the verge of a breakdown, and found herself tackling housework for the first time at the age of 46:

'My own perpetual temptation is to go on doing some housework when in my real, moral opinion I ought to be doing some writing, precisely because housework demands nothing of my higher abilities. Tradition sees to it that I am tempted to feel virtuous when I have cleaned the floor and wicked if I sit at my desk with the floor dirty. However, I know that though dirt is not nice, my writing, even if not that of a genius, is far more use to the world than having a clean floor. I think this business of housework as a temptation – as an excuse for not buckling down to more demanding work – is a point worth mentioning.'

Husbandly attitudes came in for a fair amount of resentment:

'My husband moans about the unsatisfactory nature of his job (teaching in a tough secondary modern school which requires him to be more a prison warder than a teacher). I can sympathise but he doesn't consider that I find my present position a damn sight less satisfactory and am likely to find it unsatisfactory for a fairly long time to come, whereas he is free to find another job. We have similar backgrounds, working-class family, grammar school, university, but I don't feel we have equal opportunity to follow our own interests.'

'Rather than put up with attempts at emotional blackmail by my husband – he's tired, muddle upsets him, moping about, ostentatiously tidying up, suggestions that perhaps he might find time to sweep the stairs, and other remarks designed to prod me into fresh activity – rather than all that I'll do what's really necessary. Anything for a quiet life, but I'd like to get in touch with the Women's Lib movement.'

'Most of us are so conditioned by the arrogant male attitude that we feel intellectually, morally, physically and sexually inferior to them. So nobody made us take the job? Perhaps not. But did anybody ever take the trouble to tell you what was involved? Has any man said to you, you may change your job if it doesn't suit you? Not likely. This privilege seems reserved for the other sex.'

Some husbands, though, were truly sharers:

Mrs Gabrielle P. of Manchester: 'If my husband takes time off he manages the home just as efficiently as I do. What we both resent is that society forces him to nurture his ambition as it compels me to stifle mine. We both want to be with our children in their early years; we both want careers, but he is deprived of one joy while I am deprived of another.'

Mrs Valerie P. of Cheshire says that she and her husband shared all housework, having a thorough clean every Thursday. While he cleaned upstairs, she cleaned downstairs. As upstairs entailed less work he also did the garden. Cooking was also divided between them. She made soups, stews and casseroles and he did the more precise cooking such as grilling and boiling. 'I must admit, however, that he follows this to its logical conclusion and refuses to spend time in such useless exercises as opening doors for me, helping off with my coat and so on. I think I am getting a better bargain than most women.'

In very many *Guardian* readers homes, regular housework schedules of the old type had been abandoned. Few polished silver, still fewer turned mattresses; few cleaned windows regularly. (One single woman reported that she often cleaned a window in the middle of the night because it caught her eye when she was on her way to the loo.) One reader issued an awful warning against too much polishing furniture which, she said, 'eventually chokes the wood. It is hidden under a layer of polish, dust, polish, dust, until at last when you lay a finger on it it retains the mark.'

A Preston reader said that after nearly twenty years of marriage in the belief that if the place looks tidy it looks clean, she made the discovery that one can do an astounding amount in 30 minutes. 'After I've done my absolute basic I give the house a little treat if I feel so inclined. I polished all the living room furniture one day and another took the cobweb brush round the whole house before the pinger said, 'Time's up'.

There were some readers who disliked the idea of engaging paid domestic help. 'It is our home, and though just now and again when I am desperate I would like to escape from it, the things in it are ours, and I would not wish them to be cared for always by others.'

A reader who had had a mother who was a probation officer and didn't enjoy housework or child-minding, declared that she had never 'liked the idea of paying incompetent dullards to do any of the jobs I felt I could do better. We had enough of them at home. In fact part of me has become such a prig that I would as soon pay someone to sleep with my husband as to clean our house!' But she had perfected a technique, learned from an American foster mother a variety of 'professional' methods and short cuts:

'I don't mend sheets – when they tear I rip them up for dusters. I don't sweep under the beds until the moths pop out. I use old tights to dust the mirrors upstairs. I never sew on buttons until my husband reaches for the needle and thread. He has now carted off needle and thread to sew his buttons on at work. He hasn't taken his pyjamas in yet.'

Final Awful Warning: 'An old friend's Aunt Minnie, when urged not to wash up before going to bed said, 'But a burglar might get in during the night and see the pots on the sink.'

5   Hard Times

Perhaps it is good to be reminded that there was a Miners' Strike in 1925 (and indeed a brief General Strike) and that *Manchester Guardian* readers reacted much as they did to the Miners' Strike of 1985. And that there were three million unemployed in the early 1930s, and no Welfare State to lessen the hardships of life on the dole. And to be reminded, too, that hard times are not always the result of national economic stringency.

THE WORKING-CLASS WOMAN: HER SCRAPS OF LEISURE

Leonora Eyles

Leonora Eyles (1889-1960) was a novelist and feminist. Her non-fiction books included Women's Problems of Today, Feeding the Family *and* Careers for Women.

A working-class woman, wife of a bricklayer, once said to me 'In all my married life I've never had a day off except for confinements, and then I did get a chance of feeling a lady for a week at a time'. Another one told me that she had been to Margate for four days. 'But I didn't enjoy it. Dad borrowed the money out of a loan club and I couldn't rest, thinking I was having a holiday without paying for it.' The same woman, a very intelligent woman of 50, a Londoner, saw my grate full of pine cones and thought they were a new sort of asbestos. She had never, except for this Margate visit, been out of London in her life, and had never seen pine trees, although here we are not 20 miles from wonderful pine woods.

Sunday afternoon, when the weekly orgy of cooking is finished, is the working-class woman's rest day. Her husband goes to sleep on the kitchen or parlour couch; she lies down on the bed usually with a baby beside her, while the other children play in the street or go to Sunday School. I wish some public-spirited girls with time on their hands would start Sunday afternoon play centres in working class districts to give mothers a real rest. For this Sunday afternoon sleep many of them almost live all the week. And many of them have said to me that one of the advantages of breast-feeding a baby is that 'you do have to sit down for twenty minutes then, and you can pick up a paper or a book sometimes'.

The home-keeping working-class woman sometimes gets a visit to the cinema – and falls asleep as soon as she gets there. If you go in the afternoons you will see row after row of women sitting with several tinies under school age, and usually a baby on their laps, nodding to sleep in the warmth and the soft light and music. The older children are kept quiet by the thought of the attendant and his uniform who will 'come and fetch them' if they make a noise. The baby is lulled by his mother's arms. So the mother sleeps.

Some of them go to mothers' meetings once a week, but these are losing in favour of Co-operative guilds and political women's sections which are more in touch with their lives and needs than the old-fashioned religious meetings. The political woman gets out more than any other woman – she goes to her meetings and she goes canvassing from door to door during elections, often trailing a little family with her as she does it.

Some of them buy holidays on the instalment system, paying every week into a club from the week they return from holiday to the next. But the mother gets little rest even then. The lodgings a working-class family can afford are uniformly bad; one bathroom to twenty rooms is a pretty fair average, with bad cooking and overcrowded bedrooms, so that they usually say 'Well, it's nice to go away but it's grand to get back home again'.

But it is to the factory or other worker that one's sympathies most turn. She has to rush around the home in the morning, doing all she can to set things to rights and make a meal ready for the others before she leaves. She shops during her dinner hour, and she comes home in the evening to more housework. I have seen women being addressed by trade union officials at

65

a meeting at the factory gates after work and dropping asleep with sheer weariness as they listened. A fair average day for a factory worker is this: up at six to get son off to work. (The husband has had no work for two years, which explains why the mother has had to turn out.) Clean the kitchen; wash six shirts and some house linen; put ready a stew and a pudding for the father to cook; go to work at eight. Return at six; get tea for the family; shop; wash up; bath the children and attend to their heads which have become dirty through neglect; mend stockings; iron three of the shirts and some of the other clothes wanted for next day; go out and buy fried fish for supper, when there comes ten minutes gossip in the fried fish shop with neighbours; clean the gas stove which the husband has left very dirty by letting food boil over; twelve o'clock bed – her sleep disturbed three times by the baby.

And here is the day of a woman of 45 who cleans offices and whose husband has been out of work for a year: get up and put his breakfast and her daughter's ready at half-past-six. Seven o'clock, at the office where she keeps clean four rooms and six flights of stairs. Ten o'clock – at a flat where she keeps house for an elderly invalid and his son, doing all their shopping and cooking and cleaning for 12s. a week, the office cleaning bringing in 30s. Two o'clock – home and cook dinner; housework and mending for the old man, who pays extra for this. Three days a week she goes to clean up for two business girls who have a little flat and leave the key with her. Five o'clock, at the office again until eight-thirty. Home and do any jobs left undone – washing up, cleaning, mending. Then bed at about eleven. She never goes to 'the pictures' and on Sundays, sometimes, she goes to sleep. Yet she is so cheerful that she took it as a proof of the goodness of God when I asked her to come three afternoons one week to help with removing. She asked 2s. 6d. an afternoon and because I gave her 12s. 6d. for the three afternoons she went home and made me an enormous cake to get out of my debt.

THE MINERS' WIVES (1926)

'L'

Now that the tragedy of the coal mining industry seems to be ending, may I, as a woman reader, express on this page devoted to the interests of women, the admiration which is universally felt for the wives of the miners? All through these months of dispute and uncertainty they have had the largest part to bear. They have taken no part in the politics of the crisis, and anything there may have been in it of excitement or exultation has passed them by. Their task has been to keep their homes on means growing daily more straitened and precarious. Anyone who has recently visited a colliery district knows how immense and heartrending this task has proved. In all the denials of starvation among the miners' families it could never be suggested that shortage of boots, clothes and household linen, together with hunger that would seem very like starvation to most of us, have not been terribly widespread. The sight of the pinched and half-clad children in many mining villages is proof of that, even without the statistics supplied by school teachers and local authorities, and a knowledge of the mentality of the working-class mother makes one realise that however poorly fed and clothed her children are, she herself is in a much worse plight. All types of political opinion have expressed approval of the orderly way in which the men have met this crisis, and it is difficult, surely, to overestimate how much it is due to the brave endurance of their women. Yours etc.

LIVING ON THE DOLE: ONE OF THE THREE MILLION (1933)

'M.K.'

Some people think that the unemployment pay can be made up to a reasonable income by aid from the Public Assistance Committee, or they will say that the unemployed have relatives to help them or other resources of some kind. While it is true that the poor help the poor to a great extent, so many of them are in the same plight nowadays that not much assistance can be obtained in this direction, and the operation of the means test has cut out any casual addition to the total income.

For the benefit of these people and because those more charitably inclined may like to know how it is possible to manage on the 'dole' (and 'manage' is the right word), I have ascertained the exact budget of a family of my acquaintance, showing how every penny of their income is accounted for. The family, consisting of man, wife and two children, 7 and 5 years of age, receive a total income from the unemployment insurance of 28s. 6d. per week. This is the actual expenditure of the household every week, the menu being varied as far as the narrow limits of the money allowed for food will permit:

	s.	d.
Rent and rates, three-bedroomed controlled house	12	6
Gas, used for lighting kitchen and scullery only	1	0
Coal and coke, one bag each	2	11
Wireless, batteries etc.		6
Candles, matches, soap etc.		6
Total	17s.	5d.

Eleven shillings is thus left for food, and is expended as follows (breakfast and tea consist each day of toast and margarine):

	s.	d.
Bread (10 2 lb. loaves at 3½d. each)	2	11
Milk 1½ pints each at 3d. a quart	2	7½
Tea 1 lb. at 10d. a pound		10
Sugar 2 lbs. at 2¼d. a pound		4½
Margarine 1½ lb. at 4d. a pound		6
Total	7s.	3d.

Dinners (3s. 6d. available)

Monday: Baked beans on toast, 1 lb. at 5d.			5
Tuesday: tin of herrings			4
Wednesday: hotpot, ½ lb. steak at 1s., 2½ lb. potatoes at 5 lb. for 4d.			8
Thursday: soup, ½ lb. steak at 1s., 2½ lbs. potatoes			8
Friday and Saturday: 1 lb. beef sausages at 8d. 5 lb. potatoes		1	0
Sunday: hotpot as above			8
	Total	3s.	9d.

It will be noticed that the diet is scanty and monotonous, that the only allowance for entertainment is the wireless, that clothes, insurance doctors' bills and other necessities are totally unprovided for. The husband has only been out of work for fifteen months, so the clothes problem is not yet acute, the children having been provided with shoes from a school fund. The wife suffers almost as much from the curse of compulsory idleness as the husband. She has no materials for baking, sewing or decorating the house. Cleaning materials must be used with the utmost care and, in short, it is as difficult for her to keep her courage under such circumstances as it is for the man to maintain his confidence in his own skill through long periods of worklessness.

This particular couple present an average case of the ups and downs of working-class married life since the War. They have been married eight years, and in that period they have had, including the present, three spells of unemployment. The first, coming shortly after they were married, was of eighteen months duration but was not too bad, said the wife, as she obtained work at her own trade as a boxmaker and the means test was not then in operation. The second, a period of ten months, was terrible. There were then the two children to be considered, and as she was not used to managing on such a limited income they ran into debt, not seriously, but enough to prove a hindrance when the husband again found work. Now she is determined to keep straight but it is a heartbreaking task. Renewals are altogether out of the question, and everything must be kept down to the barest minimum; illness or any other probable emergency would be a dire calamity. According to Mr Chamberlain, these people have little better to expect for another 10 years, as their best working years must be dissipated in just 'passing the time'. They can anticipate a future almost as devoid of hope, for under such straitened circumstances, however thriftily inclined, they can make no provision for the usual decline of earning power in old age.

ENOUGH TO EAT: THE COMMITTEE AGAINST MALNUTRITION

Catherine Carswell

Catherine Carswell was a novelist and journalist. A friend of D.H. Lawrence, exchanged the manuscript of her novel Open the Door *with his* Women in Love. *Wrote frequently for the* Guardian Women's Page *in the 1930s.*

Before the present industrial depression there was a most welcome rise in the standard of health throughout the community in England. This was brought about in two ways – the authorities were alarmed by the fact that during the war only one man in three was found upon examination to come up to the low standard of health and physique then required for foreign service. At the same time cheaper and far more varied foodstuffs were placed within the reach of the working population. Anybody who has kept an eye upon the street markets of London and on the cheaper food shops has marvelled at the prodigal choice of fruit and vegetables and other wholesome foods that are offered at wonderfully low prices.

But it has more and more become a case of starving amidst plenty. For, with so many unemployed, those upon the dole, besides many who are employed but earning small money, find themselves unable to take advantage of either variety or low prices. Recent research presents us once more with serious malnutrition and with a shocking discrepancy between the diet and consequently the health, of middle-class persons and the working population. Recently the Nutrition Committee of the British Medical Association went into the matter and reported that the minimum costs of diet required to maintain health and capacity were: adult man 5s. 10½d., adult woman 4s. 11d., child 2s. 8d. to 5s. 10½d. according to age.

Now a few people have got together – medical men, scientists, social workers and interested individuals of different callings – and under the general title of the Committee Against Malnutrition are setting themselves to look into the matter all over the country and to keep the question as much as possible in the public eye.

While recognising that nutrition standards can be maintained and improved only by an increase of wages and relief or a transformation of the financial system, the Committee does not undertake to initiate such a campaign, but only to collect carefully authenticated facts and make them public. It has been ascertained, among other things, that boys of 15 in four well-known public schools are getting about half as much food again – and in a more nutritious form – as boys of the same age in South London districts, the average weights showing a discrepancy of 15 lbs. to 20 lb. in favour of the middle-class boys.

What is true of boys and of men is truer of women and children. Women of all ages, especially expectant and nursing mothers stand in special need of not merely ample but correct food and it is precisely the correct foods that they find it most difficult to afford within the family budget. As often as not the mother keeps herself short of proper nourishment in her efforts to provide the maximum for her menfolk and growing children. But by doing so the babies suffer as well as the mothers and while anaemia is a condition that has almost disappeared among women of the middle and upper classes, it is still rife among the working women and their babies and children. Among the illnesses directly resulting from malnutrition are tuberculosis, diarrhoea, vomiting, bronchitis, throat trouble and general weakness.

71

Three London districts and twelve industrial cities have been examined by the Committee Against Malnutrition and the recent increase they have found in the diseases mentioned is striking. In particular there has been an increase in tuberculosis in Sheffield and other badly hit areas. Prevention here is not merely better than cure, it is considerably cheaper.

In one Scottish town it was discovered that 'most of the women complained of few, if any, symptoms of ill-health, but this was due to the fact that they had become accustomed to living subnormal lives and had really forgotten the joy of good health. Yet in a country district where a farmer was anxious to provide delicate schoolchildren with free milk he was informed that by so doing he would render himself liable to imprisonment. Under the new Milk Marketing Board's regulations he can pour away his surplus milk, or he can sell it at 6d. a gallon to be made into luxury items of synthetic ivory, but he cannot let those who need it most have it for nothing or for what they could afford. Surely such things want looking into?

THE BAD SPELL (1962)

Betty Thorne

Betty Thorne's first contribution to the Women's Page was a 'letter to the editor' which so impressed the editor that she asked Mrs Thorne to follow it up with an article. After that articles, always hand-written on pages from a school exercise book, arrived quite often, describing life in a two-up-and-two-down back-to-back house, with husband and six children.

We have just come out of a 'bad spell' or what they call 'a struggle', but what the Chancellor of the Exchequer calls a 'financial crisis'. You must understand that we have never been one of those well-adjusted families who make their budget and then quite happily exist within it. Unfortunately I can 'tell the difference' and I give my children butter. I'll go one week-end and buy the big lad a pair of 'good' shoes and at the next week-end it will have to be a pair of plastic sandals for the little lass. Then it will be the football match money –

1s. to go in, 8d. bus fare, 4d. programme each and 7d. for the cheapest lolly sold on the ground. Multiply by three and it's 7s. 9d., when they all really do need to get their hair cut.

Like other families in our circumstances we 'pay at the week-end'. Earlier on, other money troubles have arisen and we have obtained credit from the local shops – what the 'haves' call an account, but we call running up a bill. This has very definite drawbacks, for you never seem to get back to paying for what you have when you have it. It is impossible to go to the cut-price shops because all your ready cash has gone paying off last week's bill and it is amazing the way those few extravagances, cream buns all round or trying the new line in meat pies, can zoom the bill up at the week-end.

Well there comes a time when you know that to ask for any more credit is 'sticky'. In this position my husband lost several shifts' work and it was his week-ends off which meant no double-time shifts. Then it started. The kids had to go back to school, and because they had kicked shoes, sandals and sneakers out during the holidays I had to send them in 4s. 6d. slippers. The headmaster's policy is to say a few words to the child for the parents' benefit so that the child gets shoes. To forestall the few words I spoke to the head, saying I would have them in shoes as soon as possible. In answer I was made an offer of free dinners. I suppose I should have been grateful, but I felt angry. Then the final notice for payment of the rates in the form of a summons due in 14 days. Previously we have always cut everything else and managed to pay in that period, but not this time. Two gentlemen arrived one morning with briefcases and told us we had incurred court costs. They looked round with practised eye. 'Is your television set on rental?' It is. 'Well, there's not really anything here. . . . Another fortnight then, but make certain it is in by then or else. . . .'

Actually, this was good news. Another fortnight and we could manage.

It did not end there. An employee of the Electricity Board arrived to disconnect the supply. I could not face candles and cooking on the fire so I 'refused access'. This is serious. He said that in the afternoon they would be down to take the pavement up and disconnect. It would then cost about £14 to

73

replace and all the neighbours would know, or a joiner, policeman and officials would make an entry and I would have their wages to pay.

By that time I was a nervous wreck. I went down to the accounts office and asked for more time to pay, and when I was given this the relief was immense. A lot of emphasis was laid on what the neighbours would think, in pressing for payment. Well I know what they would think and I am fast reaching the point where I am not bothered.

While I was waiting to see the official at the Electricity Board an old lady was having her interview before me. Actually the place was full. I tried not to listen, but in the semi-privacy of the room that was impossible. She was about 5s. short of the full amount for her account and she asked for time until Thursday when she drew her old age pension, because she did not want 'anybody coming to the back door'. This would really have upset her.

Perhaps I am realising now what one fatherly official told me. 'You cannot go on bashing your head against a brick wall indefinitely'.

Then again, Mr Micawber knew the only reasonable thing to do but he could not live like that. Is it just responsibility I lack?

OUT OF THE SLOUGH (1965)

Rose Kosmyryk

Rose Kosmyryk is a courageous Lancashire woman who married a Pole whose health was never good, so that she has had to make herself largely responsible for the further education of her daughters. She was a frequent contributor in the 1960s.

Why dirty a fifth dinner plate when sharing out a quarter of liver? Why boil a fifth egg if it will go round the whole family tomorrow in pancakes or a cake? How many mothers have not found, at some stage or other of bringing up a family, their own proper nourishment whittled away by rising cost of living?

I never dreamed I was letting myself in for such a long siege, however, after Father died. The house had been reduced to a shambles, the garden a wilderness, after our day and night preoccupation during the last few months of his illness. We were all exhausted.

In a small house nothing is hidden. Many times the children must have feared for Grandad's, even my own, safety on the stairs. Many were the days when my husband felt unable to go to work, with resultant loss of earnings. We were drained, like the house. Carpets, bedding, furniture, had all gone west without hope of replacement until the most modest of funerals had been paid for.

Financially we were in a desperate state. I had to earn some money, yet husband and children needed me at home until we had regained some sense of security and emotional stability.

I had always expected to return to nursing, once the children were well settled at school, in order to relieve my husband of the whole financial burden. Anxiety about his own health and dread of the future never left him. I hoped to convince him that he was good for years yet, while I took over as inconspicuously as possible.

My first tentative efforts towards part-time nursing came to nothing. I felt that I never wanted to see a sick person again. Conditions and earnings were no help in overcoming my revulsion against the very smell of hospital. Illness during the winter made me realise that any job I undertook would have to make allowances for family health, and I was already aware of the illusion of part-time work – much effort for little financial return.

In the end I learnt to juggle with intermittent jobs which allowed some choice of timing according to home commitments. Difficult though it was we managed to hold our own in spite of constant ill health, increased rent, fares, fuel and above all the rising cost of food and clothes for growing children. Without Father's pension as a balancer of overheads my earnings never managed to get us past the hand-to-mouth level. It was always a question of judging how empty was the coal cellar against how near was the electric account's final warning. Shoe repairs meant a milk bill left. Once behind, it means going without to get level. Food was our only 'never never'.

The hardest thing of all, though, was to feel oneself thought feckless because family life and education were put before material show. Only the immense courage and determination my mother had shown for our education in the 1920s and the support of my many wonderful friends, helped me to plod through the 1950s to the 1960s.

Yet where is progress when a first generation gets through grammar school on bread and jam, and the second does it on the more elaborate version, toast and marmalade? Dog's bones and cow cabbage à la Trude Schulz are fine for nutrition, but they don't do much for morale. Second-hand uniforms cannot hamper first class brains . . . lack of protein and privacy can.

Nevertheless we were making headway when all my jobs faded out. A final crisis startled me into asking for help. I had to admit defeat in spite of all our efforts. In this Welfare State I found that there is no help for a family whose father is working, however reduced his earnings and disproportionate his stoppages and fares. A mother whose family depended for bare necessities on her earnings could no more afford to be ill than her mother could before the days of the National Health Service. This made me so angry I began to see the purpose of this long siege of poverty if I could learn to look back at it objectively then use the experience on behalf of people less articulate. The publication of the Younghusband Report gave me the idea that I might be able to use my qualifications and experience in a wider world than hospital if I could get appropriate training. Providence took me to a local day training college to enquire what went on there and what was my academic status . . . if I had any at all.

The opportunity of taking a three-year course of training to be a teacher came as a completely new idea, and one that took some getting used to, when thinking of the initial hurdles. The eventual advantages to a family of our nature became obvious if we could survive the three years training. Cold-water common sense and pangs of conscience about the shortage of nurses and midwives, and wastage of my training when my earnings were required immediately placed me in a cruel dilemma. I felt that I ought to be nursing and earning.

The understanding kindness and practical help I received

from the training college restored my confidence in my ability to cope when I realised that background support and guidance were there if needed. I came to see that the health and cheerfulness of the whole family depended on my writing off my 18 years of nursing as a stint not of my own choosing.

Now I could recognise in myself the eternal student, the enthusiast for learning, a natural enquirer after the truth. Here was a wonderful opportunity for further education and a new career, in which the girls and I would provide mutual support for one another while I learnt how to give other children the good start my own had benefited from in their infant and junior schools.

But I have not forgotten the darker days, and I hope my family will understand and forgive my referring to them now. We who are lucky must not forget those who through no fault of their own have not even their most basic needs.

6 The Way We Lived Then

Few, if any, women readers of the *Manchester Guardian* in the 1920s and 1930s told its Women's Page about the way they lived. Other people, professional writers like Elyn Walshe, told the story for them, as in the touching 'Life of a Lady'.

It was very different in the 1960s. Readers like Betty Thorne, wife of a Sheffield steel worker, told their own stories vividly, often unforgettably. Betty Jerman's 'Like Sardines in Suburbia' made such an impact that it led to the formation of the National Housewives Register (see p. 81).

THE LIFE OF A LADY (1933)

Elyn Walshe

Last week there died two ladies who for more than forty years had been working in offices. They were unknown to each other although they had led the same sort of life. This life was one of monotonous toil, with rare and unsatisfactory holidays, but in each case it is said that their one desire was to keep their jobs to the end – which they did.

When they were young we may hope that they had a good time at home with brothers and sisters and friends, and enjoyed all the amusements and recreations which young people, even if badly off, can enjoy together. But they had to do something to earn their living and already, in the early 1890s, it was perceived that not every young woman with a fair education can teach. In fact it was already known that unless a young woman wants to teach or nurse she had far better leave these occupations alone. Already there were a great many young women in offices and it was still an advantage for that calling to be not pretty and a 'lady'. Professional men and merchants seldom employed more than one girl, and they disliked the thought of that girl attracting to herself the attention of the male staff. And a 'lady', it was considered, would be more trustworthy and conscientious than other types of girls.

Both these young women found posts in the City of London and started out in life to do shorthand and typing for nine hours a day for 25s. a week, on which stipend they lived for several years. It was then possible to find, in the inner suburbs, a bed-sitting room for 5s. or 6s. a week, and they lunched on tea and buns. Their other meals were equally inadequate, unless some friend invited them to a meal on Sunday.

In those days there were not, even in the large business houses, the sports clubs, operatic societies and other social amenities which are now so general. The recreations open to these young women included tennis in the parks, books from the free library, bands in the parks, free, or almost free, lectures and outings to such places as Kew and Richmond Park on Saturday afternoons or Sundays. From all these they were cut off by the unfortunate circumstance that they were 'ladies' and, therefore, could not find suitable companions to play tennis or go for walks, or attend public places. A 'lady' could not walk alone in the evenings, and she could not possibly go to the theatre alone even for a matinée. There were no other 'ladies' in their offices and the men were not 'public school' and therefore any friendliness they might show must be severely snubbed. It was not so much the idea of being ashamed if they should by an almost impossible chance encounter their uncle the Canon, or their cousin the Admiral in such unsuitable company. It was their own ingrained feeling that they were entitled to the same company and consideration as their sheltered young kinsfolk and if they could not have it they would have no other.

About ten years after these women came to London there were started several residential clubs for such people as they, where a hundred or more professional women would live together and share amenities with which they could not hope to supply themselves on their salaries. Both these women went to live at such clubs, but they had never learnt to 'mix' and they could not do so now. After ten or fifteen years they were hardly known by sight to the other members. They spent their evenings either in their rooms or in the washing or ironing room or, very rarely, sitting by the fire in one of the public drawing rooms. They condemned the energy shown by the other residents. Some were out every evening and some were downright noisy. Either these members were not 'ladies' or (still worse, if possible) they were 'fast'.

Neither of these ladies ever had more than a fortnight's holiday in the year and they either stayed with a sister-in-law or took her riotous children to the seaside, or spent fourteen sober days with an aged aunt or uncle. They never went abroad, because they never found the friend who was able and willing to go with them at the right time. They were before the days of pension or endowment funds and had to try, on a salary which in forty years mounted to some four or five pounds a week to provide for old age, in case it came. They hoped it would not, for they could never hope to provide for it.

During the war they took responsibilities and did work which had previously been done by men, and in the evenings they washed up at canteens and hospitals. When the war was over they reverted to their former status in the office, and even then worried themselves terribly over the thought that it might be their duty to resign and make way for an ex-serviceman.

It was after the war that they were both overcome by that craving, known to every woman at some time, for a little home of their own, and just at that time several societies were formed to cut up big houses into tiny flats for women. They settled down in two such flats and in those flats they lived exactly the same life as they had lived since they were twenty. They never entertained or went out in the evening; they never were free to stay in bed in the morning, or have their breakfast in bed; they had no friends or companions. They took no interest in public affairs so far as it is known.

The ladies died, still in harness, ladies to the last, but never once, in forty years, human beings. They felt it was impossible for them to be both and they chose to be ladies.

SQUEEZED IN LIKE SARDINES IN SUBURBIA (1960)

Betty Jerman

Betty Jerman was a member of the London staff of the Guardian *when it had only a small Fleet Street office. She contributed many articles to the Women's Page, particularly on children's needs and holiday diversions. This article was the spark for the formation of the National Housewives Register (see p. 225). In 1981 she wrote the history of NHR, 'The Lively-minded Women' and is one of the organisation's trustees.*

The decision was for a new house i.,e. post-war not pre-war. The vision was architect designed, detached, in a large garden. The reality was semi-detached, designed by a speculative builder and a garden smaller than my mother's lawn. Our house stands in a short road. The owner of a large garden with a lot of frontage easily sold the plots on which three bungalows were built. Beyond these a stretch of wooded garden was left. From the road it dipped sharply into a valley and then rose as sharply to the back gardens of other houses. It was such difficult land that many builders turned it down but an enterprising firm got to work with mechanical equipment and managed to squeeze in six semi-detached houses. One of the firm admitted it would have been nicer to build four, but they only just cleared a profit as it was.

So we have the advantage of an already settled area with the shops within easy walking distance, a private nursery class round the corner, schools, churches, pubs, doctors, a hospital and other necessities.

The house has more in it than we could have hoped for if we had built it ourselves. . . . We have full central heating . . . cupboards everywhere . . . ample floor and wall tiling where needed. The whole house is designed for minimum housework and minimum maintenance. Where then are the flaws?

First the garden. It is about as private as a field. If we replaced the open fences with solid fencing it would block out the sun and light from half the garden.

Then the noise. Our living room is on the attached side. The

81

next-door living room is on the other side of the wall and they have an immensely powerful television set. One evening I asked my husband to turn down our radio. It was not even on! I was driven to write a note asking if the television could be turned down. The effect was odd. The entire family affected not to see us and the son, about eight, literally stopped dead in his tracks and retreated at speed if he saw me walking along the road. This behaviour stopped after a couple of weeks and now we just put up with the noise.

One hot night last summer, around 10.45, the man who sold his garden for development and who still lived in the large house could stand no longer the bellow of rock 'n' roll coming from the open window of one of the bungalows. He did not swear, but he shouted things like 'You selfish lot' at the top of his voice. People heard him from streets away. It was the big topic of conversation next day, but not with the occupants of the bungalow. Finally he telephoned them. He has moved. I do not blame him.

Acceptance of the third flaw seems a dreary prospect. Whatever happens to people when they retire to the outer suburbs to raise families? Were they always like this? By comparison the inner suburbs, now with the exception of small fashionable pockets, largely decaying houses or blocks of flats, seem to bubble with vitality. The setting is attractive enough, with open fields and forest and a few large old houses with sufficient land to lend for local fetes. There is a farm so that our children can see real cows. . . . The prospect is pleasing, especially if you have only to see it at weekends and evenings, but I have to stay here all day too, and the whole thing falls down on two counts – food and thought. Asking in the grocer's for Patna rice I was told 'We only sell rice', and I hear women order 'half a pound of "cheese" '. Maybe the hailed post-war revival in English cooking has been somewhat exaggerated.

And does no-one read? There is no proper bookshop. I can get a well-reviewed book from the public library almost at once. And it is a waste of time starting to discuss some writer's viewpoint on an interesting topic. Unless he or she has appreared on television no-one will have heard of them or their ideas. There are exceptions, of course, and they tend to be women who regret they were never fully trained and educated for a profession.

It is not lack of money that causes the stagnation. Some local households have got to the stage of a second car and a private school for the children is the norm. True the argument does not apply that a child can benefit as much from a fine new state secondary school as from a primary school since the primary school looks like one of the first ever built, but I am not convinced that sending children to private schools is entirely based on getting them a better education. This is 'keeping up with the Joneses' country.

No, this example of suburbia is an incredibly dull place to live in and I blame the women. They stay here all day. They set the tone. Many of them look back with regret to the days when they worked in an office. Their work kept them alert. Home and child-minding can have a blunting effect on a woman's mind. But only she can sharpen it. If only once in this suburb I could go to a house where a dinner would be served comparable to one an unmarried girl friend would 'throw together' after a day at the office and hear such conversation across the table, then I would think there was hope.

The fresh air, the comparatively open country make this a good place to bring up children. But I can't help wondering what effect the mental atmosphere will have on our children.

LIFE IN OUR STREET (1960)

Betty Thorne

John, my eldest boy, aged eight, has just burst in the back door with 'Can I go to the pictures tonight, Mam?'

'Yes, if you don't go this afternoon.'

'Aw mam –'

'You're not going to the pictures twice in one day and then while you are at home wanting to watch television all the time.'

'O.K.,' says John, knowing there really wasn't much hope but it was worth a try.

I have four children younger than John. We live in a pretty dismal part of Sheffield in a two-up, two-down house that opens at the back into a communal yard. I left grammar school when I was 15½ years old. I left because I wanted to and now would not change my decision though I want my children to have all the education they can get. My husband is a steelworker in a local factory where he works too hard in excessive heat.

With five children and a small house, bed space is a problem. Our family, as usual, is unusual because we have a two-tiered bunk bed. With the children being so young we can accommodate the four boys in the front bedroom which is the largest, two in the bunks, one in a single bed, and the youngest boy in a cot. Soon we shall have to get two more bunks. The baby girl sleeps in the small back bedroom in a cot, with myself and my husband sharing a double bed.

It was quite a shock to be informed in a fatherly fashion by a minor official at the local health department that we didn't qualify for overcrowding yet as our living room was a possible bedroom. Most parents would just not think of giving up the front bedroom as it is the main one and so automatically theirs.

The usual way to save space is to sleep the children in double beds. In our early married days we had a room in a house where there was a family of five. The house had four rooms. The parents and two young children slept in a double bed and a single in the front room. The boy, aged about 17, slept in the kitchen-cum-living room. We had the back bedroom. The front room downstairs was, of course, not used.

Now that our children are growing out of infancy they are entering broader worlds of school and the street and outside influences are becoming more and more important to us and I am forced into an awareness of the pattern of family behaviour around me.

The wife seems to be the dominant figure of the family. She is content in reality though forever grumbling about 'him', his laziness, his ineptness, and his peculiarities – but never that the housekeeping is insufficient or any mention of personal relationships. She is content to sink herself into 'keeping things nice'. This is the ideal to which she utterly devotes herself. Anyone who doesn't is looked upon as 'different'. A constant changing of detergents to find out which gives the whitest wash, really hard work and time given to the front of the house so that everything gleams, and an unceasing watchfulness of her part of the yard and belongings against others; these are some of the ways with which this devotion is shown.

The husband is an ornament or a nuisance alternately. It is the done thing for him to dry the pots, the done thing to change the baby occasionally, to take the children for a walk, also to go for a drink, a day's fishing, or just out. The children have to fit in. They are important because they represent an unknown factor which has to be controlled. They are urged to behave nicely, taught to speak 'proper', to carry a handkerchief, not to answer back. 'A good hiding' is the answer to revolt.

Husband, wife and children together form a family that represents a pleasing picture, clean and shining, polite but friendly towards each other. But what do they really know of each other and each other's needs?

The wife has a social life of her own but rather a limited one, composed mainly of visits to all kinds of relations, and, of course, chats with the neighbours. Conversation is usually restricted to the kiddies, the house, and 'Did you hear about Mrs Brown down the street?'. Husband and wife never seem to have a chance to get to know each other beyond handing over the housekeeping money with perhaps a box of chocolates and, on her part, seeing that he has a clean shirt when he wants to go out.

When the husband comes home from work, commercial television is a great standby, for the children as well. It really is a marvellous soporific, as we have found out. This makes conversation unnecessary at home but in the pub or club it abounds, with the all-absorbing topics of football, fishing etc. The children, when they are not at home watching television, are usually out playing in the street, where the games now sound like versions of Robin Hood, The Lone Ranger, even to the extent of 'Well, we will have two Lone Rangers, then'. Even the little ones don't play at house any more but are generally Indians.

This pattern doesn't seem to bring any real benefits to our family. I enjoy my children and I want to know them and help them, not control, command and subjugate them. When they can't go to the pictures twice in one day, roam the streets at night, or, if fetched in, watch 'M for Murder' or 'Dial 999' they want to know why. Just saying 'Because its rubbish' or 'You need your sleep' isn't answer enough. They think I'm depriving them and it's hard to find an easy answer. But on the credit side they are never short of somebody coming to play with them and they live quite happily with one another in cramped conditions.

My husband and I have quarrels, sometimes really serious ones, because of the set-up. I say 'Mrs Brown's husband does this, why don't you?' and he also has his grievances. But we do talk to each other.

LIFE ON THE FARM (1965)

Ann Willatt

It was Sunday, all the tractor men were in their homes and foreman keeping an eye on the stock. I changed out of trousers and wellingtons and was glad of the civilised feel of nylon stockings and a wool dress. As I handed the tea cups to our guests, who were on the staff of a large local university, the conversation, logical, intellectual and remote, ranged round agriculture, I found it irritating and longed to break through the abortive but cleverly spun web of words with some practical statement about the day-to-day necessities of managing a farm.

Then the farm office bell rang. I left the tea party and found foreman in the office. 'Sorry to bother you when you've got company – but you know those ten heifers that are due to calve to the old Hereford bull?'

He had no need to say more. Hampered by the tight wool skirt, I followed him in the darkness and rain, across the yard into a loose box where he became more articulate – 'The bull was too big boned for these heifers, I told you so at the time. In any case the calf's the wrong way round – these here are it's back feet.' I went into the house, telephoned the vet, changed into old trousers, and calling out to the tea party 'I won't be long,' ran down the corridor to the back door. The university accents faded and were drowned in the hissing rain as I shut the door behind me. The vet came at once and attached a fine cord to each of the calf's protruding back feet, and the two cords to a stout rope.

Foreman and I pulled the rope when the vet told us to. It cut into our hands and our feet slipped, but the calf remained with only its little back hooves and legs showing as far as the hocks. We haltered the heifer and tied her tightly to a metal ring fastened in the wall, otherwise we would simply pull her across the wet floor. The sense of urgency in the loose box, and an awareness of the warm dark night and pouring rain outside gave the episode a peculiar quality, so that a year or two later in the light of further experience I can still see it clearly. The dangling electric light bulb left the beams of the loose box shadowy and mysterious and lit up the heifer's chestnut flanks and the curious khaki rubber of the vet's overall. He turned to me suddenly and said 'You all right? Don't mind the job?' While he and foreman leant for a minute against the whitewashed wall and mopped their heads, foreman answered for me.

'She's all right – it's just that she hasn't enough weight about her.' I was surprised to see that only ten minutes had passed since I left the tea party. The vet fetched a block and pulley; it took a few minutes to rig up, and while they were doing it the men chatted about the difficulties of getting a wrongly presented calf alive. It had become essential to me that this particular calf should be born alive, and I told them so. We set to work again and the pulley made it easier. The heifer was quiet now, and we could only hear ourselves breathing as though we were running. When at last we got the calf the men both said 'It's dead'. They dragged it into a corner near the door, wiped their hands on a towel and folded up the ropes. The vet was brisk – 'Did you say this heifer was the first of ten to calve? Ring me any time you're bothered.' He saw us as good potential customers.

I was staring at the dead calf – I thought it twitched and gasped. 'Foreman – quick it's alive.' Like lightning foreman and the vet bent over it. We all rubbed it with sacks and wisps of straw. We put it in front of its mother and she licked and licked it. In a few minutes it was on its shaky legs – a curly coated Hereford bull calf, as like its father as a replica toy.

I went back to the house, trying in the short space of darkness to readjust to the donnish atmosphere of the tea party, but it was impossible. The cups were still there in the lamplight, and everyone looked at me with surprised expressions. Their conversation of the previous minute was suspended. They were staring at my hands, so I looked down at them myself and saw there was blood on them.

Then somebody said something about how interesting it would be to 'try farming as a way of life'. They seemed worlds away, and all I could say was 'We've got a calf and it's alive.'

LIFE IN A DYING STREET (1966)

Moussia Babenco

Some kind friends arranged for us to occupy the upper part of the house in which they were then living in Cressgarden Terrace. They warned us laughingly that the street was on the wrong side of the tracks and that the local council wanted to buy the house for redevelopment purposes; but in the excitement of moving from the provinces to London and into a cheap flat with elegantly proportioned rooms and a sideways view of the Thames we hardly gave a thought about the situation or the future.

Our house was one of a long terrace built by Cubitt in the 1840s. Like the rest of the street it had seen better days and had been shaken and damaged by the air-raids of 1940-1. Workmen who came to do repairs said it was a 'palace' compared with its neighbours, but agreed that the whole street had served its purpose. No one regretted that it was to make way eventually for skyscraper flats.

Most of the Cressgarden Terrace houses had been divided into two or more apartments with an occasional owner-occupied dwelling which still seemed to remember when the street had been highly 'respectable'. In 1957 all the houses had the sooty covering common to that part of central London under the shadow of a vast power station's chimneys.

Our failure to grasp the simple fact that the street had no future caused us to get involved in a scheme of redecoration which must have puzzled the neighbours who had long abandoned their houses to weather and soot. After a time we realised that there had been no new arrivals in the street for a very long time. We were very odd birds.

In spite of the reservations they must have had the neighbours accepted us and once the council became our landlords and we had been issued with their rent-card and been sounded for their rent rebate scheme we had a never-failing subject for small talk . . . what 'they' were going to do with our houses and with us . . . and when. The women I spoke to – mostly mothers of young families – knew that their street was doomed but refused to face the fact that the whole area was scheduled as slum property and that they were simply units in a scheme affecting, over the years, perhaps as many as 2,000 families in that part of London. They even tended to blame the council for having set their eyes on the street, for 'nobody touches their houses now they know they're going to come down'.

In common with our neighbours we had been told by the rent collector that we were to be moved – 'decanted' is the official term, I believe – into one of the new flats which were under construction some distance away. We accepted this destiny without difficulty, having no prejudices one way or the other about becoming council flat tenants and, in any case, we had no idea where we might be when the Last Post sounded for the street.

Our neighbours, however, found it hard to accept the idea of living in council flats and seemed to feel a slight loss of caste was involved. They nourished the illusion that before the evil day they would have found themselves a place of their own. No one showed the least gratitude at that stage for the very modern and pleasant accommodation the council was prepared to offer them.

They also grumbled endlessly against 'them' – the council – although we found our relations with them smooth and were touched by the consideration shown us in the matter of repairs. They would even issue distemper if the tenants wished to do a little internal decorating. Nobody did especially after the autumn of 1958 when rumours went the round that 'they' were going to demolish the street sooner than it had been expected and that 'they' would move us all into the new flats at a week's warning and that 'they' would pass us by if we happened to be on holiday when the call to better things sounded.

At this stage one or two families moved away into their own places – the exceptional ones – and their empty flats were not re-let. Then the first families began to be 'decanted' and as the number of inhabitants dwindled away over the weeks a blight fell on Cressgarden Terrace. Gradually it reverted to its 1941 appearance and at night, instead of light shining from scores of windows and the sound of radios and the sight of families at their evening meal, there was an only occasional light here and there from the rooms of odd survivors of the great sweep.

By this time the aspect of the street by day had become appalling – the backdrop for a realist ballet or play. All lower windows were boarded up with wooden shutters or zinc sheets while the upper windows were mostly smashed by the scores of boys and girls who now roamed at will through the deserted houses and gardens. Their stone-throwing became a menace and one was obliged to shriek from the windows to prevent it. In the evenings and at weekends the sound of breaking glass was background music to every activity. The council made no effort at all to protect the remaining tenants. One evening our kitchen electric-light bulb was smashed by a well-aimed piece of plaster.

This period of enduring the death of a whole neighbourhood became utterly demoralising and those neighbours who had at first turned up their noses at a council flat were now hanging out their tongues for the call to the housing office interview, the prelude to their removal. Against a darkening horizon of shattered windows and debris-littered pavements we discussed the position and the fate of our neighbours. 'They' now assumed monstrous proportions for the fact had emerged that 'they' were backed by all kinds of arbitrary powers. 'They' had tried to get an old lady to move into an old people's home; 'they' had moved one old soul for the seventh time; 'they' were absolutely impersonal in their dealings with the 'decantees'; 'they' had taken so-and-so to court because she had refused the rooms that had been offered her.

It was clear that for 'them' the rehousing of the inhabitants of Cressgarden Terrace was something between a military operation and a fumigation with DDT. It was not reassuring.

When we were almost the last people left we were told one day that as we were comparative newcomers to Cressgarden Terrace and to the council's area we were not entitled, under a council rule, to post-war accommodation and we were offered rooms in a converted house or a pre-war flat without lift or bathroom. It was also suggested that as we did not appear to be the usual council flat tenants we might like to make our own arrangements. It thus came about that we found our own place and although the only people who had welcomed the council's plans to rehouse us we were the only ones who did not eventually move into their accommodation.

We thought we had been badly treated but a visit to the council's housing office and a few minutes' wait in the reception-room soon convinced us that we had little moral right to be jostling in the queue for the new accommodation which appeared to be nowhere near meeting the requirements of the local people. The sight of a middle-aged lady weeping in the office of a not unsympathetic official seemed to symbolise the hard realities behind the destruction of Cressgarden Terrace.

Our last morning there had all the drama we could wish for. A short time before we drove away the street was ripped up by all the public utilities in creation and gas, water, and electricity cut off. We had, it appeared, escaped the bulldozers by inches. We have since heard that the council is to redevelop another area of some four hundred dwellings. The people involved have all our sympathy.

7   On the Dark Side

There is nothing so very unusual in the experience narrated here by *Guardian* readers. But 20 years or more ago when these articles were published, it was very rare indeed for ordinary women, not professional writers or journalists, to 'tell all' about the dark side of their lives.

FIFTY THOUSAND AND ONE (1963)

'M.M.D.'

Fifty thousand illegitimate babies were born in England and Wales last year. Like many other parents I read this neat, sad figure in the papers recently with a tremor of alarm. Could any family, however enlightened or respectable it considered itself, be immune? This, I said to myself, was being silly and unrealistic: Jane, our elder girl, had discussed pre-marital relationships with me only a few months ago and had told me quite spontaneously and firmly that she did not believe in sexual intercourse outside marriage. Our younger daughter, still at school, I had also spoken to frankly on the subject, realising that there is no excuse for mothers who are too delicate minded to speak openly of the facts of life. Surely there was little need to worry? So I spent a few moments sympathising with the unfortunate fifty thousand and then forgot them.

Two days later Jane, who shares a flat with two other girls came home to tell us that she was pregnant and that she and the father of the child had no intention of marrying. They had thought themselves in love, but when it came to spending a lifetime together they realised it would not work out.

Looking back on my first reactions to this news I remember confused feelings of anguished pity for Jane, desperate anger with the man who had shared her pleasure but would not have to share the painful results of it and a sense of the terrible injustice of things that Jane who I believe to be a simple, unpromiscuous girl should have to go through this while thousands of other girls who 'sleep around' should get away with it.

She was nearly three months pregnant, too far gone to consider 'doing anything about it' even had she wished it, which she told me firmly she didn't. She intended to have the child adopted as soon as it was born. This, unexpectedly, since I have never considered myself a particularly maternal woman, was another source of anguish. The thought of a child which was a part of our family being given to strangers appalled me. Without any hesitation we offered to adopt the baby ourselves and bring it up until she married or could take it herself. At first it seemed she might agree to this proposal, and my mind was filled with the thoughts of the child and how, at the age of 54, I should cope with it.

But the next time she came to see me Jane said positively that she was going to have the child adopted; we were too old to bring it up; it would be fair neither to the child nor ourselves. Since then I have tried not to think of the baby and my own feelings but to do only what is best for Jane and the child.

The three other children were told that Jane was having a baby. The two boys aged 18 and 20 and Fiona at 15, accepted the news with sympathetic interest, but no show of disapproval or alarm. None of them seemed bothered about public opinion. We are an agnostic family, and there was no thought of Jane having 'sinned'.

Fortunately Jane had already completed her training course and after the child was born she knew she would have no difficulty in finding a good job.

In the meantime, what were we going to do about public opinion? Should we be bold and let everyone know she was expecting a child, or should we try to conceal the whole affair? Had we been going to keep the child there would have been no question of concealment, and this is the course I should have preferred. Since, however, the baby was to be adopted there seemed no point in proclaiming the facts in our locality. So we compromised, and told the people we know to be our friends, except those who are too elderly and shockable; the rest we will leave to find out for themselves.

Jane's plan was to stay with family friends in the provinces for the months during which she could work, and then come with us to our country cottage for the last couple of months. She could have the baby in the cottage hospital and immediately she left hospital the child would go to a foster mother until adoptive parents could be found.

In making these arrangements we have been helped and advised by an excellent organisation which looks after the welfare of unmarried mothers and their babies. The laws of adoption are strict and must be carried out through an authorised body. The people who run the organisation Jane chose are efficient and sympathetic. They suggest courses of action suitable to individual girls and help them to carry them out. They provide a foster mother to take the child as soon as possible, and later find adoptive parents whom, after intensive searchings, they consider as well matched to the child as is humanly possible. The father of the child has agreed to pay part of the cost of the expenses incurred, and Jane will receive financial assistance from the state before and after her confinement.

It will not be for another three months that Jane will be faced with what must be the biggest and hardest decision of her young life. There is no compulsion either way. If she decides that after all she cannot bear to part with the child she knows that we will help her to look after it.

Like every mother in this situation, I have wondered since whether there was anything I could have done to prevent Jane getting herself into this mess, or to prevent Fiona getting herself into a similar one in the future. If there is an infallible remedy I am afraid I don't know it.

In our household sex has always been spoken of frankly. I tried to impress on Jane when we were discussing it together that though I cannot regard a decent sexual relationship even outside marriage as sinful I do know that such relationships can and often do lead to a great deal of unhappiness. I warned her that if she felt she must have such experience she must use a contraceptive.

But girls of Jane's sort don't go round with contraceptives in their pockets. Not yet, anyhow, and quite honestly I don't know whether to be glad or sorry.

Isn't it time that society faced the facts of contemporary life and changed its attitude to illegitimacy, as it has done, for example, in the Scandinavian countries? A young man who drives a car recklessly and kills or injures someone as a result does not have to spend six months carrying the body of the dead or injured on his back. If he did, society would censure him more strongly than it does now. But the girl who loves recklessly, injuring no-one but herself, carries with her the visible results of her recklessness, and because of this she is not forgiven.

If society will not help and protect these girls it is, I believe, all the more reason why their own parents and friends should do everything possible to break down the prejudice and hypocrisy that adds to the distress inherent in such a situation.

SWEET REASON (1964)

Betty Thorne

At the top of our street a double-decker bus ran over the legs of a two-year-old girl. John saw her '. . . in a puddle of blood, Mam. You should see the white bones, all broken; it made me sick.' I saw the crowd. 'It's a little girl', they said, and I couldn't find our Kathy. I was frightened, really frightened, but Kathy was there, her four-year-old eyes full of the horror. Then I saw the child, just two years old, a white face and red blankets being lifted into the ambulance to take her to hospital where she died several hours later.

The people standing by wanted to help, anything that could have been done, but the ambulance men saw to the little girl, the police saw to the traffic. There was nothing we could do, so out of the helplessness, frustration and fear came the re-establishment of normality. Those who had seen it told their tales, the opinionated started by laying the blame and a nearby voice said 'Perhaps we'll get our new houses. They'll have to widen the road now.' This was horrible, but it was true. The road wasn't wide enough for buses, works traffic, stationary vehicles; any rehousing would only be incidental to road widening.

I went to see one of my neighbours. They are known as Labour Party people. She isn't a pushing potential councillor but just steadfastly Labour. When I suggested going to see our MP she gulped but agreed. The danger of the road she knew only too well. She told me how, some time previously she had written to the chief constable when another child was knocked down. This resulted in a traffic count by the police during a quiet time of the day and though they said the stationary vehicles delivering were dangerous, the amount of traffic did not warrant any immediate action and anyway the road was due for widening some time in the future. So we agreed that until such time as the bulldozers came along we needed safety measures. She didn't know where to contact the MP but the local councillor was a regular visitor at their home and she would ask him.

The councillor called several days later when already the sense of tragedy was dulling. He knew the road and he knew the Watch Committee. He told us of other danger spots that he had attended to, and it began to seem discourteous if not downright ignorant to go on pushing to see our MP. We discussed measures, re-routing of buses, railing, one-way streets and he wrote them all down in the back of his black book.

Some weeks later he called again. He believed in keeping people informed of progress. The Watch Committee had the matter in hand; they had realised that in 1966 World Cup football matches were to be played in Sheffield and that this particular road would be on the route to the football ground. The road would have to be widened before then.

That was the last time I saw the councillor. Several months have passed and I have made no attempt to contact him. My emotions are not so strong: a football match will accomplish what a two-year-old's death has failed to do. The road has a long history of near misses, minor accidents and at least one other child's death. Who is going to be to blame next time?

A little old lady lives across the street from us. One day in the conversation of the shop she said how much she enjoyed a bit of home-made cake, but that now she was on her own she didn't bother baking. One Saturday when I'd done our baking I sent one of the kids across with a few patties. She gave him some coppers, and this has gradually built up until now each week-end she brings an apple for her apple pie; at Christmas a jar of mincemeat for mincepies. In return for the finished product she sends a shilling for the meter and a penny each for the kids.

I once went across when she was going through one of her deaf periods, making conversation very difficult, but apparently this didn't matter. All she wanted me to do was listen.

We started off with her pet hate – the landlord. All these years she'd never been behind with her rent and now he wouldn't do a thing; just waiting for her to die so he could sell the house. One by one we went through the neighbours. She had years of knowledge. Then the photographs came out. She was left a widow with five children. No family allowance in those days, and the photograph that struck me was a seaside walking snap, taken on the working men's club annual outing. A young woman in one of those suits, arm in arm with a well set up young fellow, hardly recognisable as the bent little lady in the everlasting clean pinny and head square, touching my arm and saying 'Come again. I'm always in, and then we'll have a good talk.' I said I would and meant it, but I haven't been. There's a programme on telly I want to watch or the kids aren't in, too much to do. One day, perhaps this winter, those curtains across the street aren't going to be opened. I'll feel guilty for a day or two, but it will pass.

A man came and knocked on the back door one Sunday just after tea. 'Are you busy?' Yes I was; kids to bath, ready for school in the morning. 'It's all right, then.' But something in his manner made me ask 'Anything the matter?'.

'It's the wife – bleeding.' I knew she was seven months pregnant so I went. He'd sent for the doctor but he was a long time coming and she'd been getting worse. I'd been called there at the birth of her first baby so I knew what to expect. I'm classified as 'scruffy', but they are worse. She was in bed, obviously in pain and ill. The two little girls were running up and down, the dog was yapping, the fourteen-inch telly blaring away.

I took the children round to my willing husband and went back to stay with her until help arrived. She seemed to grow weaker as I stood there, not knowing what to do, but eventually a midwife, doctor and ambulance arrived. After I'd seen them off I brought the children back to their Dad. He said 'Your Mam's gone to hospital for a bit so you'll have to look after your Dad. You can manage that, can't you?'

The oldest one, for all her six years, looked up at him and through her tears she said 'No'. She was frightened and bewildered. During the following days while their Mam was in hospital I really tried to help, kept my eye on them in the yard, had them in to play, took them shopping with us. One cold morning I went in and they had no fire, so I offered to lend some coal. 'Can't pay you back, you know'. I gave him some, but how could I keep on unless I was willing to be without myself? Trying to comfort, I said that the staff had been very good to me when I was in that hospital but – 'We lost our first in that place. I told them to take it out of the incubator and give it a chance but they wouldn't, and it died.'

I could have offered to do their washing but we have such a lot already and anyway they never did look really clean. I could have cleaned round for him, but there looked so much to do and he was a healthy enough man and he wasn't at work.

Their Mam came out of hospital but she'd lost her baby, and I'd lost my chance to help. I'd done something, but once again, not enough.

By the new year the rates bill will be here. Willie will have his cough back. 'What's on telly?' and well, what can I do about it anyway?

Sometimes the sweetness of reason sickens me.

LEARNING TO BE A WIDOW (1968)

Mary Stott

'Learning to be a Widow' is included in this section because this article, together with the last chapter of Mary Stott's 'Forgetting's No

Excuse' has brought her continuing response over the years and began a continuing involvement in the National Association of Widows.

It may come suddenly or far, far too slowly, but from the day we are born death is a certainty. So why do those of us who are agnostics or atheists and cannot believe in any kind of personal survival shove the thought of death into a dark cupboard and refuse to look at it? Why do people even say 'How morbid!' when one talks quietly or with tension-easing jokes, of hearses and wills and estate duties?

This is about learning to be a widow and it is for men as well as for women, but people who think such an article is either exhibitionist or depressing had better stop here. It is intended, simply and rather urgently to help with the hard fact of life that the chances are much higher than evens that a woman will survive her husband. Women who don't face this, or whose husbands don't, are in for a far harder time than those who do. To start with three practical points:

It is best to accept quite early in one's married life (a friend of mine came back from her honeymoon a widow) that it is necessary to make a will and to leave all family and household documents tidily in a place known to both. You need birth certificate, marriage certificate, the name and address of the building society, national insurance number . . . and all sorts of addresses and particulars. Do you know where they are? No woman should have to cope with the hell of scrabbling blindly through drawers and pockets to find these things when she is distracted, numb, or exhausted.

Every woman should have money of her own that she can get at quickly, even if it is no more than £50 in the Post Office. The most thoughtful and far-seeing husband may crash his car just before pay day when funds are low, and anyway, his money may not be immediately available to his wife. How does a woman pay the butcher or buy food for the people who will come to the funeral unless she has ready money? Has she to humiliate herself by borrowing from her friends, or to trudge to the Ministry of Social Security, which may only be open from 10 a.m. to 4 p.m. and be closed on Saturdays. Employers should immediately offer help, even if it is no more than an advance on wages, to every employee, every employee's widow.

Given that to the very young death is an outrageous thing, a denial of meaningful personality, an impossible idea to accept, it should not be so once the first uncle or aunt, let alone the first parent, has died. From that time on the thought should be explored, gingerly at first, and then more openly, and often with laughter, for jokes are no less funny for being macabre and help to make intolerable jobs just about tolerable . . . summoning the undertaker, getting the death certificate, arranging the funeral. People want to say goodbye in dignity and fellowship and the only place to do this yet is in a church. Most ministers of religion understand the strong need for this kind of help and give it generously. But if one knows beforehand which minister, what form of service, it is one strain the less, and a help to one's friends.

The other things are harder to say: It has happened. The human being with whom your life was inextricably bound up is now, incredibly, an undertaker's job. You are liable to be alone in the house in the middle of the night, or be knocked up by a well-meaning policeman. And so, of course, you may be terrified, helpless or entirely out of your mind. The thing to hang on to is that human beings are basically kind. The newest neighbour, the merest acquaintance, will make your telephone calls, summon help, prop you up with tea or brandy until your own people can be with you. You have only to raise a finger and someone will cope for you, glad, grateful to serve your need. This is something one can absolutely rely on.

Most widows manage bravely until the funeral is over – and should be told so because it helps. But then what? Alas, no one can say. Not only are we all different people, differently equipped, suffering in different ways and degrees, but none of us can know in advance how we shall react to grief and shock. The strong and capable may suffer a total collapse of the will to live. The gentle, even the flabby, may find a life force exerting itself almost right away. One woman may need to hide, one to run to friends, one to stay alone where she is. One may clutch at work, one be incapable of it. Thinking ahead about this won't help much and shock may numb the wits for quite a while. One does as one must.

But one must find one's own way back, as the numbness wears off. One must fight the thought 'Why did it happen to me?'. However appalling it was, it was worse for someone else. So your husband died on a business trip to Bulgaria, or collapsed in the loo, or you saw him walk under a bus, or you were driving the car, or you called the doctor too late or you saw him wrestle agonisingly with death for days, or linger, unconscious or senile for weeks or even months. So it was beyond bearing. But other women bore this and more. Lapses into self-pity and into a kind of hatred for the carefree, the untouched, are inevitable, but to make self-pity a way of life is unreasonable and almost unforgivable. There are so many of us and none of us is entitled to think 'No-one suffered as I suffer'.

However smug and trite it may sound, it is true that the best therapy is ungrudgingly responding, as soon as one can, to other people's needs, accepting that they have their lives to live, their troubles to cope with. In time of grief and loss one is driven to lay a burden on one's friends, for one has a great and continuing need for support, company, affection, practical help, but it helps a great deal if one can spread the load and remember not to lean too much on any one shoulder, not to ask too much, and manage to give a little, here and there.

This, I think is what one ought to learn during one's married life. The most devotedly loved wives are not by any means always the most desolate widows. What he was, what he gave you, what you became because of him, what you learned in the way of unselfishness, what you earned together in the way of friends, may well be enough to see you through.

NEVER ARGUE WITH A DRUNK (1968)

Anon

It is early evening. You are sitting at home, watching television. Suddenly the door bursts open. Enter your husband, swaying. 'Are you still here?,' he shouts. 'I thought I told you to get out. Leave my house, you silly bitch! Go on, get out.'

This kind of scene is familiar to any woman married to a boozer. Equally familiar are the sounds he will probably make the next morning. 'I'm terribly sorry, darling. Please don't leave me. I know I'm a louse. I've brought you a cup of tea.'

Which does he mean? The only way to avoid schizophrenia is to face the fact that you are living not with one man but with two. Which is going to come through your front door at night? Met men forecasting the day's weather for the British Isles have an easier job than the boozer's wife trying to predict the condition of her ever-loving in the twelve hours between 9 a.m. and 9 p.m. Will the evening prove wet or windy? Mild or bitter?

But there are pointers if you are prepared to look for them. For instance, if he wakes up in the morning and says 'It's a terrible bore, but I've got to meet Charlie Farnsbarns on business tonight at 5.30. But don't worry. It'll only be one drink and I'll be home about 6.30.' You know perfectly well what happened on nine out of ten evenings when Charlie Farnsbarns was involved so you can translate his remarks to read: 'I am meeting Charlie Farnsbarns at 5.30. After three or four doubles in the York Minster we shall proceed on a circular pub crawl ending up where we first started.' You can now safely assume that at about eight or nine, Mr Hyde will clump up the stairs, give you a piece of his mind and fall flat on his face.

Or he rings you about five in the afternoon and says 'Hullo darling. Have you had a nice day? What's all the news?' This means he has a premonition he won't be in any condition to hear your news by the time he gets home, and is checking to make sure he isn't going to miss anything important. So come the evening, it will be Mr Hyde again. And so on.

Friday night is danger night. The domestic week-end looms ahead so on Friday morning when he says 'Thank God it's Friday, you've no idea how much I'm looking forward to a quiet weekend with you', you can be pretty sure that a final end-of-the-week fling is on the cards. Other danger spots are: the evening before starting a new book (or any other new project). The day after starting it. The day after finishing it. Any time in between when things are going particularly well. Any time in between when things are going particularly badly.

The day before a visit to relations (yours or his). The day after same.

On the other hand, after a real bender, lasting three or four days, serious alcoholic remorse is likely to set in, which means at least 48 hours off the hard stuff and you can look forward to one, or even two evenings with your Dr Jekyll.

So here you are, married to a boozer. Nobody can help you. It is no good ringing the doctor or the police. You are on your own. I once rang Alcoholics Anonymous to ask their advice. 'Does he really want to give it up?' they said. 'If not, there's not much you can do about it. But we'll send you some leaflets' – which never arrived.

Drinking is one of those things like homosexuality, drug addiction and cancer, the causes of which just aren't yet known, though there are theories galore. Dominating wives and mothers are often blamed, but there are plenty of dedicated boozers about with timid mothers and mousy wives, so it is impossible to generalise. Insecurity? Everything nowadays seems to be attributed to it from divorce and delinquency, to rags-to-riches success. So we are no farther.

The first rule to learn is *never argue with a drunk*. Otherwise they can turn very nasty and start throwing things. You may feel like throwing something yourself. My advice is, don't. Your husband is almost certainly bigger than you and you can't win this sort of contest. You'll probably end up screaming for the neighbours or locked out on the lawn in your nightie.

What drunks want is to be loved, and when they are at their most unattractive, smelling of drink and with ash all over their coats, that's when they want to be loved most of all.

Every drunk has a silver lining, and the nights when Mr Hyde comes home and passes out can be turned to financial advantage. One characteristic of drunks is that when under the influence they scatter their money about like confetti and never remember where they've been or who with, let alone how much money they had on them when they got home. This gives you a chance to add a few pounds to the housekeeping. But make sure he really is out for the count. A good test is to put on the lights on. If he sits up and shouts 'Put those bloody lights out', put them out and try again later.

Proceed with caution and remember that as in birds' nesting, it is fatal to be greedy. Don't take all the eggs else the bird may become suspicious and decide to move its nest egg to a safer place in future. And do try a bit of finesse. If a pile of crunched up notes is lying on his dressing table, and coins are strewn all over the floor, don't try to tidy up the mess. The whole art lies in leaving things as much as possible as you found them. A natural effect is the thing to aim for.

Any qualms of conscience you may feel at this pilfering should be quelled at once. After all, who are you robbing? Only the distillers, and they are unlikely to grudge you a few quid for the benefit of yourself and your family. You are going to spend the money on food, a new dress to boost your morale, or on having the ceiling mended.

All the boozers' wives I have talked to agree that it is the sheer unpredictability of the husbands' behaviour that really gets you down. One of them told me, 'I don't even expect him to give it up, but if he'd only say to me "Look, from now on I'm going to be drunk on Mondays, Wednesdays and Fridays, so make your own arrangements", I could probably adjust to it.' Unfortunately boozers don't seem to have any control over their actions in this respect, but it does seem to depend to a very great extent on the people they meet during the day.

This uncertainty not only makes life nerve-racking. It tends to rule out any social life in the normal sense. The last 'normal' dinner party I gave was some years ago when the guests' departure at midnight coincided with the arrival of Mr Hyde who wanted to know who on earth were all those bloody people cluttering up the doorstep.

The answer is not to give up parties altogether but to try to confine them to friends in a similar predicament who are perfectly prepared to find their host gay and welcoming, having a pee in the garden on the way in, or inert and lifeless. The latter would seem to be an ideal situation, as the party can then continue uninterrupted. But not so. Just as you sink back in your armchair in the belief that the body is safely bedded down for the night it is quite likely to reappear suddenly like a skeleton at the feast and order the visitors out of the house. If this happens, on no account groan or lose your temper. 'Hullo darling,' you should say, 'come and sit down and have a drink.' This always works like a charm, and after snoozing in a chair for a few minutes he will announce that the conversation is boring him to death and will go quietly back to bed.

Why do women stay married to drunks? Probably because when sober, or up to the moment when they down the Fatal Glass, they are charming, kind and amusing. Or perhaps it is the fascination of trying to figure out what makes them tick. Anyway, the chances are that you wouldn't leave your boozy husband. I wouldn't.

Wife No. 2: The trouble with boozers is that they go in stages of roughly ten years. At 30 you can have the children tucked up in bed, or quickly distract their attention away from the room where daddy is 'having a rest', or even walk to the park. Even when they are not asleep when he comes home full of paternal affection, trips, literally, up for a good rough and tumble, and you hear screams of laughter growing ever more hysterical, you can brightly call 'Supper ready, darling.'

At 40-odd you are no longer a 'silly bitch' but a silly old bag or a bloody old cow. Somehow much more hurtful, it emphasises your own self-doubts and you begin to feel all men see you in the same light. But it is really the situation with the children growing older which is the hardest. The hurt in the boy's eyes on a night when he was just waiting to tell his father a particularly good piece of school news, his father had come home 'nasty' and picked on some minor lapse nagging on ceaselessly about useless, idle people who take everything, etc. Later I crept up to his bedroom and said 'Daddy doesn't mean what he says. He'll be sorry tomorrow, he's had a very hard day and lots of difficult men to deal with; it's just that we're close to him and he takes it out on us.' But the innnocence was gone. 'You mean he's sloshed?'

At 40-odd 'Darling, I'm a louse' has worn thin, even to his own ears. Instead there are terrible scenes because it has to be somebody's fault, so you are everything that's horrible. Boozers are boozers because they always have an excuse.

Again you have to explain to the children, trying to make excuses for him, too, because you don't want to make them insecure, or to lose all respect for their father. Try to explain that sometimes a man's world is a jungle, they fight to survive and keep the knives out of their backs, and they sometimes drink to get the energy to keep going to keep the younger men down.

But it is the ten years I see coming I dread, from observing older boozers. When their health begins to fail they become stupefied or disgusting. All charm goes, for their drinking companions as well as the family. You just wait for the stroke, the coronary or liver, whichever comes first. The children leave home and you hope they've made it as whole people, not more insecure casualties.

Of course, I expect I handled the whole thing wrong. For instance, I hated to hear boozers' wives nagging in public and vowed never to do this. Now I see it at least makes an excuse for them to be able to blame their wives – 'You see how I'm placed, old man, who can blame me?'. So I bottle it all up in public and bottle it all up in front of the children and when I let go it's so vitriolic I frighten even myself.

Of course many would say divorce or separation would be better for all of us, but I am convinced it was precisely his own parents' separation and guilty feelings that he had driven his father out in defending his mother that is at the root of my husband's insecurity.

My son says he thinks that the older generation are hopeless. They make such a mess of things; young people have so much more sense.

VIEW FROM THE OUTSIDE (1968)

Anon

I was sitting on a sunny but rather chilly beach, sorry for myself because my friends were an unconscionable time a-coming when the thought began to take shape, 'I don't *have* to go on living. It's quite easy to stop.' It was nothing like the anguished, angry 'LET ME OUT' impulse to jump from a high building that everyone must know who has been suddenly bereaved. It was a gradually pervading awareness that living is a sort of habit; a habit I didn't much care for, since though by then I could function quite usefully, sensibly and even kindly,

I was involved only at a superficial level, I didn't really *care*. I hadn't got anything to care with. I was completely hollow inside.

I saw myself quite clearly as an Outsider. It was rather interesting, in a chilly sort of way. Everything looks so different from outside. Why, I asked myself, should survival be a duty? One has obligations, obviously, and they must be fulfilled. But when that is accomplished? A duty not to cause pain, guilt and grief? Need there be guilt, and is not the clean grief of death easier to bear than the attrition of affection when the parent grows old, dependent, outrageously demanding, senile?

'You owe a duty to your God'? I have no God. 'It is a sin to take your life'? Sin is a meaningless word to me. 'You must fulfil the pattern; you will go when the right time comes'? That is nearer to my thinking. I see a pattern in the universe, the many universes. It seems possible to me – because I have experienced briefly, in the garden or on a mountain top, the feeling of one-ness with the All – that there may be a life force, a pervading spirit, into which I shall merge at death. But it seemed a little silly to imagine that it would make the slightest difference to such a vast pattern, incomprehensible to our space/time conception, whether I joined the mainstream now, voluntarily, or through some very unpleasant illness 20 years on.

The Outsider looks at people who believe in personal survival, especially Spiritualists, who believe that the Others are waiting to welcome them, and even communicate with them now, with astonishment. If the Other were waiting there, a hairbreadth away, behind a curtain, should I not run to him, to be folded in his arms, to be a whole person again? 'Oh no,' they cry, horrified. 'That would cut you off from him.' Why? They cannot tell me why.

The Outsider looks at the fear of death with pity. From the time a dog died on my knee with a relaxing of the muscles and a little sigh, I have not feared death. The Other went as simply, and for me it could so easily be a blessed, final sleep. The awakening? Perhaps no awakening, but annihilation is preferable to a half life. Facing my Maker? An incomprehensible but not a terrifying image. And the idea of merging into

107

the mainstream of consciousness is interesting; not less interesting, you might say, than going on a journey to China or Peru.

The thing that separates the Outsider from his fellow-men is that he has stopped thinking that it is obviously better to be alive than dead. He ceases to admire the 'courage' of people whose will to survive is at the expense of those who have to tend them. The will to live is a force of nature, very powerful in the young; if it weren't so the human race would not have survived. But one comes to feel loathing for the clutching at life of the old and decrepit out of fear; and of the terror of many otherwise well-balanced citizens that some over-zealous doctor might snatch their heart from them before life was truly extinct. The will to live only equates with courage when it is a will to continue to serve the needs of one's family, friends and fellow-man, or one's God.

I became an Outsider about three months after the Other died. I had expected a certain bleakness, but this was an aspect of bereavement I hadn't known about or been able to imagine. Now I understand how common it must be. It is not beyond the bounds of rational thinking that when over the years two personalities have become integrated, the psyche of the one may be mutilated by severance from the other.

My father, an apparently healthy man, died within a year of my mother. I was glad for him and now I envy him, because I understand how and in what degree the loss mutilated him. The hard-pruned healthy young rose may put out strong new shoots, but if the stock is old and the winter frost keen, the rose may die, as he did. Or put out only suckers, weedy second-class growth, as it seems I begin to do.

Now, after a year, my friends are pleased with me. I have put bulbs in the garden, daffodils, tulips, scillas, ixias. They see it as an affirmation that I shall enjoy the flowers next spring. I appear to be functioning on all cylinders. They must be saying 'She is getting over it very nicely'.

Getting over it. The things one did because they were there to do, the things that filled up the hours, blanketed thought, helped to keep the door shut against the intolerable, plugged up gaps in some fashion, are beginning to take on a little meaning, a little purpose. That is the way it goes. Time heals, they say. New life floods in, they promise.

For the reassurance of everyone the story should end on this soothing note. But it doesn't, yet. I still don't much care for the habit of living, especially this second-class, second-hand living and I dread that the habit may again become so strong that it may over-ride a rational assessment of when, for me, enough is enough; when it is time to go.

I wish I could stay outside.

BUT WE PLANT TREES (1968)

Eva Figes

Eva Figes is the author of many highly-regarded novels and also of a powerful anthology, Patriarchal Attitudes. *She contributed frequently to the* Guardian's Women Talking *feature in the 1960s.*

The human race is a curious phenomenon. I suppose it is fair to say that the great majority of us have long rejected the idea of Divine Purpose. We tend to think that life is a terrible joke, that we are born to suffer and die, and that the little happiness we find is only just enough to make it all bearable, the proverbial carrot to keep us going to the end.

And yet we do not live as if we believed anything of the sort. We plan, we build, we project into a future which we can never hope to see even if we wish to, and I find the fact that we should do this, and continue to do it, so extraordinary that I am beginning to wonder if it is not this characteristic above all others, which distinguishes us from the lower mammals. Conservative moralists may tell us that things are not what they were, that we are selfish hedonists, undisciplined and irresponsible, but the facts belie this view. It is true that we have stopped Empire-building, that Darwin gave an ironic twist to the Victorian concept of progress, that we feel no-one is going to reward us beyond the grave for what we do on this side of it, and that therefore any sacrifices we make should be practical and for our fellow-man rather than ascetic and for our mortal souls.

But in spite of all these changes in our attitudes . . . there are men planting trees which will never be harvested in their lifetime or the next generation. . . We are paying taxes to build roads and libraries and swimming pools which will not be for us. . . . The more I stop to think of it the odder it became, this striving to build, construct, keep things going, perpetuate the race. One thinks of the antheap, the beehive, but though our complex social behaviour is the result of intelligence and not of instinct, it might just as well be instinct for all the difference it makes.

8 Fashions and Feminism

The urge towards self-adornment seems basic in human nature. How much is due to the desire to attract the opposite sex is for all of us to ponder now and then. And why *fashion*? Why a compulsion to conform to some new style of dress, hair, make-up or jewellery? That compulsion has greatly lessened in the last decade or so, and long or short, full or skimpy, plain or fancy, are a matter of individual choice, except among the very young. One cannot imagine women of the intellectual quality of Dame Mary Scharlieb, Dr Maude Roydon or Mary Stocks getting so worked up today about a fad of fashion. And if Naomi Mitchison, happily still alive as this book is being compiled, reads what she wrote in 1929 she is likely to smile gently over her youthful agitation.

It should be remembered also that in the 1980s things do not look quite the same as they did in the 1960s and early 70s. Perhaps Gillian Tindall and Jill Tweedie would write slightly differently today?

FASHIONS AND FEMINISM (1927)

Winifred Holtby

Not long ago I happened to be present at a conference attended by several hundred women from all parts of Great Britain. They were for the most part practical, conscientious women, who perform useful, unostentatious service in their own localities. Not very many of them were young, and most of them, I imagine, were married. The conference was interesting in many ways and I could not understand why, as the meetings continued, my own spirits became more and more depressed.

Then towards the end of a session I chanced to look along

the rows of delegates, in search of an acquaintance from the North of England. I saw line after line of dark velour coats with dreary rabbitskin collars, line after line of unbecoming hats which were mostly laden with trimmings which were fashionable five or six years ago, line after line of heads with rather untidy hair, of sallow complexions and listless, unlovely figures. And just then the meeting ended and we all streamed out to lunch. There was a mirror in the entrance hall and in it I saw the reflection of a youngish woman in a black velour coat, cut rather long, and slung negligently across stooping shoulders. Her nondescript blue hat was faded, its ribbon no longer in any sense an adornment. Her stockings were mud-splashed, her impractical shoes a little worn at the heel. She gave a general impression of dowdiness, lethargy and neglect. 'That's it,' thought I. 'That's what's wrong with the conference. It's utterly inartistic. How can she bear it?' But as I moved forward, to my horror the young woman moved also and I realised I was staring at myself.

The sequel to that conference was a visit to Regent Street, and the purchase of a coat, frock and hat which I could not afford; I had my hair waved; I acquired lizard-skin shoes and silk stockings and nail polish and complexion creams and I did with limited time and money what could be done for that young woman. But when the first fine careless rapture of my extravagance had passed I realised that this frenzied reaction was quite unconstructive.

Since then I have been thinking hard about the problem which at some time or another has to be faced by all working women. Ought we to abandon an interest in our clothes? Does appearance matter, or is it only a concession to the old ideal of the parasitic but respectable courtesan?

Obviously today a large number of the women who undertake public and professional work decide that they have no time to be bothered about clothes. Some definitely disapprove of attempts by women to appear attractive. They agree with Olive Schreiner – that very great and far-sighted feminist – that 'an intense love of dress and meretricious adornment is almost always the concomitant and outcome of parasitism'. They lament the time, money and thought expended upon the futilities of shopping, upon changing fashions, and women's magazines.

Discussions about the leisured woman, whether in the press or at the *Time and Tide* debate in the Kingsway Hall, invariably emphasise that aspect of her influence which leads the typist girl to spend money which her brother would spend upon a beef-steak lunch, on silk stockings and georgette dresses. We feel that fashions are set by the arbitrary dictation of Parisian or Viennese firms, to exploit the income and the attention of the wealthy and the idle, but that they steal the leisure and the food, the thought and the exercise of the girls who are earning their living, the women who might be performing valuable service to the community.

Therefore many of the most thoughtful women of today, in their own personal action, fall into the helpless acquiescence of Olive Schreiner herself. Her husband, in his biography of her quotes from a letter written by a younger woman who had deeply loved and admired her. 'I did not meet "Aunt Olive" until 1915', she writes. 'Then she, her niece and I, dined with John at the Holborn Restaurant. She had on a bottle green coat and skirt without pretence of fashion or distinctive style and a hat that left me gasping, because it was a fussy arrangement of straw and lace and (I think) of battered roses. Perhaps nothing would have emphasised better her attitude of despair towards modern women's dress.'

This attitude of despair has its dangers. It encourages belief in the most pernicious of all excuses for inaction, 'We can't have the best of both worlds'. Under the tyranny of that dilemma women have been told that they cannot both marry and have a home and have a career outside the home, that they cannot preserve both domestic and professional efficiency, that they cannot maintain a decorous and exquisite standard of taste in their own appearance and in their possessions, and at the same time perform useful service to the public. And only a few of the very brave or the very wise have yet replied to the proposers of the alternatives 'We will have both'.

We want the best of both worlds and we believe that we can and ought to have it. Civilisation should not be less beautiful because we are working to cure its imperfections; the performers of public work do not lapse into committees through despair of finding joy in the rich arts of living, and it is a pity if they should look as though this were the case. The knowledge that she has no need to feel ashamed of her appearance is a help, not a hindrance, to a woman undertaking responsible work.

But the appearance should suit the occupation. We have done much in the last ten years to destroy foolish traditions of dress. Our skirts are short, our hair for the most part shingled. We neither lace tightly nor hang mounds of voluminous material about our hips. Fashions still change with chameleon-like rapidity; the waist of today may be the bust of tomorrow; we still watch anxiously the news of the latest styles from Paris and Monte Carlo, and the working woman called suddenly to appear among her leisured sisters of fashion too often acquires an inferiority complex in consequence.

We need to carry the war into the enemy's camp. We want clothes in which we can dress ourselves quickly and comfortably, and which we can wear all day if necessary without feeling awkward. We want clothes designed for the modern wife who does her own housework, for the woman on the committee, and the girl in the office. And we want to feel that in them we appear as charming, as chic and more entitled to self-respect than the ladies whose photographs today we admire so wistfully in the illustrated papers.

THE RETURN OF THE LONG SKIRT (1929)

Muriel Harris

Muriel Harris served as the first Guardian *fashion correspondent but she wrote on a wide variety of subjects, often from Paris.*

In considering the future of any fashion, such as that of the long skirt, it has to be realised that there is nothing too absurd, too uncomfortable, too grotesque, to be adopted with alacrity, provided that the social or fashionable conditions are propitious. Not sport, not transport, certainly not hygiene or aesthetics can stay the progress of the long skirt if once the long skirt becomes the hall-mark of differentiation, or provocation, of talk in general. And this it certainly has become. . . .

While it is not likely that the woman golfer will adopt a tweed train or the motorist a leather crinoline, fashion has far more subtle methods of coming into her own. And not the least is the suggestion that the woman who does not adopt her, far from being superior and more attractive is, perhaps, just a little bit of a crank. Certainly she doesn't bother much about dress. . . . The wearers of long skirts are momentarily attracting all the attention, and arguments concerning the really sensible and classic clothes evolved by the modern young woman no longer meet with a really warm response. . . . In the intimate matter of dress social prestige is involved and a fashion which has social prestige on its side is bound to win. . . .

The only way of saving women from the long skirt is to praise it universally, so that within the shortest possible time ready-made long-skirted models may be had on the hire-purchase system. And if a distinguished physician could be found to say something about the advantages to hygiene, since long skirts swept the carpets as well as vacuum cleaners, it would probably be doomed. Until then, however, the long skirt seems likely to prevail.

'Talkback'

The distinguished women who wrote about the return of the long skirt included Mrs H.M. Swanwick (suffragette and peace campaigner); Miss Horniman, founder of the famous Gaiety Theatre, in Manchester; Dr Maude Royden, one time editor of the suffrage paper, *The Common Cause*, famous preacher in Nonconformist churches, and one of the organisers of the pre-war 'Peace Army'; Rose Macaulay was one of the greatest novelists of the era; as was Naomi Mitchison; E.M. Delafield is best remembered for her *Diary of a Provincial Lady*; Mrs J.L. Stocks – Mary Stocks, who became the Baroness Stocks of the Royal Borough of Kensington and Chelsea – had a profound influence on her times as feminist, educationist (she was principal of Westfield College) and broadcaster.

Some of the young girls' dresses have recently been decidedly on the short side; they were neither pretty nor suitable, and certainly tended to give rise to attacks of rheumatoid or at any rate muscular pains in the lower limbs. I should like to see day dresses lengthened to somewhere about the middle of the wearer's calf; but I decidedly deprecate a return to the long skirts that were fashionable before the war: they were unhygienic and apt to sweep up all manner of germ-containing dirt. I really cannot believe that the majority of Englishwomen will tolerate the pre-war long skirt for day wear.

Dame Mary Scharlieb

It is all very well for fashion designers and mannequins and actresses and ladies with motor cars to sweep along with adorable, flower-like furbelows, but we common folk have enjoyed the freedom and cleanliness and security of shorter skirts and I hope we shall stick to them for common life.

We may have to face the possibility of being called 'dowdies' or even 'freaks'. But I am proud to think that I didn't mind that even when I was a young, ball-frequenting girl. In those days we were threatened with a return of the crinoline, and I remember Mr William Morris encouraging my school-fellows and me to sign an 'anti-crinoline' declaration. I think we all kept our vows, and never lost a dance.

The real test of one's endurance arose, however, in the hottest part of the struggle for the vote, when it was evident that one could not allow oneself more than one 'cause' at a time. So in order to appear womanly at all costs we endured the preposterously uncomfortable fashions that may be seen in any old snapshot of our manifold public activities. In skirts reaching the gound and measuring several yards at the hem we marched in the mud. With gigantic hats precariously poised on piled up hair we carried large banners, ourselves defenceless in the gale. To me, I confess, these imbecilities never appeared to be womanly. I submitted to them because the mob required them before it would listen, just as I submitted to the dangerous long skirt and many a fall when I was one of the first women to ride a bicycle in the streets of Manchester. Even so, one was pretty frequently pelted or pulled off one's machine until royalty took to bicycling; if one had worn the modern tunic one might have been torn limb from limb, and one wanted to live. But do not let us suppose that the short skirt is needed only for sports. It is needed particularly in the house, for a mother carrying a baby or a lamp upstairs, for a maid carrying coals, for a nurse carrying a tray.

I like to see women playing pranks with clothes, or no clothes, provided they look pretty, but to insist on all women following the fashion at the peril of being called 'freaks' seems to me to be snobbery. I hope we are growing out of that.

Mrs H.M. Swanwick

I, being an average female, shall wear blindly and blithely whatever is 'being worn' regardless of the suitability of my person or purse.

Lady Lavery

If women be so silly as to return to the old custom of sweeping the streets with dragging skirts they will deserve all the sarcasm which will be showered on them. The present younger generation is ignorant of *our* sufferings; the misery of wetted boots from our muddied petticoats and the worry of cleaning the filthy garments. For evening wear it is a different matter – a train is of stately appearance, but it used to be difficult to dance in one with grace. It may be a relief to see a few inches less of ugly legs, but the worst of them does not carry home much mud!

Miss A.E.F. Horniman

I think that skirts for day-time wear should not be longer but shorter. Long skirts for walking seem to me to be unsightly and are both dangerous and inconvenient. I do not think it matters in the least what people wear in the evenings, provided that the skirts do not touch the ground, which is a dirty habit.

Rose Macaulay

To the hungry and sensitive generation produced by the war and post-war conditions, long skirts have an undoubted sexual appeal, as they promise that their wearers will be gentle and kind and comforting. It is after all a well-known fact that ministering angels always wear long (white) skirts. However it is not perhaps always advisable to be kind to young men, or so we are told. There is, therefore, much to be said for the short skirt, revealing the hard, glittering modern leg. But as to doing what the fashion designers, who are neither psychologists nor artists but, like the rest of us, out for their own pockets, want us to do – well, surely we have got sense enough to smile sweetly and go on wearing what length of skirt our own individual sense of expediency or brand of sex appeal make advisable from time to time.

Naomi Mitchison

The fashions which we have been wearing now for some years have left us as free as people wearing clothes can possibly be. No high tight collars round the throat, no constriction round the lungs and waist, no hampering of movement around the knees and ankles. Skirts reaching to the knees or only an inch or two below, hamper the movements no more than a Highlander's kilt. Such dresses can be made with a very small amount of material, with a minimum of trouble and in the minimum of time.

Of course it is true that, as with any fashion, women may go to the extremes and choose frocks which accord neither with their figure nor with their years. But the short-skirted simple frock has these enormous advantages: (1) It is beautiful, since it neither cramps nor over-emphasises nor distorts the human figure. (2) It creates beauty for it creates health. Anaemia, once regarded as almost the normal condition for women, has practically disappeared. Women not only look younger, but from the real point of view they are younger, because they are healthier. (3) Any woman of any intelligence can look, and does look, very nearly as nice as any other woman. Of course there is still a difference between the supremely and superbly expensive simplicity of the best dressmakers and the little dress made by a clerk or a factory girl at home. The difference, however, is much less than with a more elaborate form of dress. And the great mass of us do look very much alike, as far as social difference is concerned. I suppose there are people whose innate snobbishness makes them regard this as a drawback: I cannot believe that the great mass of women will regard it as anything but a very great advantage not willingly to be sacrificed.

I wish that among your great and intelligent public some woman may be found with leisure enough and goodwill to organise us into a great movement of protest against the attempt to impose upon us the elaborate untidiness of the fashions with which we are threatened; against their lack of beauty, simplicity and hygiene. Thousands – tens of thousands – would rise up and call her blessed.

Dr Maude Royden

Concerning the conspiracy which seems to be hatching among 'fashion designers' for the reintroduction of longer skirts I will begin by asking 'Who are these fashion designers?' Nobody really knows the answer. One can only suppose them to be a secret international organisation (a Fourth International more virulently anti-social than the Third) with headquarters in Paris and agents in every European capital except Moscow. The vileness of their motives is demonstrated by their behaviour. They are actuated solely by the desire for a quick retail turnover of new clothes. They show consideration neither for the steady fortunes of the textile industry nor for the health and economy of the consumer. They are now about to decree new shackles for emancipated womanhood. We have at last raised our skirts from the mud. We have set in train the cult of the good leg. We have become economically and physically mobile as never before. Cabs are no longer necessary for the protection of evening dresses – or trunks for their transportation. Hands are freed from the business of skirt-holding, ankles and calves from the flip-flap-flop of redundant and often mud-soaked draperies. We have evolved a type of clothing which is not merely hygienic but also democratic. Never before has it been so difficult to distinguish a factory girl from the unoccupied daughter of an urban landowner.

And now we are asked to revert to trains and bustles which only the rich will be able to buy and the cab-crawler to wear. And we feel vaguely that there is a kind of omnipotence about the 'fashion designer' which must bend us uncomplainingly to his mysterious will. But I fear I have demonstrated my

119

unsuitability as a protagonist in this controversy. Never a fashionable woman, I am now middle-aged. It is easy enough for me to say as I do say, that I will never approximate my day dress to the mud of Manchester, and that if I cannot dine out without wearing a train, hoop or bustle, I will choose rather to stay quietly at home. The unperturbed 'fashion designer' will appeal over my irrevocably shingled head to younger, smarter women who are more vulnerable to the appeal of contemporary elegance. It is for them to dig their heels in and wage a defensive fight for an element of physical freedom which, quite seriously, seems to me as well worth defending as the political freedom embodied in the Franchise Act of 1928.

Mrs J.L. Stocks

I cannot bring myself to believe that just when we were so happy, hopping, skipping and jumping through our declining days we are to be re-swaddled round the legs in order that these foolish children may experience the thrill of a horror they have never known, for the mere fun of the thing. They were short-coated from the day they were born; they wore shorts and pyjamas in their seminaries for young ladies, they danced through their first season in what we should have called an apology for a ham frill; and now because they want to dress up as something else they are going to make us all play at being Jane Austen or a mermaid or the Mother of the Gracchi . . . we are all to go trailing about again as we did in those distressing years of our early married life, spending our days in clutching and stumbling and dropping our parcels, and our nights in making sordid renovations to repair the damage involved in crossing some portion of the one-way traffic. There will be time for them to outlive their youthful follies and elapse into their bathing clothes or whatnot; but there will be no more earthly dressmakers for us. We shall die entangled in the chariot wheels of our children and disappear, game to the last in the height of fashion, clad in premature winding sheets.

The Hon. Mrs Dowdall

It will be a real misfortune if we are all to revert to mediaevalism and the days of 'the Queen of Spain has no legs'. The majority of Englishwomen have got nice legs and I can see no reason whatever in favour of concealing them. It is a truly terrifying thought that in our present energetic life we should ever have to board an omnibus, cross a London street or play efficient tennis burdened by the additional responsibility of keeping a long skirt off the ground.

A progression ending in women wearing knickerbockers would be preferable to a retrogression ending in their returning to long skirts.

E.M. Delafield

FOOLISH WOMEN (1934)

'*A Physician*'

Before all the unpleasant features of this winter are forgotten let me recall one outstanding impression. That has been the number of women who have attempted to withstand the weather without woollen underclothes. After determined sunbathing and slimming last summer they have thought to come unscathed through a trying winter. Judging by my case records, they have paid in full for their temerity. Some have suffered enough ill-health to make them think hard whether or not the risk is really worth taking.

This underclothing habit is not confined to young girls, who might be excused through ignorance; I have found it in patients approaching 40. So many have been overtaken by one complaint after another, generally of a catarrhal nature or infectious disease that I cannot believe it to be mere coincidence. The more robust have suffered little but their weaker and generally older sisters have failed lamentably in the struggle against ill-health this winter. What has been so vexatious is that it has been those women who earn their own livings who have had to give up, in some cases for long periods. No employer welcomes illness among his women workers and small blame to him. He puts up with it because he knows it is one of the misfortunes of women. Those women who wish to make sure of retaining their hardly-won posts would do well to pay more attention to this clothing aspect of health, particularly at the end of the winter.

Women, we are told, spend no less than twelve million pounds a year on silk stockings. Before the cold weather is over it is to be hoped they will see the wisdom of spending more on woollen underwear. Those who are subject to faults of circulation, such as chilblains, or to chest complaints are looking for trouble if they deliberately wear inadequate clothing. At this time though the wind is cold I see children abroad half-clothed, presumably because the sun was shining when they came out. I refer to well-to-do children of six years and upwards, who wear no covering from their ankles to near their hips. Whether their parents hope, by so misclothing them to harden their unfortunate children I cannot say, but the risk in my opinion is unpardonable.

In close competition with this under-clothing business one often finds another crying evil, underfeeding by women. A breakfast so meagre that it has to be supplemented by a mid-morning coffee is followed by a hurried lunch. Tea, fortunately, is a movable feast, or these slimming, wilting creatures would drop. This is not a question of economy or need. Thanks to the modern vogue of slimness at all costs, a common topic of conversation among young women today is the amount they have lost in weight. They are penny wise and pound foolish, at any rate where food values are concerned. Chemists, sellers of patent foods and of cooked foods, are making their fortunes out of such folk.

The illnesses ensuing upon under-clothing and under-feeding are all too obvious to those who have the merest inkling of physiology, but I dare to write no more – I must now be so unpopular. Fortunately for the race some of the younger women are still bent on clothing and feeding their bodies rationally. That remains as one crumb of comfort for the doctors. Nothing but the doctor's bill will cure the others of their foolishness.

COLD LEGS (1965)

Prof. A.M. Boyd

In spite of the increasing popularity of sensible warm clothing among teenage girls there are still many girls who do not avail themselves of the gaily patterned thick stockings, attractive 'bloomers', well-cut trousers and high boots which are readily available. I have seen many girls in nylon stockings, or even bare legs, and short skirts shivering in bus queues. These girls, I am told by my assistants, wear practically nothing under their skirts. They are therefore virtually unprotected in cold weather from the hips downwards.

The disastrous effects of prolonged exposure to cold are not sufficiently widely appreciated. Exposures to temperatures as high as 50-55 degrees F (average summer temperature 55 degrees F) can cause damage to the tissues. The result of exposure to these temperatures is unlikely to have serious effects unless the circulation in the legs is 'poor' and there is a family history of hyper-sensitivity to cold. A tendency to cold legs and feet and a rather 'poor circulation' – 'just like mother's' – is extremely common in girls. Hundreds of thousands of girls with an inherited tendency to cold extremities live in poorly heated houses, stand in cold bus queues in order to reach cold factories or offices where they sit with inactive muscles until it is time to repeat the cold bus queues etc. on their way back to inadequately heated houses.

The effect of chronic exposure to cold – erythrocyanosis frigida crurarum puellarum – are usually noticed in the late teens. The back of the calves of the legs and the outside side of the legs are an ugly bluish colour in cold weather and an even uglier beefy red in hot weather. The minute pits in the skin produced by the hair follicles, and scarcely visible normally, are much enlarged, giving the skin a very coarse appearance. Swelling, at first confined to ankles and feet, gradually spreads up the limb. The swelling, due to accumulation of fluid in the subcutaneous fat, disappears with rest, in the early stages, but later on becomes replaced by increasing quantities of lumpy fatty tissue until the leg becomes grossly enlarged and shapeless. Cuffs of fat covered by coarse skin overhang the ankles and shoes. In very severe erythrocyanosis the lumpy fatty masses may liquefy and burst through the skin, leaving painful and intractable ulcers.

Erythrocyanosis was first observed after the introduction of silk stockings and short skirts. It was originally called 'silk stocking disease'. It was never seen in the days of red flannel petticoats, woollen bloomers, woollen stockings to the groin, boots to the knees and skirts to the floor. Erythrocyanosis frigida is not seen in men on account of the protection of tweed trousers and underpants.

This very distressing condition can be completely prevented by adequate protection from cold in teenage girls. This is especially important if there is a familial tendency to chilblains and cold extremities.

The fashion houses and couturiers have made their contribution and suitable clothing is available at prices all can afford. It now remains for the ghastly effects of exposure to cold to become more widely appreciated by the working girl and also by headmistresses who not infrequently send girls home for wearing 'slacks'.

Finally, a warning to young men contemplating matrimony – look at your future mother-in-law's legs in order to observe the trend.

Yours truly

(Professor) A.M. Boyd,
Department of Surgery, Manchester University

LARGE GIRLS AND FEMMES FORTES

Alison Adburgham

Alison Adburgham is a distinguished fashion writer and author of many books, including Shops and Shopping *still a much quoted textbook and* A Punch History of Manners and Modes.

In fashion, as in life, there is never anything funnier than the facts. Certainly the facts of the visit to Woburn Abbey of Mme Mag Cornou, president of the Club Sympatique des Femmes Fortes de Paris, to launch the Linda Leigh Large Girls' Club, need no embroidery. They are rich in genuine jewels, of which the most precious is that overheard across the strawberries and cream at luncheon: 'I have looked after the bigger woman in Ilford for twenty-two years'.

We must, however, take the facts in their proper sequence. Mme Mag Cornou is a blonde model with 60-inch hips and weighs 222 lbs. To give a comparative picture, Victorian Mr Banting, the originator of the Banting diet, weighed 202 lb before he started his diet and was so fat that he had to go downstairs backwards. Mme Cornou flew to London Airport; or rather, since we are being accurate she was flown to London Airport. Thence she was conveyed to Chiswick Polytechnic Sports Grounds. No time, alas, for sports, because a helicopter and the Duke of Bedford were awaiting her. The helicopter took off without difficulty and made an unforced but no doubt relieved landing on the lawns of the Duke's Bedfordshire house.

Whether Madame's descent from the helicopter was in the style of Mr Banting's staircase descents, or whether she was able to face the music is not known, because the music had not yet arrived: the coachload of journalists and photographers from London, having gathered in Bayswater for cocktails at the uncocktail hour of 9.45 a.m. was still on its way. When it did arrive, Madame, soft-hearted, warm and obliging as larger ladies are, ascended once more in the helicopter to make a second touchdown. All this in spite of having been on a trip up the Seine the night before with 500 *femmes fortes*, their husbands and their sweethearts, which had not ended until three o'clock in the morning. Late nights are nothing to *femmes fortes*, and she looked in blooming perfection like a gorgeous peony. Now the reception was under way in the entrance hall and Madame was under fire from a volley of questions, which bounced off her harmlessly enough since she knew no English. Her bilingual smile carried everyone with her and any gaps in understanding were filled in by an interpreter. We learned that there are 5,000 members of the Club Sympatique des Femmes Fortes. We were told that *femmes fortes* can be just as *coquettes* as their slimmer sisters and that they tend to attract younger and *toujours jolis* husbands. We learned that *forte*, when applied to *femme*, means well-built rather than powerful; and we hoped that the husbands have no cause to learn differently. We were told that the peony-coloured nylon dress and loose matching coat were bought *pret-à-porter* in the Champs Elysees.

It is doubtful whether a dress of such yardage and hippage could be bought ready-to-wear in England; and one of the objects of the Large Girls' Club is to make a better selection of big sizes available in the shops. Other objects are 'to give an opportunity to girls of all ages who are generously proportioned to get together and generously exchange views on their problems in fashion and beauty'. The club will run its own newspaper in which the girls will voice their views on all subjects, and tours will be arranged by area presidents. The target membership figure is a quarter of a million. The target weight figure was not given.

From champagne in the hall the party proceeded across the lawns to champagne in the Sculpture Gallery. This proved to be an artistically satisfying setting for the parade, during luncheon, of Linda Leigh fashions worn by five well-sculptured and corseted Junos and one fuller-figure Venus. There were speeches. The Duke of Bedford courteously thanked Linda Leigh Ltd 'for inviting me here today', saying how he had enjoyed the fuller figure fare, and indeed everything. 'I adore nice round plump natures. My wife spends her whole time trying to be long and thin. I get depressed by plates of lettuce.'

Photographs were then taken of His Grace with one arm around Mme Cornou, as far as it would reach; the other around the almost equally comfortable form of London model Mrs Eve Coles.

Perhaps that is a good moment to draw the curtain; perhaps, indeed, we should have drawn it earlier because as someone sighed, 'The trouble is, the Duke of Bedford kills any story now'. Whether or not he killed this story, he certainly made Mme Cornou's day, adoring, as she did, every minute his arm was around her. And it was not only Mag's day that he made. To meet our most shameless aristocrat was a real break for the buyer who had looked after the bigger woman in Ilford for twenty-two years.

THE WAY WE LOOK (1969)

Gillian Tindall

Gillian Tindall, regular Guardian *Women's Page columnist in the 1960s is also the author of many novels. She writes: This was written, I believe, in 1969, and was a*

*piece for that time. While I would not now particularly
disagree with any of it, I wouldn't think it needed writing
anyway: its originality has been eroded by a general social
consensus against 'sexism', its points have become
truisms. Perhaps this simply indicates that I was right!*

*In fact, such is the ungainliness and ungraciousness of
much New Feminist style that, if I were going to write on
this subject today, I would probably be more inclined to
stress the old-fashioned virtues of Looking Nice and
Behaving Prettily. . . .*

There has been a certain amount of trouble about my
photograph. The editor thought the one used on this page was
'too grim'. (By the time it was reproduced in his newsprint I
was inclined to agree: it did look a bit spectral.)

All the same, I slightly resent the implication that I
shouldn't be shown looking grim. From time to time I write on
fairly grim, or at least serious subjects; surely it would not be
suitable for me to beam ingratiatingly on top of a piece on the
population problem or cruelty? No one suspects a man of
being nasty because he looks serious, furrowed or straightforward old. I'm not an actress or a girl in a tooth-paste ad.
Why can't I look cross and old, too?

This may sound a frivolous complaint, but it has its serious
side. For women whose life-style is based on their looks and
who gain their greatest satisfaction thereby, life from about 35
onwards must be a slow, concealed purgatory, and I don't use
the word lightly. The last thing any responsible person should
do is to encourage women to stake so much on an inevitably
diminishing asset. Yet how a woman looks is given an absurd
and irrelevant importance by people who should know better
and in some cases secretly do.

Tough male journalists among whose qualities gullibility is
not usually numbered, almost consciously transform themselves into old softies ('See, I'm nice really') when interview-
ing a young woman upon her views. These views may be
entirely serious, she may herself hate the idea that they could
be attributed to her age and sex – but she is liable to find them
reproduced interlarded with wistful asides about her face and
figure.

127

Imagine the howl of derision that would go up if a woman journalist wrote of a male novelist's magnetic eyes or hairy chest! Yet we have a male television critic, usually a model of straight thinking, furrows and all, eulogising a pop star not (apparently) because she is Good Box as because she is 'astoundingly good-looking' with 'large and lustrous eyes'. In the same paper, a day later, there was Brigid Brophy complaining that people write to her to tell her they don't like her hair style so her views must be nonsense, or, alternatively, to enquire with ghastly playfulness why 'an attractive woman like her wastes her time writing?'

There are a number of topics on which, I think, Miss Brophy and I do not see eye to eye, but here I am 100 per cent with her. She is not a film star, her appearance is not part of her stock in trade (as it arguably is for a pop singer) so why should people feel free to comment on it? It's just plain rude. No-one asks Kenneth Allsop why, with his delightful gamin hair, he bothers to be a television personality. No one but a few obvious boors and anti-Semites makes personal remarks to Bernard Levin.

Several men to whom I have said this say: why complain? Your appearance may be nothing to do with your ideas, but if it can get you extra kudos and thus help you to put your ideas across, that's all to the good, isn't it? I see their point – but I must, in careful disinterest, point out that this illogical advantage can work the other way, too. I mean, if you are a marvellous ideas woman but happen to have buck teeth and an enormous bottom, your looks aren't going to help if any significance is placed on them.

But my real objection is that what appears as merely fulsome praise for a young skin is actually, quite often, a subtle form of disparagement. The underlying suggestion in the indulgent comment on face or body is that the mind beneath need not, perhaps, be taken entirely seriously. Rather than attacking 'on the level' unacceptable views that happen to be propounded by a young girl, it is easier to make slightingly facetious references to the mini-skirt or the flowing hair. There is a hint of Keats: 'I am inclined to class women with roses and sweetmeats.'

This is not sour grapes. I have had my fair share of supposedly disinterested and intelligent men smiling with paternal concupiscence down my front at parties, and I really – no really – do not welcome it. I'd rather be Baroness Wootton any day. In fact I am looking forward to middle age on the theory that by then I can really be just me, and as formidable as I like, and not find myself suddenly cast in the role of some chance acquaintances's sex object. It takes a while for a woman to learn that superficial sexual appreciation is no particular compliment, but once she has learnt it, she is not fooled. Real personal appeal, after all even on a sexual level, has so little to do with external appearance.

If you think I am exaggerating, here is a specific example. When my last novel came out, one reviewer (for a provincial paper, but that's no excuse really) spent lines and lines contrasting me with another woman novelist published the same week – and I mean contrasting us, not our books. He compared our two jacket photos: we both had centre partings, readers were, I am sure, enthralled to hear; we were both wearing dark jerseys. He refrained from saying 'Miss X looks older than Miss T but her bosom is bigger' – but really, if he had said that, would it have been much more impertinent, in the basic sense of just plain irrelevant?

The test of this is to imagine disparate male novelists being reviewed in this manner: 'Brian Moore has more hair than Julian Mitchell, but his tie is not as nice'; 'Graham Greene is, of course younger than J.B. Priestley, but he does not go to such a good tailor'. Instant offence.

I think, however, that women themselves must take a certain amount of blame for this state of affairs. If they didn't go on quite so much about 'the sex war' and about how unequal and unfair their lot is, they might find that men put less emphasis on specifically sexual roles also. After all, if you want to be treated as 'a person as well as a woman' you must behave as a person and not keep nattering on about 'women's problems', as if men didn't have any.

The idea of one sex imposing a role on the other is prone to exaggeration: rather each sex tends to take its cue from the other: influence is a two-way process. I don't know what other readers felt about a recent article by Margot Naylor about her facelift. My own feeling was a mild disappointment that this distinguished financial journalist should worry about looking old, as if she were an insignificant person with no abilities as compensation. She argued her point persuasively in terms of holding an important post and *therefore* not wanting to look like a great-aunt. But looking like a great-aunt only matters if you and other people think it matters, and if you don't think it does then your confident attitude may go a long way towards persuading others to the same point of view.

You wait till I'm the only woman novelist who looks like a Greek granny. I'll show 'em.

'Talkback'

I was delighted to read an article by Gillian Tindall with which I could whole-heartedly agree. After reading the *Guardian* series on beautiful women I felt thoroughly angry and humiliated. (No, not even subconsciously do I long to be Ava Gardner or an Italian earth goddess.)

Girls seem to realise quite quickly that behind a handsome facade often lies a load of old junk. Don't men learn this, or do they honestly not care whether the pretty dolly they are escorting is worthless? Are men as genuinely uninterested in personality as it would appear? . . . In my experience even intelligent sensitive men are honestly amused that women can find it degrading to be regarded as a sex symbol.

Mrs Mary Williams
London SE9

If women make a feature of their 'fronts' is it not with the object of having them looked at, or down? I should have thought that it was obvious that much dress-design aimed at being sexually attractive; if so, why complain?

S.F. Yeo
Hexham

Gillian Tindall must be very naive if she really does not know why men persist in regarding us as sexual objects even when we have other claims to notice. It is because they have money and power over us. If women had the money and power then young men would try to be appealing and attractive.

In my time, I have had some notably impecunious admirers, to the dismay of my mother who was sure they were after my money, had the admirers been wealthier than myself she, like any other mother, would have been well pleased.

It is unrealistic to inveigh against a social patterning that casts women in the role of sexual objects while at the same time making use of that patterning to obtain for oneself a legal provider and father for one's children. Women cannot have it both ways.

Women like to exploit their sex appeal when it can be useful to them and to have it ignored when it cannot. This is not honest and not fair to men. Why should men struggle and compete among themselves to win us, to own us, protect us and provide for us, if we will not admit that we are desirable?

A woman's professional success does not enable her to choose a husband from among the personable youths in the ranks of her subordinates but the nurse still dreams of marrying the doctor, the secretary her boss and the girl student her lecturer. Men cannot use their youthful charm to provide for their future; women can and do.

Meg Lynn
Hull

FEMINISTS AND THE RIGHT TO BE UGLY (1970)

Jill Tweedie

A Scottish father with Calvinist knobs on is the parent most likely to nip the first delicate buds of vanity in his daughter. My own Scottish father, if nagged to comment on my appearance, invariably replied that he supposed I looked better than a slap on the belly with a wet fish, or that I might pass with a push in a crowd with the light behind me. Human nature being what it is I managed to salvage enough vanity to get along with, though that early conditioning did make for a later ambivalence with the opposite sex: if a man compliments me on my cherry lips I think him boorish for overlooking my mind and if he says nice things about my mind I think him a cold fish for ignoring my cherry lips, which leads to alarums and exists all round.

Such an upbringing ought to make me feel at home with today's militant feminists who disdain make-up and other artifices designed to enhance their sexual attractions, on the grounds that these have for too long been the instruments of slavery. There's no doubt that it is humiliating to be dependent on so arbitrary a thing as physical appearance for any success or comfort in life, and many a girl has envied her brother for his freedom to operate in a haze of scruff and sweat where she is under constant pressure to groom herself like a Cruft's exhibit.

132

Apart from anything else, grooming oneself is a boring occupation and demands a more persistent dedication than I, at least, can muster. Once, overcome by a sudden desire for champagne and adoration, I presented myself at a model agency. An exquisite person looked me over, said go away, get your hair done, manicure your nails, iron your clothes and then come back. But I never did. Somehow champagne and adoration seemed too puny a reward for a lifetime of tweaking and peering at myself and I have now settled for looking like the curate's egg – good in patches, depending upon whether vanity or sloth has the upper hand that day.

One of the many Women's Liberation manifestos floating about London these days not only rejects positive grooming but demands the negative freedom for a girl 'to be able to be as funky in dress, body etc. as a man' and, after years of being urged, on pain of sexual ostracism, to keep myself as hairless, germless and odourless as a boiled bottle, by advertisers who believe, along with Saint Augustine, that women are vessels of uncleanliness, I see their point. As far as I am concerned, a natural slut can languish unwashed, hairy, germy and odorous, if that's the way she wants it, and other people should grin and bear it from her at least as much as they would with her male equivalent. And if a mother is going to impress hygiene on her daughter, she should do the same with her son.

In the past, a girl's face was her fortune and without some physical attractions she forfeited some of the necessities and all of the luxuries of life. Now, if a woman wants security, she can just about manage to provide it for herself and it seems eminently logical that the present revulsion of some women from self-titivation should coincide exactly with their maturing economic autonomy. But, as usual, logic appears to have little to do with it, because men are now taking more interest in their appearance than ever before and men have always had economic independence. All they have discovered is that being a meal ticket is not a sex symbol as it once was, and they are falling back on the oldest behaviour pattern of them all – roll up, roll up and look at lovely me.

Feminists also complain that, as women, they are expected to look attractive to all men, rather than just to the one man they choose and, certainly, this peacocking role is part and parcel of attracting and keeping a man. Many men are a good deal more interested in proving their masculinity to other men than they are in the woman herself and the need to feel sure their choice is applauded by other men too. One man I know goes doggedly out night after night with a series of inter-changeable beauty queens on his arm and though in the silence of his lonely room they bore him to distraction this is apparently a small price to pay for the public envy of other males. I doubt if jettisoning make-up is going to cure this hardened case and anyway, beauty queens need outings, too.

In fact I doubt if jettisoning make-up will cure anything, though it may make a passing point. Women are far more introverted about their appearance than men and they need, on the whole, to think themselves desirable before they can arouse, or even feel desire. At the age of 10 I wreaked havoc in the heart of a neighbourhood lad by setting my cheeks aflame with pink chalk, scoring my eyebrows with black crayon, stuffing two pairs of socks up my jumper and nursing a blind faith in my own uncanny resemblance to Rita Hayworth. The blind faith did it, and the fact that I looked uncannily like a deranged ten-year-old went unnoticed by either of us.

9 Toward Personhood

From the beginning – from Mary Wollstonecraft onwards, one might say – feminists discussed the nature and extent of the differences between men and women. (Mary Wollstonecraft wrote, in 1792, 'I earnestly wish to see the distinction of sex confounded in society, except where love animates the behaviour'.) These discussions went on throughout the periods covered in this book – from the early 1970s onwards the new feminists tended to *emphasise* the differences, so as to urge the importance of a specifically female contribution to society.

THE PERSONAL PRONOUN (1928)

Winifred Holtby

The other day my business took me into the office of a certain socialist editor whom I did not know very well. The circumstances of our meeting had not been wholly fortunate and at first our conversation went haltingly. But as we both became really interested in our subject the editor lost his constraint. He pulled out his pipe, lounged with his feet on a chair and began to call me 'brother'.

At first the unexpected title amused and almost disconcerted me. Then, as I realised its implication, I became unusually pleased. For we had grown so much absorbed in the business before us that my new acquaintance had lost all sense of my identity, I was no longer a rather troublesome young woman who might or might not be of use to the particular cause he was sponsoring, I was 'brother', an impersonal creature, drawn into that comradeship of 'those who want to get something done', who are like the angels in heaven, without sex or nationality.

It occurs to me that at certain periods of absorption in a piece of work, which is one of the most agreeable of all human experiences, the personal pronoun fades out of our vocabulary. To the really busy man or woman sex for a time becomes just gender, masculine, feminine, or neuter. And after a certain point of interest has been reached even gender loses its significance. He, she or it, brother, sister, it matters very little. We have become for the moment agents of a driving power far more important than our individual idiosyncrasies.

The abolition of sex would not be desirable, even if it were possible, but I have sometimes wondered if abolition of gender might not be convenient. In a society where occupation and character is no longer finally determined by sex what does it matter whether to address an editor or a lawyer as 'Dear Sir' or 'Dear Madam'? the dairy worker may with equal efficiency and probability be either he or she. The gardener, the spinner, the stenographer, the lecturer are in their work without sex differentiation, yet continually the little personal pronoun obtrudes itself, demanding recognition for their forgotten sex.

I am not a philologist and I do not know how far a modification of our grammar is either possible or desirable. If we lived in France or Germany, where even knives and pillow cases have their gender, the case might be grammatically more complex but socially much easier. But we live in England, where our language recognises only three sorts of creatures, he, she and it. Tables and stones and mountains share one gender but men and women are irrevocably divided. Save for the awkward 'one' who occasionally performs actions, the neutral 'we' or the unintimate 'they', when acting alone the human being must be he or she, man or woman, sir or madam, inescapably, perpetually. Letters from strangers signed only with initials cause nerve-racking hesitations and usually end in a reply being sent to – Esq, whereupon they become a source of indignation or amusement to the recipient.

It would seem that for business purposes and the workaday world we need a new personal pronoun, personal without gender, neutral but not neuter, something more definite than 'one' and less distant than the German 'mann'. We need also a noun; but 'comrade', 'colleague,' 'friend' all imply stages of intimacy too particular for ordinary purposes. We want a form of address courteous yet sexless, a neutral but not a neuter form of sir and madam. Sadam and mir would not do. We must devise something better. I make no suggestions. Every attempt in my own mind slays itself. But I am sure that here is a fruitful occupation for philologists.

The real problem of the professions and the industries, the arts and government services is to find the best person for the best work. It does not matter whether that person is masculine or feminine. It matters very much that he (she) should not be neuter. Philogists to the rescue! Find us an alternative and half the difficulty about women in the world of business will have vanished.

THE CURE OF SOULS (1928)

Miss Ellen Wilkinson, MP

Ellen Wilkinson was first elected to Parliament in 1924, for Middlesbrough East, later sitting for Jarrow. She was Chairman of the Labour Party from 1944-5, Parliamentary Secretary, Ministry of Pensions 1940 and Parliamentary Secretary, Ministry of Home Security 1940-5. In 1945, as Minister of Education she became a member of the Cabinet.

Dean Inge rather took people's breath away the other day when he boldly advocated the admission of women to Holy Orders. This seemed the latest expression of modernity, the one ditch to be conquered by the fully enfranchised woman. But we are all so busy discussing what Miss 1928 will do next that we are apt to forget that hardly any of these 'problems of the modern woman' is really new.

The discussion as to whether women should be ordained ministers seems to be nearly as old as the Christian church. Some historians believe that Phoebe of New Testament days was as much a deacon as St Stephen or St Philip. The word 'deaconess' had a very definite meaning in the early Church. Bishop Collins says 'There can be no question that deaconesses in the early days were really ordained. The technical phrases of ordination are used of them in precisely the same way as of men.'

In the Middle Ages, women had enormous influence in the Church. The abbesses of the great convents played a part beside which the role of the most widely-advertised modern woman seems very small indeed. They controlled very rich and powerful organisations and many had the same rights as a bishop with the exception of the power of administering the Sacrament. They were women of high intellectual ability, and the fame of some of them has come down through the ages. St Hilda, an abbess of Whitby, was renowned far and wide for her theological lectures. Certain abbesses in Germany ranked among the independent Princes of the Holy Roman Empire, and sat and voted in the Diet as members of the Rhenish Bench of Bishops. Cistercian abbesses in Spain held civil and criminal courts and issued licences to priests which authorised them to engage in the cure of souls. There seems to be no service that these great ladies of the mediaeval church could not render except the administration of the rite of the Sacrament, and of course that excluded even the most powerful of them from the ranks of the actual priesthood. St Thomas Aquinas produced what seemed to him the final word on the subject when he pointed out that women's long hair could not receive the tonsure. I wonder what he would think of our Eton crops!

In modern times women have not enjoyed the power and position which they held in the mediaeval church, though there are exceptions. The Quakers 250 years ago placed women on complete equality with men, but then, they do not have an ordained priesthood. The Salvation Army also recognises no difference between the sexes in Christ's ministry. The work of the Salvation Army women makes a heroic page in the history of women's service. True, they have never been advertised, as have women in more spectacular posts but when people talk to me of this or that form of activity being 'not fit for a woman' I think of those unknown heroines who have faced alone the horrors of the foulest dens, not only in their own country but in the unspeakable slums of far Eastern ports, secure in the security of their faith.

The Wesleyan Church has always been rather stiff in its

attitude against women as ordained ministers. George Eliot drew the character of her woman preacher from that of Elizabeth Evans, a Wesleyan Methodist who had left that body because of its refusal to allow women to preach. In 1803 the Wesleyan conference decided that women preachers were 'undesirable and unnecessary' but that if a woman thought she had 'an extraordinary call from God' she might 'address her own sex, and those only'. It took 115 more years before women were recognised in 1918 as local preachers. The resolution to allow their ordination has recently been decisively defeated.

The report of a very influential committee appointed by the Archbishop of Canterbury on the mission of women in the Church, which was issued in 1919, paid a high tribute to their work. 'It has slowly become recognised,' said the committee, 'that the influence of women in State and Church for moral and religious progress is of incalculable value. The names of Hannah More, Elizabeth Fry, Florence Nightingale and Josephine Butler illustrate this.'

What then stands in the way of women's ordained Ministry in the Christian Church, especially in the Protestant Churches? Much of the controversy centres round the Communion table. To the Protestant the Lord's Supper is not a mystic rite, but a reverant commemoration of our Lord's suffering, and a rededication of the communicant to His service. Is there anything unsuitable in receiving the elements of that service from the hands of a devout and noble woman who, after careful training and examination, is recognised as having a vocation for the Ministry?

St Paul is always quoted as though he had said the last word that could ever be said on the subject. I rather imagine that that very practical and sensible man would have been not only surprised but very impatient if he had been told that his hints to certain communities in Corinth, where the zeal of a few women had outrun their discretion, were to be taken as a final instruction to all Christian Churches in the very different conditions existing two thousand years later.

When we turn from the Communion table to the other activities of the Church, we find that the organisational work is already largely in the hands of women under the supervision of the ordained man. In the relations with the flock there is some work that can be best performed by men and some that would be far better done by women. When I see the embarrassment and difficulties of young ministers attempting to deal with numbers of young girls in their 'coltish stage', between the ages of 14 and 17, I feel that sensible women would not only do this work better, but with the added prestige of ordination would have more influence with them, just as a man knows best the way into the hearts of the youth.

It is, of course, true that there is nothing to prevent women from doing this work and many of them are already very successful, but there is other work that in the present organisations of the Churches must fall within the province of the ordained minister. The consolation of the sick in the last hours of earthly life, the spiritual leadership of a church or parish, all the devout and specialised service which we include in the phrase 'the cure of souls' can be well done by carefully trained persons who have given evidence of a vocation for such ministry. This vocation is not the privilege of one sex only. Such vocation is of the spirit, and in the realm of the spirit sex cannot and should not exist.

SECOND FIDDLE (1932)

'E.W.'

We have Mr H.G. Wells's word for it: women must be content to play second fiddle. They have had 14 years of political freedom in England and 15 years of complete equality with men in Russia, and in neither country have the women beaten the men. Therefore they can't, ever.

Well, of course, the women of today were bred in the bad old days, when women were classed with criminals and lunatics, and that may have something to do with their failure, so far, to become Shakespeares and Lenins. What the women of tomorrow do may confound Mr Wells's arguments. Or, on the other hand, it may not, for they will have been brought up by the more old-fashioned women who still have vestiges of the old slave mentality. It may be reserved for the women of the day after tomorrow to throw up a Beethoven or a St Paul or a Julius Caesar. Fourteen years is not a long time in the evolution of a whole sex, as the man who wrote the *Outline of History* ought to know.

Besides, political equality was never supposed, even by the most excited Suffragette, to be more than a preliminary, and, indeed, it has proved to be just that. The war helped in other ways to free women. It is almost unbelievable today to recall that shortly before the war women in industry were terribly upset at the bare suggestion that they might be under forewomen instead of foremen in the cotton mills. They had no confidence in their fellow women. But some confidence has grown up now.

Principally there is a great deal to be done by women for other women. Mothers, for instance, still put their sons first and relieve them of countless small cares and duties which their daughters must undertake as a matter of course. It is still observed by schoolteachers that the girls who win scholarships are handicapped by household duties from which their brothers are free, saved by that 'protective selfishness' of the young male, sedulously fostered by their mothers. Consequently, girls are more liable to breakdowns in critical years. And almost all women who work outside the home have to fritter away a good deal of their so-called 'leisure' on small jobs of washing and mending which almost all men find some woman to do for them.

No landlady on earth ever proposed to mend the stockings of a woman lodger, whereas many (not all, we know) do make some pretence of darning the socks and sewing on the buttons of their men lodgers. Women are trained to fritter away their time and efforts and sedulously guarded against any concentration of their energies such as is absolutely essential for the production of good original work. And this is the doing of women and constitutes an enormous handicap.

Women believe in their menfolk; they do not believe in their womenfolk – with very rare exceptions. It is considered admirable in a mother to sacrifice herself for her son (even for a wastrel son) but the mother who sacrifices herself for a daughter, however, brilliant, is rather despised by other women. And the daughter who allows it is definitely despised.

She is condemned by all her female relations and friends if her mother washes and mends for her, considers her in planning the meals and spares her the hundred and one little domestic duties that make up life for most women. And this attitude cannot fail to affect a woman's mind from her infancy onward, even if she has The Vote.

The conclusion of the whole matter is that Mr Wells, and nearly all the men, and women, in England, see what they want to see. Women are too useful to be spared for fame. They must not be encouraged to step out of their sphere of helpmates and themselves become great. And it is true that for most women a subordinate position will always be their role. One reflects at this point that in this the sexes are equal. Most men will continue to occupy subordinate positions. There has, after all the ages of man's pre-eminence, been only one Shakespeare.

Until every gifted woman has some devoted personal adherent (man or woman) who believes in her, adores her and thinks it a sufficient career to make her path smooth we shall not have made the best of women's talents. And until women believe in the possibility of women's genius, no woman will be pre-eminent. It is all very well to say that 'genius will out'. Women start with an inferiority complex, bred in them throughout the ages and fostered by all the other women they know (and by Mr H.G. Wells). This is a handicap so immense that it is enough to stifle any genius.

STANDING UP FOR OURSELVES (1932)

Vera Brittain

Like her friend Winifred Holtby, Vera Brittain began writing for the Manchester Guardian *in 1928. She was already beginning to be well-known but won continuing fame for her* Testament of Youth, *published in 1933.*

The other day I was taken severely to task by a contributor to a newspaper for stating in an article that recent literary work by women illustrated the long-repressed power and orginality of the female sex. Women, stated my critic, are still, in spite of their political victories, imitative and 'pseudo-male'. Their success in literature, the very fact that they write books at all, implies a mere treading in masculine footsteps, while in other spheres once monopolised by men they are simply 'slavish followers'. Why, demanded this intrepid masculist, don't they form a 'Woman's Party' for the propagation of reform in 'feminine' affairs. Why don't they tackle such problems as housing, maternal mortality, the forlorn dreariness of domestic service.

Neither this article, nor its singularly uninformed author would have seemed to me of any special importance were it not for the fact that they do represent an obstinate and widely held belief. Largely through ignorance of publications, of political origins, of the inter-relation of social movements since 1918, the general public still remains under the strange impression that everything of importance from rebellions to changes of habit is, and always has been, initiated by men. In actual truth no decade has ever seen a revolution in the social habits and values of a people so profound and yet so subtle as that which occurred in this country through the influence of women during the ten years that followed the war.

To dispose first of this matter of literature: it is of course arguable that no one is original who follows any occupation which has ever been pursued by somebody else. In this case there has been no originality in the art of writing since it was first developed from the primitive alphabet by the fathers of civilisation in Mesopotamia, and men authors are as imitative as women. If we carry the argument to its logical conclusion in every department of human activity, we shall find that men are the 'slavish imitators' throughout the whole field of economics and industry since – in the words of Professor Veblen in his *Theory of a Leisure Class* – 'virtually the whole range of industrial employment is the outcome of what is classed as women's work in the primitive barbarian community'.

But granting that prehistoric man did not exhaust even humanity's capacity for imaginative achievement it is manifestly unfair to class as 'imitative' some of the most important work – of the type that would once have been called 'masculine' being done by women in fiction today. My critic maintains that the examples I gave of powerful novels by

143

women, Naomi Mitchison's *The Corn King and the Spring Queen* and Phyllis Bentley's *Inheritance* – and no doubt he would add Sigrid Undset's *Kristin Lavransdatter* – are written by 'disguised males'. Yet few writers, male or female, are more consistently original than Naomi Mitchison. I doubt if the most inveterate anti-feminist could find a masculine model for the long novel that so nearly won the Feminine-Vie-Heureuse Prize. Phyllis Bentley, perhaps, owes something to Arnold Bennett and to Hardy, but no male novelist has ever made quite the attempt she is making to place a great industrial community, with its historical and industrial background upon the literary map.

But even if it could be proved that, in any of the arts, young women are more influenced than young men by the work of the great masters, no just and faithful observer could deny the direct influence of the Women's Movement upon political and social life, so quickly and thoroughly has it permeated, that the older generation has already forgotten what it felt like to live in a man-ordered world, while the younger generation has never known.

Far from being imitative, the suffragette campaign itself initiated methods of publicity and propaganda which have ever since been imitated by others. Apart from the 'direct action' which is the final stage of nearly all rebellions against the existing order, many modern publicity campaigns have derived their inspiration from those spectacular processions, those picturesque mass meetings. Women, in fact, have largely developed the present art of advertising which has vitalised and electrified the commercial and industrial world.

It seems strange that any man or woman today should still believe that women have failed to use their political power to urge reform in the spheres peculiarly their own, for the record of Parliament since 1900 gives the lie direct to any such theory. Between 1900 and 1918 only four Acts were passed which affected the welfare of women as such. Between 1918 and 1929 16 Acts were passed directly concerning women as wives, as mothers, and as members of the domestic professions, apart from many others enfranchising women and giving them the right to enter 'male' professions.

The very personalities most prominent in the feminist

movement joined it, and later used its results, to further social reform. Mrs Pankhurst herself confessed in her *Memoirs* that 'the poor unprotected mothers and their babies' in the Manchester Workhouse 'were potent factors in my education as a militant'. Her daughter Sylvia has made herself a specialist on the subject of maternal mortality, while among the constitutionalists Miss Eleanor Rathbone is the leading authority on family allowances and Mrs Corbett Ashby has become the insistent advocate of such peace and order in international relations as woman has maintained in the home.

Such a list could be prolonged indefinitely but the widest results of the women's movement are more subtle, more diffused, less easy to tabulate. Mrs Oliver Strachey has summed them up in one sentence in her book *The Cause*, 'A hundred years ago a girl could go nowhere unprotected: today there is nowhere she cannot go.' The changes which have given women the right, if they wish, to live alone, work alone, travel alone, eat and drink in public alone, are now so completely and universally accepted that we have even completely forgotten that it is solely women to whom they are due.

CRUMBS FOR WOMEN (1935)

Anon

There seems to be an indestructible belief on the part of the present government that all women are nurses, teachers, or in government offices. Nurses, teachers and government officials, it seems, are delighted to be thrown an MBE or so, and so they receive a handful, and there the matter ends. While nurses and teachers, especially those sanctified by the Government are indispensable members of society, they are not alone there. The government might be informed, indeed, that there are in this country a good many more women than men and that they have more than three occupations, and that the MBE is inadequate when compared with the alphabet of stars bestowed elsewhere by a grateful national government. In case the government had never heard of such a thing, there are women who run newspapers; there are women who are distinguished historians, even if they do not teach. There have been women novelists during the last year or so who have been at least as grammatical as men, while women politicians are not unknown, and even some who have been more useful to the Government than is measured by an MBE. Women social workers take a high place and there are even women county councillors and women magistrates whose services are by no means negligible. There are, in short, plenty of women in all the occupations for which men are rewarded from which to choose for more than the few crumbs of honour which drop from the rich man's table. The CBE of Dr Catherine Chisholm is perhaps among the most gratifying of the awards, but in weighing it against those awarded to her brothers her side of the scale decidedly kicks the beam.

STRICTLY A FEMALE FEMALE (1967)

Catherine Storr

In addition to contributing to The Guardian, Nova, *and other women's journals, Catherine Storr read medicine in Cambridge and London and worked for the NHS for fourteen years. She is the author of several novels and over thirty books for children.*

'I'm so plain and he's so funny.' This is the cry of a little girl on seeing a contemporary little boy in the nude for the first time. It is quoted by an American gynaecologist, J. Dudley Chapman, in his recent book, *The Feminine Mind and Body* (Vision Press). He explains disarmingly, in the introduction that he is no psychiatrist, but that an obstretician becomes 'mother, father, and confessor all in one, and if he listens he can learn more about a woman than can any "expert" in the behavioural sciences'. On the other hand there is *Feminine Psychology* (Routledge), a book of collected papers by the late Karen Horney, a Freudian-trained analyst who approaches the problems facing women through her dealings with their minds rather than through their bodies.

I've started with this quotation, because it expresses in

146

everyday terms a theme which was first propounded by Freud, and which crops up as often as one of the motifs in Wagner's *Ring*. Penis envy is its technical name, and it explains half the feminine ills and dissatisfactions in terms of the woman's wish to be a man, her conviction that she was originally equipped as well as he, and her vain striving to regain that pristine state of equality.

The early Freudians apparently regarded this myth literally, as fundamentalists did the story of Adam and Eve and the Fall, believing that every girl infant saw and coveted the penis, and followed this with fantasies of having suffered castration, generally at the hands of a parent.

It is true, of course, that women today are desperately trying to find their place in a world which is man-orientated. Karen Horney points out in the paper called *The Flight from Womanhood*, that our philosophies, our laws, our hypotheses about the nature of the universe and about the human body and mind have all been expounded by men. We recognise, thanks to another man, that in the observation of any phenomena the eye of the observer forms a part of the phenomena being observed. Therefore the criteria by which we measure behaviour bear the imprint of the male mind.

There are areas where this doesn't seem important; would a woman have come to different conclusions about cell structure, nuclear physics, the importance of DNA? I don't think so. But in the determination of one's own role in relation to the opposite sex – or of the potential of either sex – how could one expect objectivity? One couldn't, it wouldn't be human. I'd go farther and say it would be wrong. So we are faced with the conclusion that most of the theories concerning the development, the establishment, the rewards and the desirability of the feminine role have been observed, interpreted, and explained by men; and God help us if men are going to tell us how to be women. Are we to tell them how to be men?

So we come back to penis envy. And, being a woman, I'm now in the same difficulty that I've just described. I can't be objective about any scheme involving the male-female relationship because, whether I like it or not, I'm not outside it. I have to be personal, to say what seems true to me, now. 'Penis envy' has been used in the past to explain many of the aspirations women have felt in a world dominated by men, all the claims to share the advantages, educational, social, financial, emotional, which have been to a great degree monopolised by men. But what Karen Horney points out is that many of these advantages are real; they aren't fantasies. Since women have been admitted half way, so to speak, isn't it natural that they should want to administrate, to teach, to preach, to fly, to run businesses, to govern, to create things other than children?

Some women want these things as men want them – because they are interesting, demanding, satisfying. Some women, I believe, are better wives, mistresses, mothers, because they can express the whole of themselves in a variety of activities. There's a time and a place for everything. We might look askance at the husband who could write a first-class article on the current political crisis during the birth of his first child. But though for a woman the care of the children probably takes first place while they are young there is still, in the present-day world, opportunity for her to engage in activities which affirm for her that she is a person socially as well as domestically viable. This isn't envy, which I take to be the desire to steal from some other person something he possesses, it's the desire to share, to be admitted to an equality of interests which can enhance, rather than diminish the mutual acknowledgment of an essential, anatomical, rewarding, enchanting difference.

Both Karen Horney and Dr Chapman deal with this aspect of feminine psychology. As you'd expect, Karen Horney is the more sophisticated; she has the courage to challenge Freud's assumption of penis envy as being the driving motive in the lives of most women; she suggests that boys and men may also suffer from a feeling of inferiority in the face of woman's power to create life; she questions the persistence of penis envy beyond the natural childish longing for a piece of valuable equipment which need not survive a recognition of the potential of womanhood.

Dr Chapman is somehow very much more naive; many of the Aunt Sallies he inveighs against no longer exist in the European scene; when he advocates early education in sexual matters, or protests against the view that sex is 'unclean', 'not for the nice girl', for instance, I find myself impatient. This is not what we need to be told now. But it may well be that these things can't be said too often or too simply. Dr Chapman's conclusions are totally sympathetic. He and Karen Horney advocate that women should be women; in competition with men only where competition is enlivening and stimulating, aiming at being not second-rate men, but other human beings, with qualities of their own to offer.

After all – and this is my thought, not that of either of these experts – we may be unadorned outwardly: but as every gynaecologist and psychoanalyst knows, we make up for our plain exteriors by being inside, for the benefit of the next generation, most fearfully and wonderfully made.

NICE GIRLS FINISH LAST (1971)

Jill Tweedie

One of the more crippling aspects of being a woman – and an Englishwoman to boot – is the continual and largely unconscious compulsion to be nice. Nice and kind, nice and fair, nice and tidy. Nice. Always ready to understand the other point of view. Always careful not to give a wrong impression. Always reacting rather than acting, responding to outside pressure rather than inward need: human chameleons so sensitive to the surroundings that a change in attitude is a near-uncontrollable reflex mechanism. And if, in some aberrant moment, inward need erupts like Etna, great lavas of guilt immediately inundate the wayward ego and drown it in remorse. Just as the white man pounded the black man into submission, beating him over the head with the Christian ethic, so men have hypnotised women with a masculine code of behaviour and stood back, relieved and amused to see the poor things take it all so seriously.

It would be a tragedy if the still embryonic Women's Liberation Movement in this country sank without trace into the amniotic fluid of niceness, but already I detect some signs. The women directly concerned with organising the March 6th demo, though they point with pride to the massive WL movement in the US, seem not to have learned very much from the performance of their American sisters. They bend over backwards to be fair. ('We must be very careful not to assume that if a woman is refused a job it is sexual discrimination' – why? It's not our job to worry about fairness.) They talk too much about wanting to be taken seriously; they say too often how much they deprecate extremes and shudder with refined horror at bra-burnings and at SCUM and WITCH. Not at all the image we want, they say, metaphorically crooking their little fingers and adjusting their petal hats. We don't want to go to gaol, or, worse, be laughed at.

The tendency among these ladies is to sneer at the Germaine Greers of the movement and, indeed, it is easy enough to carp at sweeping generalisations and lack of careful factual research. But anger, neurosis, insights, obsession and extremism is where it is at and women will have lost the battle before it has begun if they reject all this and concentrate their energies only on concrete injustice. Reforms like equal pay, equal job opportunities, free contraception, better nursery schools, have needed implementation as long as I can remember, and armies of hard-working, dedicated women have been pushing them forward as long as I can remember, too, and a great deal longer. *The only new ingredient Women's Lib ever had to offer was the intellectual recognition of an imprisoned psyche and the realisation that when that inner battle is fought and won, concrete injustices crumble at the roots.*

And that is not done by being nice. American liberationists did not surge into life thinking of the other chap's point of view or making constant efforts to be fair, moderate, cool and ladylike. They succeeded by being prejudiced, unfair, immoderate, uncool, and devastatingly unladylike and they came up with the only symbolic image of the movement so far – bra-burning. A small and risible thing, perhaps, but their own. Yet even this causes a throwing up of hands, in England – one girl commented last week, among general agreement, that she hoped no-one would freak out that way on such a serious demo.

In fact the whole point of bra-burning seems to have vanished from some English liberationists minds. Have they forgotten that hilarious though it may be, the bra is a presentation pack, two breasts, gift-wrapped, to please the customer, with as many human variations as possible camouflaged under the implacable stitching? And by rejecting bra-burning (or any other symbolic act in favour of the concrete) they reject anger almost before it begins. Ah yes, there was a faint smell of burning there a while ago, but we're glad to report that it's now well under control.

American Women's Liberationists go to extremes, but I cannot personally think of any widespread injustice that has been remedied by plodding worthily down the middle of the road, smiling and smiling. The argument against extremism, however non-violent, is that you risk alienating people who might otherwise support your cause, but does this hold water? Where have all those potential supporters been over the last 2,000 years? Nodding sleepily in their corner is where, rousing only to growl about extremism when disturbed by a particular extreme. But by actively alienating some people (or not caring if you do) the debate is immediately polarised: furious reactions prod previously uncommitted women into action and if you are sure of the justice of your cause it must be better to have people thinking of it with initial anger than not thinking at all. As to the fear of derision, that *is* anger in another guise.

Another hurdle for nice, reasonable English ladies is to realise that nice, reasonable English gentlemen are, to some extent, the Enemy. There are, for instance, very few women 'free' enough to pursue a cogent emancipation argument in the presence of a man (granted he isn't the Hunchback of Notre Dame) without feeling a terrible urge to soften the hard edge, to persuade him in subtle ways that after all, you're lovely when you're angry. This weakness – a resignation to the sexual object role – must be recognised and accepted quite coldly by women and they must protect themselves carefully from it until such time as they are more secure.

Ladies, unite. Let us cherish our freaks and fanatics, cultivate our obsessions, hone our anger to a fine point and never, never, listen to anyone who says 'be reasonable'. Our own voices will tell us that too often, as it is.

10   Equal Citizens

A good case could be made for the claim that it was the *Manchester Guardian* Women's Page which, following quickly on *Time and Tide* (1920) and often quoting from it, kept feminism alive in the 1920s and 1930s, after the suffragettes had disbanded and the major battle for the vote had been won (1918). Madeline Linford, the first editor, was certainly a feminist and so was one of her most regular contributors, Evelyn Sharp, who admitted in more than one article to being acquainted with the inside of Holloway prison. In its first few years the page carried regular reports on what measures of interest to women would be debated in Parliament, and on the women candidates who were standing for election.

It is startling to discover that women in the boot and shoe trade went on strike in 1922 for a pay increase to bring them nearer to men's earnings and that this was termed 'a sex war'. And it is humiliating to read that in 1958 there were, 'After 40 years, 28 women MPs', for in 1983, a quarter of a century later, only 23 women were elected to 'the mother of Parliaments'.

'BRIEF ENCOUNTER'
Winifred Holtby

October: I went to see feminism at the Queens Hall. I saw a woman (Dame Ethel Smythe) accepted at last as a master of her art by pure virtue of merit, dominating a crowd of performers, both men and women, moulding their wills by a gesture of her arm to her own creative purpose. I saw in the orchestra men and women co-operating to produce one complete and harmonious pattern of sound. I saw that an orchestra's relation to the conductor and to its own individual

152

players is the most civilised form of society that it has ever been my fortune to observe. And I saw that when it came to the whole-hearted desire to abandon oneself to the discipline and leadership of the beat for the sake of the music it did not matter the turn of a hair whether a man or woman was performing, a man or woman was conducting, or men or woman listened. The music alone mattered and the desire to perform. And this, after all, is what feminism means.

Dame Ethel Smythe: Militant suffragette who is reputed to have given Mrs Pankhurst lessons in how to hurl a stone through a plate glass window and to have conducted 'The March of the Women' with her toothbrush from her cell window in Holloway prison as her sisters marched round the yard.

'BRIEF ENCOUNTER' (1934)

Sylvia Pankhurst

Sylvia Pankhurst, militant suffragette, daughter of Emmeline, sister of Christabel, was imprisoned and on hunger-strike 13 times. In her later years became deeply involved in the affairs of Ethiopia when it was invaded by Mussolini's troops, and the Emperor had to take refuge in England. She moved to Addis Ababa in the 1950s and died there in 1960.

April: Few people now remember John Grave, Mayor of Manchester from 1869 to 1871, yet he earned a place on the scroll of history. In the first year of his term of office the municipal franchise was extended to women ratepayers, thereby adding 9000 persons to the electorate of Manchester. When in 1870 the first Suffrage Bill, drafted by Dr Pankhurst, was brought before the House of Commons by Jacob Bright, the Manchester City Council supported it by a petition of its members, not once but on every occasion it was before the House. At the first School Board election held in Manchester under the then new Elementary Education Act of 1870, the citizens confirmed the verdict of their parliamentary and municipal representatives in favour of women's suffrage by electing a woman and a suffragist, Lydia Becker, to the School Board. So John Grave was the first returning officer in the kingdom to make an official return of a woman by the suffrages of a great popular constituency.

Lydia Becker of Manchester was one of the Pankhursts' earliest supporters. School Boards and Boards of Guardians were the first public bodies to which women were entitled to be elected.

WOMEN IN THE LORDS (1922)

An interview with Lady Rhondda

Lady Rhondda succeeded to her father's title. (Viscount Rhondda was Minister of Food in world War I), but never took a seat in the House of Lords – women were not admitted until a number of women were made life peers in 1958. Lady Rhondda died shortly before this. She was the founder of the campaigning feminist political and literary weekly journal, Time and Tide *in 1920.*

Today the Consultative Committee which represents 60 women's societies, including nearly all the non-political women's societies in the country, carried the following resolution:

> 'The constituent societies of the Consultative Committee demand that the Government shall as a proof of good faith immediately pass into law an amending Act to the Sex Disqualification (Removal) Act enabling peeresses in their own right to sit in the House of Lords.'

'It seems to me that this is a question for the government,' said Lady Rhondda, discussing the resolution with a representative of the *Manchester Guardian*. 'It was the government which was really responsible for the decision taken by the House of Lords when the Committee of Privileges reported on my petition. If the matter had been left to them the Committee's report would probably have gone through. That first Committee agreed to my petition by a vote of seven to one. It is a most unusual thing for the House of Lords to turn down or to refer back the report of the Committee of Privileges. Had not the Lord Chancellor lent his authority to the suggestion of doing so it seems unlikely that the House would have taken such a drastic step. We feel that the government must be held responsible for this action on the part of one of its leading members.

'It seems to me a very serious thing that the government which passed the Sex Disqualification (Removal) Act and held it up to women as a sort of charter of liberty, should through one of its prominent members make waste paper of the opening part of the Act which states that "a person shall not be disqualified by sex or marriage from the exercise of any public function".

'The only way in which the Government can escape an imputation of deliberate bad faith, in that they gave the impression that they were granting much more than they really did, is by bringing in a short amending Bill to that Act allowing women otherwise qualified to sit and vote in the House of Lords, and passing this Bill through all its stages.

'It is a matter of importance to women that an authoritative decision should have been given that women otherwise qualified to sit in the House of Lords shall not do so because of their sex. That is to reiterate that the status of women is inferior to the status of men. Such a decision is going to react on every professional and working woman, for on the status of a woman depend her pay and opportunity and chances of advancement in every direction. This is not, therefore, a matter that concerns only a small body of about twenty women; it is a matter which really concerns all the women in the country.

'Of course I do think the amending bill is important for its own sake. I happen to know that the majority of those who, had the report of the first Committee been adopted, would have been entitled to sit in the House of Lords, are anxious to take their places and to do what seems to them to be their duty in that Chamber, and I think it would be very useful if they could do so.

'The plain fact is that the Sex Disqualification (Removal) Act has turned out to be a 'dud'. It has not protected married women, where local authorities have wished to dismiss them;

155

it has not helped the women at Cambridge, though, it was apparently intended to do so.' Lady Rhondda then quoted the clause: 'Nothing in the statute or charter of any university shall be deemed to preclude the authorities of such university from making such provision as they shall think fit for the admission of women to membership thereof, or to any privilege therein or in connection therewith.' 'The Act,' continued Lady Rhondda 'really leaves an opening for what amounts to acts of bad faith. The local authorities have taken advantage of this: the Civil Service has taken advantage of this; and now the Lord Chancellor, who cannot, unfortunately, be dissociated from the government, has taken advantage of it.

'A sense of dissatisfaction, based very largely on the failure of the Sex Disqualification (Removal) Act has been growing among women for the past year, has been accentuated to a very marked degree in the last few months.'

WOMEN AND THE BOOT TRADE: THE LEICESTER STRIKE (1922)

Anon

The existence of a 'sex war' within the National Union of Boot and Shoe Operatives has been both affirmed and denied during the conference which is at present sitting in London. The indictment comes from the Leicester women's branch. 'The sex war within our union,' they declare, 'is forcing women to look after themselves first.'

The attitude of the Leicester women does not appear to be wholeheartedly endorsed by the women operatives in other districts. A woman delegate from Northampton, the other great centre of the boot trade, told the conference that her own constituents did not subscribe to the charge levelled at the Union, and her statement seems to have passed unchallenged. The grievance behind the Leicester protest has been only locally articulated so far, and is perhaps the less significant on that account. It comes of a refusal to acquiesce in working conditions which the rest of the women in the boot trade have accepted.

Resentment at these conditions drove a section of the Leicester women into an unauthorised and unsuccessful strike a month ago. A national agreement for the whole of the trade had been signed in February by the National Union of Boot and Shoe Operatives, representing men and women alike, and by the employers through their own organisation. The agreement set up a sliding scale by which wages were to fluctuate with the cost of living, with the result that each successive lowering of the index figure in the Board of Trade returns since that time has meant a corresponding fall in wages. When on 15 May the rate for women day-workers – which is lower, of course, than the men's rate – fell from 38s. to 36s. a week, the Leicester women day-workers struck, and some of the piece-workers, though not directly affected, left their work in sympathy. Out of 5,000 women in the Leicester branch about 1,000 are day-workers. The women outside Leicester accepted the new rates prescribed by the agreement; so did the men everywhere.

The strike lasted barely a week, and the women returned to work with virtually nothing gained, though it is true they claim to have received some concessions from individual firms. Having struck without authority they received no strike pay. Nor did they, as far as one can see, receive much sympathy from the men at the head of their Union. The Council of the Union insisted as steadfastly as did the employers themselves on the honouring of the national agreement. The General Secretary, Mr A.L. Poulton, sent a letter urging the strikers to resume work immediately, pointing out that the stoppage was a breach not only of the national agreement but of the rules of the Union, and intimating that the employers had already entered a claim for compensation out of the guarantee fund for breach of agreement.

Brief though the strike was it had the effect of putting a number of male employees temporarily out of work, and that is not likely to have increased its popularity among them.

It ought perhaps to be added that the Leicester women never approved of the February agreement. They voted against its acceptance but were overruled. The president of the Leicester women's branch, Mrs J. Bell-Richards, as a member of the Council of the Union, stood out against the proposed reductions in the women's wages but she found herself in a minority. Although the strike was directed as much against the authority of the Union – of which her husband, Mr T.F. Richards, is general president – as against the employers, she lent her active support to the strikers and attended their meetings. One understands that she has resigned from the Council since the strike came to its unsuccessful end.

THE YOUNG MAN OF TWENTY-ONE (1927)

'A Modern Girl'

In all the mass of correspondence, speeches and opinions for and against votes for girls of 21 that has collected as a result of Mr Baldwin's proposal to bring such a measure of enfranchisement before the House of Commons I have not seen or heard anything about the young man of 21. How the girl of 21 would vote, for whom she would vote, what she would vote for, and why she wants or does not want the vote – this has apparently all been settled. But how does the young man of 21 vote? Whom does he support, and why? Does he want the vote and what does it mean to him? Girls of 21 are described as 'flappers'. Is there no corresponding term for young men of 21?

Let us divide the young men of 21 into two clases, the educated and the uneducated. I think there can be no doubt that the majority of young men of 21 in England do not want the vote at all. Many of them never trouble to get their names put on the register. Young men of 21 are seldom practical, and almost as prone as many women to follow a fashion. It is fashionable with many young men at the present time to regard politics as a sordid, noisy, troublesome pursuit, lacking in philosophy and to be left severely alone.

However, I suppose the educated young man is in a minority. The uneducated voters, male and female, of 21 are those round whom the tumult rages. What difference is there really between them? How can anyone say that one is more fit to exercise a vote than the other? What are the interests of the young working man of 21? Drink, smoking, cinemas, girls, betting and football. How does that compare with the love of dress, entertainment, domestic pursuits, chldren, sport and flirtation which is supposed to make up the sum total of the girl of 21?

POLITICS AND THE MODERN GIRL (1926)

Mrs H.A.L. Fisher

Mrs H.A.L. Fisher, wife of a well-known Cabinet Minister in Lloyd George's World War I government, is remembered in the National Council for One-Parent Families as 'Lettice Fisher'. She helped to found its predecessor, the National Council for the Unmarried Mother and her Child, and fought unceasingly to keep it alive.

Is the university girl of today interested in politics? I am told that she is not. When I was one, she certainly was, and I should have said that she was for a good many years after my student days. Perhaps she wasn't really. Perhaps she was. Perhaps she still is. Nothing is more difficult than to generalise about the real interests of the young. Girls are kind creatures. They talk to their elders about the subjects they think those elders are interested in; they are frank and friendly and delightful. But whether the elders who listen and interrogate and try to learn ever have any real knowledge of what is going on in the minds of those young people is one of the insoluble problems not only of university but of life.

However that may be, this is what my young friends tell me. They say that girl graduates, take them in the mass, are really not much interested in politics. They don't want to join political associations and committees; they don't much want to hear or take part in political debates. They know more and care more about playwrights, scholars or literary lights than about politicians. Of course there are many of whom this is not true. Some girls are ardent politicians. They are probably daughters of definitely political families; they come from homes where politics are the daily food, the familiar stuff of

159

life; their fathers are Members of Parliament or leading local politicians. But of the mass I am told that they are not, as they were when I was young, ardent social reformers.

If my rather vague impressions are correct, what is the explanation? I think there is one and it is perfectly intelligible. We had real political battles to fight, real grievances to remove, real and very inconvenient barriers to break down. We had no votes, no prospect of attaining to active citizenship. Our choice of careers was very limited. We were not members of the university, only tolerated guests.

The modern girl is an undergraduate like her brother. She will in time take her degree. She will also have a vote, and although she is probably rather annoyed at having to wait until she is thirty for the possession of that vote, (her brother gets his at twenty-one, and she is perfectly conscious of being at least as sensible as, and probably more sensible than he is at that age), she feels that it is a more or less temporary arrangement. Her choice of professions is fairly wide: some careers, but not very many, are still closed to her, but not very many. . . .

What will all this mean? University women should surely be the intellectual leaders, able to help the mass of their fellow-women to think, to judge, if necessary to act. Is all this potential leadership, or most of it, going into art and letters? How much will there be for politics? If the young people of today are less filled with the burning passion for social reform than were their mothers, is it because so much has been achieved, . . . and a new social system is in process of making, inequalities are far less, chances are more evenly distributed? Perhaps these modern young people need not worry and agonise as much as we did. Their cheerful calm is very agreeable. But I wonder what they will make of the rather confused world we elders are leaving for them.

TOWARDS FULL EQUALITY (1957)

Kay Collier

Female suffrage, looked upon as a luxury when it was first introduced, is now recognised by contemporary historians to have been a necessary stage in the general movement towards greater social equality which we call progress. Certainly without the battle which women waged with the Government in order to obtain the vote, their own movement towards equality would not be following the slow but sure path of constitutional reform it is taking today.

For by forcing the Government to accept the principle of female equality for voting purposes they made it logically difficult for legislators to deny them the rights of equal citizenship in other respects. Equal citizenship, after all, implies more than simply the right to vote. But between getting the Government to accept the principle and seeing that it is implemented in all branches of society lies many years of hard campaigning. For this, however, the former women suffragists are supremely well fitted.

The principal target remains, as ever, the Government, and apart from equal pay and equal opportunity another of the current aims which are being pursued as an important matter of principle by the former women's suffrage societies is to get the House of Lords open to women peers.

The Women's Freedom League is continually urging upon the Lords that any reform must include the abolition of the sex barrier. But Mrs H.V. Horton, secretary of the Fawcett Society, hopeful about the possibility that there might be some concession on the way as a result of the last Queen's Speech, says 'We are lying quiet for the moment so far as this question is concerned'. They desire that the women peers who have inherited their titles – there are only 24 of them – may be allowed to take seats in the House of Lords, and indeed there appears to be no legal reason why a woman peer in her own right should not be allowed to sit in the House.

The Sex Disqualification (Removal) Act of 1918 says that nobody should be debarred from holding any office in the state because of sex. But the Committee of Privileges has hitherto refused to let women into the Second Chamber. Much feeling has been aroused on this question among the old campaigners by the treatment of Dame Florence Horsbrugh who, but for her sex, would, they believe, undoubtedly have been raised to the peerage. The DBE they feel, was not a satisfactory substitute.

The two societies are also pressing simultaneously for the removal of anomalies which make both taxation and insurance laws unfair to married women. They are constantly sending in resolutions to MPs and the Chancellor of the Exchequer, asking that married women should be taxed in their own right and separately from their husbands, instead of being coupled together for taxation purposes as at present, and also that married women who pay the same insurance contribution as spinsters should not get less benefit when they are ill or unemployed.

To achieve changes of this sort the principle of equality must first be soundly established in the minds of those who legislate. But there are many other minor laws operating to the disadvantage of married women which are simply the legacy of centuries of exclusively masculine government yet which only come gradually to the notice of the public through occasional court cases.

For instance, it is not generally known that according to the law of the country a wife's domicile is considered to be that of her husband, so that if he moves to New York and she remains behind, she too will automatically be 'domiciled' in America though she may never have been there. As, until 1950, it was laid down that unless a person was domiciled in this country he or she could not go to law, such a woman was deprived of all legal rights. The efforts of the women's societies, however, secured reform in this direction, but equal domicile rights are still not granted.

Equal guardianship of children also has not yet been completely achieved and it is strangely anomalous and often unjust laws of this kind, geared to the attitudes and conditions of an earlier age, which one finds reflected in the sort of thinking that prompted a passport official recently to answer a mother's inquiry about her child's passport with the singular reminder 'You have to take into account that the parent of the child is really the father'.

As Mrs Horton says 'The recognition of human beings being equal in rights and responsibilities to men has not yet been accepted'. Even the Church of England is a long way from practising the equality that it preaches. Miss Marian Reeves, chairman of the Women's Freedom League, is particularly concerned about the refusal of the Church of England to accept women preachers. She considers it 'a terrible thing for the Church to assume that spiritual truth can only come through a male vehicle', and believes that the Established Church of the land should admit duly qualified women as the Free Churches do. Women preachers in the Church of England now have to enter the Free Churches if they want to practise their calling.

Thus, even when the necessary reforms are achieved, the work of the old suffrage societies will continue against such unthinking and unworthy prejudices as these. Here, however, one might point out that such work is not considered by them to be what is generally known as feminist. 'Indeed,' says Mrs Horton, 'there is no reason why in a community of true equality there should be feminist societies at all.'

Yet true equality has still to be achieved. The purpose of these old societies is to establish that equality so that they can go out of existence. But all this, as Mrs Horton rightly says, does not have the appeal of an obvious injustice like the lack of a vote. If people ask why feminism has declined here is the simple reason. Women's franchise was a straightforward issue. Full equality is a different matter. As someone has written, the suffragettes succeeded by saying over and over again with boring regularity a very simple truth which was obvious to all and which could be reasonably denied by nobody.

Full equality is more difficult to establish than women's franchise. Women tend to feel that it will come of its own accord, so that it makes no appeal to the energies even if it makes an appeal to the sympathies of women everywhere. This is the reason why the two societies mentioned, the Women's Freedom League and the Fawcett Society have less than a thousand members between them, compared with the thousands of members they had in the days of the women's suffrage campaign.

Here, however, the words of Miss Reeves might profitably be remembered: 'My own opinion is that if there were not societies like ours women would lose all the rights they have ever gained, not through malice, but because it is perfectly natural for men legislators to see things only from a man's point of view.'

AFTER 40 YEARS, 28 WOMEN MP'S

Thelma Hunter

Today, 40 years after the Parliament (Qualification of Women) Act made women eligible for election to the House of Commons and 30 years since the right to vote was extended to 'flappers' of 21 years, there are only 28 women members, in a House which numbers 630. Strangely, too, the rate of growth to this unimpressive figure has become slower and slower over the years, and if present trends continue the number of women standing for Parliament will be stabilised at about 100 and the number of MPs at 20.

The prospect, even for the most tepid exponents of sex equality, is scarcely encouraging. Since 1929 women have outnumbered men in the electorate by 10 to 9. And, what is probably more significant, they have constituted a majority in most constituencies. Their combined vote could, if they chose to concentrate it on the same candidate, ensure his success at the polls, so that if in each constituency the candidate supported were a woman, the result would be a female majority in the House of Commons.

Few would envisage these possibilities as more than academic. Clearly, women voters seem unlikely to 'gang together' in some sinister fashion to secure a nightmare succession of petticoat governments. Indeed, early fears that this would be so have been totally reversed. It is now held, often with astonishing dogmatism, that women will not vote for their own sex, either because they have no confidence in their political abilities, or because they are jealous.

Whatever the truth of these assertions in individual cases there seems little evidence that they constitute a major element in the electoral fortunes of women candidates as a whole. In 1953 Dr H. Durant conducted a public opinion poll on the specific question 'If your party put up a woman candidate would it make you less or more inclined to vote for it?' Results showed that for 67 per cent it would make no difference and that the sex preferences which existed among the remainder cancelled out.

It is true, of course, that people often vote differently from their stated intention. On the other hand, results of the last election for which separate figures for men and women are available suggest a similar conclusion. In the two-member constituencies which returned one male and one female candidate of the same party there was no appreciable difference in the allocation of votes between the two, and when the percentage of votes cast for unsuccessful women candidates was compared with the number of women electors in a number of constituencies no significant relationship was found between the two. Conservative candidates, it is true fared better in terms of the female vote than did Labour. But this points only to the relatively well-known fact that the female vote tends to be Conservative.

This is reassuring. On the other hand, other serious obstacles do exist which go far to explain the failure of many women at the polls. Until fairly recently they have had to fight a disproportionately large number of hopeless seats. Labour candidates have apparently found it as difficult to preach Socialism in Westmorland and Hendon as Conservatives to convert citizens of Ebbw Vale and Claycross. A few women MP's do now represent high majority seats – Mrs Harriet Slater in Stoke-on-Trent North, Miss Emmet in East Grinstead and Miss Pitt in Edgbaston – and this may be an indication that the situation is changing. But an essential difficulty remains. As one woman MP points out, 'The safer the seat the greater the competition from men who are well-known and have good records.' To develop similar 'quality' requires experience, time and boundless energy. This few women can afford to give – especially if they are married and have families. They must wait until their domestic responsibilities are less demanding. And, as in most professions, unless they are exceptional, late entry is likely to prove a severe if not an insuperable handicap.

Women MPs have suggested a variety of reasons to explain the vast discrepancy between the number of men and women adopted as candidates in the first place – 613 women as against 14,619 men in the ten general elections between 1918 and 1951. They mention uninformed fears by old-timers on selection committees that a woman will be a bad bet, either because she will not catch votes or because once elected she will concern herself only with domestic matters; the persistence of the traditional view that debate and political life in general are a typical masculine activity; in certain cases sheer prejudice.

To counter or at least minimise the effects of these attitudes women may have to reassess their present role in constituency parties. Do they confine themselves too much to canvassing and money-making activities? And concern themselves too little with matters of policy? How far do they avail themselves of opportunities to serve on committees, executive and selection? Does the existence of separate women's sections encourage them to do this?

In the past 40 years the enfranchisement of women has brought feminine values, insofar as they differ from men's to bear on social and national problems. But more could be done – if they could reverse the trend and secure a substantial change in the sex composition of Parliament.

THE DOUBLE LOAD I (1962)

Lena Jeger

Lena Jeger, formerly a member of the Guardian *staff, was a regular contributor to the Monday 'Women Talking' feature, both before and after her election to Parliament as Labour member for St Pancras. She was elevated to the House of Lords in 1979.*

Into these few autumn weeks the major parties all huddle their annual conferences – between the dates when it is reckoned (who knows by whom?) that all good men and women have had as much holiday as they deserve, and the dates when Parliament reassembles, and county councils and parish councils end their euphemistic recess. It must all begin around the fourteenth Sunday after Trinity and be well over by All Saints Day.

But as usual in this man's world of affairs the women have a double load to carry. The increasing number of women delegates to all the party conferences are now making arrangements for their children, baking pies to be eaten cold for a week by deprived husbands; even, thank goodness, buying new hats. This is the time when the loyal, slaving skivvies of every party can say to hell with making the tea at the bingo party and sorting the rubbish that disgraces the jumble sales: now is the time for the reality of politics, for putting one's hand up for fluoride in all tap water, for labels on all bottles, for no more bombs or no more landlords, for no Common Market or for no more Commonwealth. Hundreds of women are busy at this moment either recovering from, sitting through or looking forward to their own chosen party conferences.

But the double load? This is not only because, unlike almost every man, scarcely a woman can walk out of her house, case in hand, without the traumatic exhaustion of writing notes to the milkman, organising the rota of childminders, pet-minders, door-answerers to laundrymen, and fixing the minutiae of her Dorcas life. But added to all this is the fact that conscientious, representative political women are expected to go to two conferences. Parties hold their separate women's conferences, as if there were still any subjects under the sun that were the affair of only one sex.

We all run our women's conferences (usually in the spring) as if only women cared about children, as if men were not parents; as if consumer protection was entirely the affair of tired little women with string bags; as if the soft-faced men who did well out of the war had nothing to do with costs and prices and profits and values; as if no man ever bought mutton labelled as lamb, or cared about how his wife was looked after at the maternity hospital.

Why do we do this to ourselves? I think one real surviving value of the women's conferences is that many over-modest women attend and cut their teeth at public speaking who would be too shy to attempt the full-scale 'real' annual conference, with its television lights and scribbling reporters. The women's conferences are, in contrast, little publicised and one can lose one's notes on why family allowances should be increased without the world seeing. Of course this is all wrong. Logically there should be separate men's conferences where shy husbands could practise public speaking without Lady Violet Bonham Carter hearing their stumblings. Another reason which perpetuates these women's conferences is that men are so greedy that they tend to 'bag' the delegate places at the real conference and so, to make that urgent speech at all, the little woman must go off on her own to her own special conference. Which has no policymaking power but at least gives some condescending man a chance to declaim about how all politicians depend on the ladies who, at any moment now, will be expected to address the mountains of envelopes, make the tea, knock at the doors.

This is, of course, all absurd double-think. I experienced the same duality when I was an MP. If you take, as I do, the simple view that an MP represents all his or her constituents, regardless of sex, age, beauty, or even politics, it is irritating to be referred to all the time as a 'woman MP' or, even worse, as 'a lady member' when nobody talks of 'man MP' or 'a gentleman member'. But you quickly find that there are special jobs for you to do. This is basically not because you are a woman but because generations of men in public life have neglected what they like to call 'women's questions'.

So the conscientious woman member has added to her normal constituency duties, to her homework on Southern Rhodesia, EFTA, Algeria and school-leavers, a lonely burden of problems that bore the majority of men. She is expected, as well as being better than average as an MP (otherwise a man would have got the job), to concentrate on widows' pensions, maternity services, and cheap milk. Preferably you neglect Southern Rhodesia, EFTA, Algeria, and unemployed school-leavers to concentrate on the price of cabbages and the quality of nappies, and then men will pat your shoulder and say that you are a splendid little woman.

For obvious reasons many widows from all over the country used to write to me (and still do) to say: 'You are not my MP but I am writing to you because you are a woman and a widow yourself and therefore you will understand what I am going through and why I cannot manage on my pension. . . .' I always want to redraft such letters, to re-address them to the MP for the constituency: 'Dear Sir, You are not my MP but I am writing to you because you are a man and an MP and a husband, and because you will never be a widow yourself and because you passed all these laws that crucify us with their earnings rules and their inadequacies and their meanness and because, as a man, you should be ashamed. . . .'

So we lumber ourselves with two conferences, two jobs, two loads of responsibility, without counting the home-front, and the job which many women councillors and political workers run as well. In fact we could be much more haughty about it all. For they all need us, they all want us. We are the queens of the ballot box and as we pack for Brighton or Llandudno we should remember, and make them remember, as they allow us to the platform.

THE DOUBLE LOAD II (1965)

Shirley Williams, MP

Shirley Williams, daughter of Vera Brittain and George Catlin, was first elected to Parliament, for Hitchin, in 1964. She held several parliamentary offices from 1966 onwards and was a member of the Cabinet as Secretary of State for Prices and Consumer Protecton in 1974 and as Paymaster General in 1976. She was one of the 'Gang of Four' which formed the SDP, and is its President.

One of the perennial questions in the debate between the sexes is the one that runs: 'Why haven't women been more successful in public life? After all they are emancipated now'.

There are several ways to try to answer this one. You can recite a lot of names, beginning with Lady Astor and moving by way of Margaret Bondfield to Barbara Castle; or you can say that we have not been emancipated long enough; or, more fashionably, that women have two lives, and so cannot devote themselves single-mindedly to either. There is some truth in this, but it can be exaggerated. After all, many men have demanding wives, or shy wives who dislike meeting new people, or difficult children. Domestic requirements impinge first on the woman, but no longer solely on her.

I think there are some other reasons for our relatively indifferent showing in public life which have not been discussed much, and which seem worth airing. One of these is the absence of prominent public figures prepared to act as

169

patrons. Last week I went to a memorial service for Herbert Morrison – Lord Morrison of Lambeth – in Westminster Abbey. In his tribute the Bishop of Southwark referred to the way Morrison had encouraged women to take part in public life. I was glad he did so, for Herbert Morrison was almost unique in this respect, and many of the outstanding women who served on the London County Council were spurred on by him.

Consider how whole generations of young men have gained their first insight into politics. The younger Conservative leadership is, to a considerable extent, Butler's creation. On the Labour side, Hugh Dalton played an immense part in selecting able young men and becoming their political mentor. There are many others one could name, some of them still in Parliament, who have fostered and nursed talent when they found it. There are, of course, obvious reasons why so few senior political and public figures try to encourage women in public life. Clearly their motives could be only too easily misrepresented.

Then there is the absence of an old school tie or an old college scarf linking one generation to the next. Belonging to the same town or the same university rarely carries the same emotive associations. It might be argued that women should assist women, but this is the hen and the egg story repeated; there are few women in public life because there are few women in public life ad infinitum.

There is no lack of supporters, but this raises another complication. Women in public life are a minority group; like most self-conscious minorities, they tend to organise in these terms, as women's groups. And this means that the woman councillor or woman MP is not just supposed to be interested in her own particular subjects, as a man would be, but also in all questions affecting women. There still tends to be a division between 'men's subjects' – finance, economics, defence, foreign affairs – and women's subjects – welfare, education, health, pensions, consumer questions. The woman in public life is free to interest herself in men's subjects; but she is expected to interest herself in all the women's subjects, and other women will almost invariably assume that she is.

This adds to a burden that tends to be extra heavy anyway;

not just because of the 'two lives', but because women are on the whole very conscientious, sometimes excessively so. Most women councillors, social workers, and magistrates must be familiar with the letter that starts, 'I am writing to you as one woman to another, because I am sure you will be sympathetic'. I doubt if letters ever begin to men in the same way. After all, 'man to man' means something quite different. Then, locally and nationally, there is not just the normal range of meetings that anyone in public life has to do; there are the others that their wives usually do for them. I wasn't surprised to learn from a very experienced secretary who had worked for a number of MPs that the women she had worked for received far more letters than the men. I should imagine this is general.

This double responsibility – to one's electors (if one is elected), or to one's case-load or to one's department, and to women as a special category – raises in an acute form the question of how tough to be. It is quite possible to be unsympathetic to the author of the 'woman to woman' letter; it is possible to refuse the extra meetings, stick closely to one or two subjects one is interested in, in fact simply refuse to take on the double responsibility. But this produces another dilemma. Women in public life are under close scrutiny. They are expected to become terribly tough, yet are denounced immediately if they do so. 'Look,' it is said, 'how unfeminine they all become!' Yet most of the women I know have not found it in themselves to reject requests for help, and most of them consequently work too hard.

The only solution is the obvious one: there have to be more women in public life to overcome the problems of the ones already there. The indications are that there will be fewer, because of a higher marriage rate and larger families, unless our society moves a long way further to adapt itself to the attitude that life begins again at 40.

11 The New Wave

It may be said that Simone de Beauvoir's *The Second Sex*, published in France in 1949 was the first sign of the new wave of the women's movement, but it was not until Betty Friedan's *The Feminine Mystique* was published that the *Guardian* began to be aware of a surging tide in the affairs of women. This was discussed by Eleanor Timbres in 1963, soon after it was published. By 1970 the tide was in full spate in the United States and Ruth Adam was one of the first people to describe in a British newspaper the impact of the National Organisation of Women. By the beginning of 1972, when this anthology closes, the 'New Wave' had totally changed the feminist image here.

FEMININE MYSTIQUE (1963)

Eleanor C. Timbres

Eleanor C. Timbres, educationist and former psychiatric social worker, is married to a former Guardian *Features editor and leader writer, Dr John Rosselli, now of Sussex University.*

The boredom and dissatisfaction of intelligent housewives, so often discussed on this page and elsewhere, has been studied in fascinating detail in America by a woman journalist, Betty Friedan, and her startling findings are set forth in *The Feminine Mystique*.

American women have been commonly thought of, by themselves as well as by Europeans, as aggressive, career minded, dominating, materially greedy and sexually frigid – in short, the antithesis of feminine. Fearful themselves of this picture, afraid of unhappy marriages and sexual maladjustment, American women after the war started to reject the idea of careers and instead have tried to commit themselves totally to the home. Femininity has been defined primarily as biological and the goal has become an early marriage to an up-and-coming man, an open-plan home in the suburbs, and four or more children. Women may attend college but do not commit themselves deeply to any interest, frequently dropping out when a suitable marriage presents itself. They take marriage courses or water-treading jobs and openly equate careers with loss of femininity and sexual frustration. In this they are strongly supported by many of the educators themselves as well as by advertisers, sociologists, psychiatrists and above all the women's magazines, all of whom say that the only deeply creative feminine role is exclusively as wife and mother, bar a few innocuous voluntary activities.

While some find happiness in being the 'creative engineer' of the home, many more are being driven to desperation by the sense of being under-used, of abilities untapped, of brains unstretched, of sheer boredom. Living vicariously through their children and husbands, they dominate the former and make insatiable demands upon the latter.

But this is not to say that the problem Mrs Friedan sets out does not exist here or that it will not grow. After all, as she says, if you are intelligent, you do not have to be educated to feel under-used.

Quite apart from difficulties in women's education, however, certain developments here look ominous: for example, the trend towards increasingly early marriages, before girls have acquired a suitable education and training, or even the experience to make a suitable choice of mate. Another problem is the population shift to the suburbs or new towns or, for economic reasons, to other areas of the country. This is a particularly knotty problem because of the difficulty the English seem to experience in making new social contacts. 'I keep myself to myself', may be said with pride, but to a social worker or psychiatrist it spells disaster when a move has to be made or grown children leave the home.

To state the total problem is not to solve it individually. Many women are undoubtedly perfectly happy and satisfied in their lives, but for those who are not there is no blanket answer. For the untrained, possible answers might be in painting, music, political activity or voluntary work of various sorts, for unlike America, where these fields have been taken over by the professional, a great deal can and needs to be done by the untrained but interested person. For the trained woman society – including the trained women themselves – could expend far great effort towards making part-time professional work an accepted and solicited part of the employment pattern – an urgent problem about which much has been said and little done. Efforts to break out of old patterns, to stretch ability and brains and to grow are difficult, even painful, but for those who persevered the rewards can be great. If you are bored and under-used you must do something about it yourself.

In these beautiful suburban areas doctors report increasing illnesses, psychiatrists' couches are filled, school authorities worry about unmotivated children, and the divorce rate mounts.

Mrs Friedan's thesis is that the crucial mistake has been to think there was an either-or choice between home and career. In this century women have discovered they are human beings and it is not possible to reduce them again to second class citizens by reducing higher education or by social pressure forcing them back into the home and away from the development of their capacities.

She presents a good deal of evidence showing that the higher the education of the American woman, the deeper she is committed to a creative line of work and the more her abilities are used to top capacity, the greater her chances for marital and sexual (to say nothing of personal) happiness and the healthier the development of her children. If she commits herself to a career or special interest and trains for it when education is easiest to get, a woman finds that it lasts throughout her life whether or not she works at it when her children are small; in any case it is there to be taken up when the children are grown and a third of her life is yet before her. It is also there in the event of divorce, widowhood or spinsterhood.

To state the obvious, America is not England, and the goal of professional careers for all capable women is perhaps not the solution at present. Higher education for women is far more limited in England, and it is correspondingly difficult for women to entertain the idea of entering the professions, though no doubt this is changing slowly.

THE NEW FEMINISM (1970)

Ruth Adam

Ruth Adam was the author of 12 novels and a valuable book on the women's movement, A Woman's Place *as well as a biography, with Kitty Muggeridge, of Beatrice Webb. Her husband, Kenneth Adam, formerly of the* Manchester Guardian *and the BBC, was a visiting lecturer at the university of Philadelphia and as a result of the time Ruth Adam spent there she wrote one of the first serious studies of the new Women's Liberation Movement to appear in a British newspaper.*

The new feminism is taken seriously in the United States. The British attitude – that we've seen it all before – has no place there. The Women's Liberation movement arouses the kind of passions which died out here in 1914 when the Huns pushed the suffragettes off the front page. In America all political argument has a lower boiling point than in Britain, anyway. But this one is about a shocking heresy – that sex isn't really all that important. No-one pretends to be detached about it, any more than about Black Power or socialised medicine.

The most powerful feminist in America at the moment is Wilma Scott Heide, the newly elected chairman of the National Organisation of Women. It is the oldest and most organised of the new-feminist associations. The more way-out groups such as WITCH (Women's International Conspiracy from Hell) and SCUM (Society for Cutting up Men) consider it conservative. Mrs Heide says it is 'unapologetically militant. We have many areas of agreement with the others, but we are more action-oriented. We are the catalyst of the movement.'

NOW was founded in 1966 by Betty Friedan, in the wake of the uproar caused by her book *The Feminine Mystique*. In it she told American women that since the war a male-dominated society had conned them into accepting the role of

175

sex-object, consumer and mother, which meant giving up career hopes and sinking into an empty middle age. She has just resigned from the leadership of NOW, though not from its activities. To the press, at least, she is still its figurehead – fiery, dramatic, aggressive, invariably turning up with something which will provide a good 'quote'.

Last month she called for a strike on the fiftieth anniversary of women getting the vote (26 August 1920). She urged women throughout the country to cover their typewriters, unplug their switchboards and sit back until their employers guaranteed that all jobs in their company – including the top ones – would be open to women, with equal pay all round.

But, from now on it is Wilma Scott Heide who is at the wheel of the National Organisation of Women and in control of its course. She comes to the job well armed against the standard anti-feminist gibes. She is happily married, with two children. (It was her husband who first drew her attention to NOW, suggesting it might be an interesting field for her.) She had already made the grade, personally, in a man's world – a point at which most career women begin to see the folly of feminist agitation for equal opportunities for all.

She is a distinguished behavioural research scientist; one of the directors of Pittsburgh and Pennsylvania Civil Liberties Union and the only woman member of the Pennsylvania Human Relations Commission. One's first impression is that she will please those who sympathise with the aims of the movement but deplore its militancy. She seems to be gentle and placid, as ready to listen as to talk, amused rather than indignant over the anti-feminist arguments that man was born superior to woman. ('Since 1958, scientists have known that all mammalian embryos are female for the first six weeks of embryonic life and that only after that do some develop male attributes. But no-one has re-written Genesis as an Adam-out-of-Eve myth yet.')

But the cosy first impression is as deceptive as Mrs Pankhurst's Dresden-china shepherdess image. On the job, Mrs Heide gives no quarter to her opponents. When she took a deputation to Congress to press for an amendment to give women equal rights before the law (on the books since 1923) the senator receiving them asked them to let a man who had to catch a plane see him first. 'We've been waiting 47 years already, Senator. I think you can attend to us now.' On a television programme about NOW she refused to start until a popular 'television person' who had been co-opted on the panel was dismissed from it. He protested that he was in favour of women's equality. 'In the church, too?' He faded out.

She does not believe that any protest group ever got concessions as a reward for good behaviour. 'We've got to learn to rub people the wrong way, to get what we want.' What they want is an end to the second-class status of women in every social institution – employment, education, legislation, the Church and the mass media. 'We live in a male-centred society and that's not healthy any more than a female-centred one would be.'

The United States is still living on its past reputation (circa the age of *Little Women*) as the country where the female sex has a freedom and an influence undreamed of in stuffy old Europe. Most Americans (at least American men) believe this themselves and are bewildered by such phenomena as Barbara Castle and Bernadette Devlin. Mrs Heide says 'The appearance of freedom is greater than the reality. The position of women here has actually declined during the last twenty years.' Although over 46 per cent of them now work outside the home, three-quarters of these are in the lowliest occupations in the labour market. They are also losing ground in the professions and in the executive ranks of industry and government. Nixon appointed only six women among 300 top level posts. One fifth of women with four years' college education have to settle for unskilled or semi-skilled jobs. In every field they are becoming increasingly concentrated on the lower part of the job ladder – as nurses, not doctors; secretaries, not executives; researchers, not writers. Mrs Heide says that the worst thing about this decline is that it is affecting the aspirations of the young. In a survey at her research institute they found that 84 per cent of high school girls aspire only to the 9 most dead-end and ill-paid occupations of all 'Women *think* poor'. They are oppressed psychologically. Sex-role stereo-typing is as harmful for them as race-role stereotyping for blacks.

NOW takes its stand on Title VII of the Civil Rights Act of

177

1964, which forbids job discrimination on the grounds of race 'or sex'. 'Sex' is said to have been originally thrown in, with intent to sabotage, by a sardonic congressman from the South. It enables NOW to bring lawsuits against employers – for instance the case of *Weeks vs. Southern Bell Telephone* which was taken as far as the Court of Appeal by a young Southern lawyer and NOW member. The company denied Mrs Weeks a job as a switchman on the grounds that a Georgia labour regulation forbade women to lift more than 30 lbs. and that their emergency fire extinguishers weighed 34 lbs. The court ruled that they hadn't proved that few women can lift 34 lbs. whereas all men can. 'So-called protective legislation is actually restrictive on women in most cases', Mrs Heide reflects. 'When I was a nurse nobody minded my working from 6 at night until six in the morning.'

Under Title VII NOW also forces newspapers to 'desegregate' their employment columns. 'The division of male/female jobs is out of all proportion to their biological differences. If half the human race is barred from the half of the jobs that are more creditable, interesting and appealing, it's bad for the individual and a loss to society.' She argues that technology has made superior muscular strength irrelevant and that the problem of over-population forbids women to make a lifetime career of motherhood. 'In this country they want 3.5 children, which is too many. But if women are not brought up to have visible alternatives they will be reproducers of population rather than producers of services and goods.'

NOW fights (with some success) for Abortion Law repeal, for day nurseries to enable women to work, organises sit-ins at 'Men Only' restaurants and carries on a continual campaign against advertising which represents women as only good for sex or housewifery. The long-term objective of Women's Liberation, as Mrs Heide sees it, is equal partnership and an end to 'game playing' between men and women. 'This sex-role stereotyping is as bad for men as for women. There is an awful expectation of any boy born into this culture. He's got to live up to an enforced image of maleness. If he isn't naturally aggressive, he's terribly afraid that means he's not really virile. Liberating women from their stereotyped role will also, in the end, liberate men.'

THE WORDS IN ACTION (1971)

Jill Tweedie

All demonstrations are fleshed-out polemics, happenings that have more to do with reinforcing solidarity within the ranks than luring spectators from pavement or box – conversion will come later, as fall-out comes. And so it was with the Women's Lib demo on Saturday. I went, unreasoningly fearful that me and my friend Ivy would be alone stomping down Regent Street, running the sneering gauntlet of Saturday shoppers. But there they were at Hyde Park Corner, all the lovely sisters, giggling and shivering, and bawdy and prim and I turned and turned again, gloating at the numbers before and behind, my motley frost-defying sex.

Because sex is all we really had in common. Odd to think, in the middle of Oxford Circus that inside our overcoats, under our mufflers, coiled within our sweaters and vests is the same intricate reproductive system – fallopian tubes, uteri, vaginas and breasts – and that is why we're here, on 6 March 1971, in the snow. When, since the beginning of time, have men ever marched because they share a particular sexual apparatus? Ludicrous, shameful, ridiculous, perish the thought.

Goodness knows, our outsides were various enough. Long and short and thin and fat, quiet middle-aged ladies in careful make-up, bare-faced girls with voices as loud as crows, Maoists, liberals, socialists, lesbians, students, professionals, manual workers, spinsters, wives, mothers. One two three four, we want a bloody damn sight more. Biology isn't destiny. Equal pay *now*. Bed or wed, are you free to choose? I'm not just a delectable screwing machine. Capitalism breeds sexploitation. *Freedom*. There were even women so politically committed that the very sight of Downing Street submerged 'Twenty-four-hour nurseries' with 'Tories Out' and 'Kill the Bill'.

And when we arrived at Trafalgar Square, the demo arranged itself into a symbol so apt as to seem planned. One girl at the mike, four girl photographers and a solid phalanx of great, grey brawny men blocking the view of the women. 'Get out,' shrieked the women, 'get away, get back,' and the men,

179

genuinely startled, got back. Communicators themselves they communicated the women's case – men, men, men, grouped at the foot of a soaring phallus with Nelson, a man, at the top.

In the crowd a tiny 'Gay is Good' placard vied gamely with a huge Women's Lib banner. 'Here, it's *our* demonstration,' said Women's Lib testily. 'It's against oppression, isn't it?' snapped Gay Lib. 'I was chucked out of my job last week because I'm gay. We're more oppressed than what you are, any day.' Women's Lib raised her eyebrows in ladylike fashion and turned back to the platform.

A middle-aged woman in fur has been lured from a bus stop to join the march. 'I'm a graphic designer and what do I read in a trade magazine last week? Some man complaining how difficult it is to get a job at 45. Huh, I've had difficulties getting jobs all my life – the moment they hear your voice on the telephone they don't want to know.'

Another woman, face flushed with panstick had a hand-scrawled notice pinned to the front of her tweed coat. 'I've come all the way from Sheffield. I can't afford the fare but I must do something for the single woman. We don't get paid nearly as much as the men but still we've got to find rooms, pay the electricity, feed ourselves. It's not fair. It's just not fair.' Behind the pebble lenses her huge eyes watered.

Then the speeches were over; vast congratulatory relief filled the square. The demonstration had happened (miracle) and it had happened well (greater miracle). Girls stood in groups, stamping and chatting. 'There was only one thing. The weather. The trade unions had such a marvellous day, and we had to go and get this.'

'Well, what did you expect, love? God is a man.'

12   Shadows of War and Voice of Peace

From our very first month (May, 1922) the *Manchester Guardian* listened to the voice of internationalism, the voice of peace, reporting a conference of the International Council of Women. In 1926 regular columnist Evelyn Sharp was writing about 'The Peacemakers Pilgrimage'. In 1923, Women's International League secretary Mary Sheepshanks wrote an article about the great American peace campaigner Jane Addams. The shadow of the 1914-18 war still hung over most wives and mothers during the 1920s and early 1930s – Vera Brittain's letter to her son on the twentieth anniversary of its outbreak is a moving reflection of the pacifist feelings that became widespread in the 1930s.

In 1933 the Oxford Union debated and passed by a large majority a resolution saying that its members would not fight for King and Country.

In 1935 the League of Nations Union organised a peace ballot. More than 11 million votes were cast: 10½ million were in favour of all-round reduction of armaments by international agreement and the prohibition of the manufacture of armaments for private profit; more than 10 million agreed that 'if a nation insists on attacking another nation the League should combine to compel it to stop by economic and non-military means' and the vote fell only to 6.7 million in answer to the question as to whether the aggressor should be checked if necessary by 'military means'. But the shadow of war loomed ever larger from 1937.

There were no such ballots in the 1960s when fears of war were again widespread . . . it was left to the women, as in the 1980s, to set up their own initiatives for peace.

THE WHITE FEATHER COMPLEX (1933)

Evelyn Sharp

It was pleasing to read in an account of last week's Fascist raid on the Oxford Union that it was not a woman's college that sent two consignments of white feathers to those members of it who voted against taking part in a future war. Though it is never wise to generalise, this may perhaps be said to show some slight growth in grace since the lamentable days of the last war, when women walked about offering white feathers to young men who were not dressed in khaki. Making allowance for the hysteria that held whole nations in bondage at that time, I think women never dropped more completely below their own standards than when, protected by custom from the obligation to risk their own lives, they brought a contemptible pressure upon brothers and lovers to risk theirs. One did not need to be a pacifist to deplore the white feather complex of 1914. As an expression of a whole set of primitive instincts that most of us at least endeavour to keep under control, it would seem to make the boasted emancipation of women meaningless.

The acid test of an anti-war resolution is applied when the usual setting is absent and the resolution is worded in blunt terms that make no pretence as to what is meant by a refusal to fight in any war. When war breaks out, young men are not enticed into armies by a brutal appeal to a love of slaughter but by a romantic appeal to love of King and Country, and unless, in times of peace, we face this issue and prove that there are grander ways of being loyal to both than by slaughtering of individuals whom we are taught by our religion to regard as brothers, we simply beat the air with our pious peace resolutions. The news that a group of university students have had the courage to recognise this truth and express it openly is like a gleam of light in great darkness; and we need not worry if they are not universally acknowledged as 'better and braver men' than the 'heroes and bravos' who send them white feathers. It takes more than one debate to turn a revolt against accepted standards into a revolution.

Pacifism is on trial everywhere. Anybody can be a pacifist

immediately after a war; nineteen years later it begins to require courage again, as the Oxford resolution already shows.

But it is our business, as pacifists, to take up the challenge as it has been thrown down and to maintain frankly that the fight to make a country worth fighting for and incidentally fit for a king to rule over, demands more courage, heroism and loyalty to a high ideal of patriotism than any war. A country in which three millions of men and women are powerless to use the hands and brains that God gave them, in which little girls learn the facts of life in hideous outrages because of housing conditions that make their homes worse than brothels to live in, is not a country to inspire love and loyalty. If the white feather stands for the greater war against those atrocities, a war which shall make both King and Country better worth defending, I should like to see it worn as a panache by every woman who calls herself a pacifist.

WOMEN AND WAR (1933)

'R'

The Territorial Army wants about 40,000 men and all over the country efforts are being made to stimulate recruiting. There are gay recruiting posters on the walls and hoardings, special meetings are addressed by statesmen, politicians, generals and Lord Mayors. It may seem that this is peculiarly a man's affair, but there is a woman's side to the subject. At the meeting I attended a general urged us to get away from 'this absorbing idea of everlasting peace and try to realise that the paradise you hope to live in in the future is a very foolish and idealistic one'. He was also certain that the women of the country could do a great deal to stimulate the young men to join the Territorial Army instead of discouraging them. The politician said he knew that the Territorials did not look as fine as they used to do in the pre-war days of scarlet and blue, but a khaki uniform was not to be despised 'and most young ladies think their menfolk look better in it than in their plain clothes'. I imagine that few women today are not revolted by an appeal on those lines. The 1914-18 war has led us to doubt the darling belief that the best way to ensure peace is to prepare for war.

Human nature itself, the unchangeable, the stock factor that is said to make war inevitable, has changed. The militarist philosophers admit it themselves, for I have never read one that did not deplore the growth of pacifism. But still the statesmen and politicians look across their frontiers through spectacles forged from classical and Old Testament facts and the half-legendary horrors of the Dark Ages. If you look at war through those spectacles, then the women are still the best recruiting sergeants. Their duty is two-fold. They must allow themselves to be used as propaganda and they must whip on their menfolk.

What was one of the strongest factors in turning the million Social Democrat pacifists in Germany in 1914 into soldiers? The *Chemnitzer Volkestimme* put it well and briefly: 'Before all else it is our duty to fight against the Russian tyranny of the knout. Germany's women and children shall not be the victim of Russian bestiality.' And here is the substance of an English recruiting poster for the same war: 'Four questions to the women of England: 1 You have read what the Germans have done in Belgium. Have you thought what they would do if they invaded England? 2 Do you realise that the safety of your home and children depends on our getting more men now? 3 Do you realise that the one word "Go" from you may send another man to fight for King and Country? 4 When the war is over and your husband or your son is asked "What did you do in the Great War?" is he to hang his head because you would not let him go? Women of England, do your duty! Send your men today to join our glorious army.'

The women behind and the enemy in front are the two universal allies of the militarists. 'They (the recruits) fancy themselves in a smart uniform and think that the women fancy them too,' writes the Revd. E.J. Hardy, chaplain to the Forces, in some admiring papers on the British soldier and the soldier's life published in 1902. 'Hence the necessity of dressing our soldiers in peace time in a way that pleases women, who influence recruiting.' Thirty years later we get the song 'There's something about a soldier' on every side of us and feminine susceptibility to a uniform urged at Territorial meetings. The more everything changes the more war and its trappings remain the same on a larger scale.

AN OPEN LETTER FROM A MOTHER TO HER SON (1934)

Vera Brittain

4 August

My dear Son,

The date on this letter is the same as the one on which twenty years ago, the Great War began for England.

You have heard me talk about the excitement, and the shouting and the scramble for newspapers, on the night when we decided that we should have to fight Germany, and you like my stories about the great white ship with the red crosses which carried me safely through the Mediterranean, in spite of the submarines, or about the miles upon miles of camps filled with soldiers near the sea in France. They are more thrilling to you than the tales of Grimm or Hans Anderson, because they are not just 'pretend stories' but true.

You did not arrive until 1927, and when you read the long story of the reason why, you will learn that between 16 and 20 years ago a great multitude of young men of all nations – the best and cleverest and handsomest that those nations had – gave up the women who loved them and all hope of marrying and having children, for the sake of something they called honour, and their country's glory. They believed then that a nation which laid down the best of its life would surely find it, and fortunately for themselves they never realised that the generation to which they belonged would go bankrupt and crippled to the end of its days for the lack of that lost life and that vanished youth.

Did the women mind? Why yes, of course they minded, but at the time they were persuaded that it was right for them to sacrifice everything which makes a country happy and brave and strong. So they watched their lovers go off to the war without crying or making a fuss. Many of them didn't even cry when their lovers failed to return, although it meant that they could not marry or have the children they wanted. Years and years afterwards a few of them, although they never forgot the soldier who marched away, married someone else, and that is why there are a number of small boys and girls, like yourself, whose mothers served in the Great War and have very long memories.

What happened to the young men, and where are they now? Well, about many we are not quite sure. We knew that many disappeared, but we'd rather not be told exactly how, and we hope that by putting up great impressive monuments to the 73,000 missing on the Somme and to the 35,000 missing at Arras, and to other thousands of missing at other places, that it was not dreadful but really rather glorious, to be smashed up into so many little pieces that you couldn't be found or identified.

Today, whatever happened to them at the time, the young men have simply become part of the soil of France or the sand of Gallipoli, or the hard earth between the rocks and the pines on the high Italian mountains. It seems strange that we made ourselves believe, all that time ago, that their dust would be more valuable to England, twenty years after, than their living presence in our homes and our schools and our churches and our political councils. It is stranger still that so many even of their contemporaries appear to have forgotten that they ever existed.

'There don't seem to be any young men coming along,' somebody grumbled to me the other day when one of our cynical elderly statesmen had let us down more thoroughly than usual at Geneva. And I felt too startled, too flabbergasted, to put the protesting query 'Don't you remember why and where those "younger men" have gone?'

For you, my son, the tale of their departing will not even be a memory. Twenty years, 200 years, even 2,000, are much the same at 7 years old. When you start to do history properly the Retreat from Mons will seem to you almost as distant as the Wars of the Roses or the Siege of Troy, and the battles during which we watched and waited and agonised will possess the thin remoteness of legends, taking shape only upon the lips of your parents. Why, even the other day you yourself remarked to a school friend 'My mother's very old, she was alive during the war.'

All the same, though you have nothing of all those years to remember, I hope that in time to come you will read and learn and think about them, for though the young men are gone, the irrational fears and passions which destroyed them are in the world still. What were those aeroplanes doing which made you so vexed last week because they kept you awake half the night with their sullen zooming? They were practising the defence of London in the next war – a defence which even the experts know we could never carry out except by a barbarous method known as 'retaliation'.

You don't hate German or French or American children, do you? You don't want to fly across the sea and bomb them, any more than you would like them to bomb you? Of course you don't – and if in the future you read about what happened after 4 August, 1914, you will know that it is not by destroying but only by living at peace with our neighbours that you and the civilisation of which you are part can hope to survive. If only you and the other boys and girls who are now 7, or 10, or 15, will one day join with older people who are working for life rather than for the death of mankind the young men whose story you have heard will not have given up their lives entirely in vain.

That you will help us, and them, to redeem the past is the chief hope which the future holds for

YOUR MOTHER

AIR-MINDED: VENTILATION PROBLEMS (1938)

'*M.R.H.*'

Danger from the air is the theme of the moment; at home, in our friends' houses, in committee rooms and theatres, wherever there is serious, or even casual conversation it sooner or later turns to an exchange of views on air-raid dangers and precautions. And all we can do is to go on accepting the situation and forcing ourselves to continue in the belief that it is good to go on living – in cellars if necessary, and gas masks.

Perhaps by concentrating on concrete things – often, indeed, on concrete – we are enabled to shun the real horror of facing our own acceptance of fear and what seems a positive and dangerous anticipation of calamity. 'Cellulose paper over the window' is one way of sealing it' 'Now if,' someone else goes on, 'you could make a concrete room under an ordinary cellar there might be a reasonable chance of having a bomb proof chamber.' 'But what about the problem of ventilating a sealed shelter?' An answer is immediately forthcoming in this latest parlour game, 'If only the due number of people, according to the cubic measurement of the shelter, occupy it, they say you could live quite comfortably in a sealed shelter for about 15 hours.' There is an uneasy laugh.

Whatever precautions may be taken and provisions made, it is always suggested by someone, most of us, 'when the time came', would prefer to take a chance, to take the risk of being killed in the open rather than to go to earth in some cavity wherein a place was reserved for us to wait while our immediate world fell about our ears. This prospect, we have to assure ourselves, is now a normal feature of civilised life.

A child, we are told, when we are given a subscription for the NSPCC, has come home from school in a state of fear crying because 'they all say there is going to be a war and we shall all be killed'. . . . In vain we are told occasionally that dangers of general annihilation are probably exaggerated and that with modern methods of defence casualties from an air raid would probably total no more than those on the roads on any Bank Holiday. But whatever we plan or learn, whatever precautions we take, it is with a feeling of humiliation that we recognise at odd moments that the danger from the air has already come amongst us.

THE EVACUATION OF CHILDREN (1938)

'I'

The evacuation scheme recently produced bears the appearance of being a hurriedly produced masculine solution to meet a dire need. One end of the problem, getting the children out of the towns, reveals the masculine mind competently at work on a matter it understands. But the reception end of the scheme and safeguarding the children while they are out of their parents' care are left in the air.

I live in one of the proposed billeting areas, where almost every house has been booked to take one or more children. A local committee would know that some of these houses, by reason of the habits or character of the householder or his wife, are not fit for the reception of children. Near me there lives a frail old lady, with a maid, who is booked to receive six children. . . . The burden of responsibility for other people's children in such desperate times and at the risk of possible air raids in our own district – for our immunity is only comparative – is too heavy to put on individual shoulders.

How unpractical and unimaginative are some of the people who have these evacuation schemes in hand is shown by the pronouncement of one of them that he supposed that, say, six babies or three toddlers could be managed by one woman. . . . So far as the reception of the refugee children is considered, all that is known is that so many are allotted compulsorily to each household. It might have happened that we had two or three hundred children brought to us, but so far as anyone knows there is no provision for food or bedding, and it is no-one's business that these essentials are to hand.

THE CHEATED: WOMEN AND WAR (1938)

Winifred Peck

They have been reflecting over their grudge against life for twenty years; they are writing of it now in a hundred memoirs. They are the women who were young at the beginning of the Great War and are now middle-aged, the women who have never forgotten or forgiven the four years' super-tax of misery on their golden youth.

Twenty-five years ago they were snatched from ballroom floors, from wind-swept moors, from sunlit gardens, from the careless gaiety of their gilt-edged world, to work of the grimmest and hardest nature. Not one woman of forty to fifty today but bears some scar in her heart for husband or lover who broke his faith with her to keep faith with that other bride, honour, across the seas. The unmarried scrubbed in hospitals, scoured in canteens, tapped out their fingers on

189

typewriters or lost their freshness in munitions. The married produced and reared children in the discomfort of camp-following or solitude at home, living only for those leaves from France when the very kiss of greeting held all the agony in it of an imminent farewell.

And now, as war clouds hang over Europe, those same women look at their children, in their twenties now, hardly able to believe in their misery that they look, perhaps, on another generation of the cheated. In their own youth they were too proud to bewail the lot of women. How could they, when it was for men to face the real horrors of war? But death today, mothers tell themselves, will threaten their girls as swiftly as their boys. And if not death, but life, awaits them, we see for them a dark horizon of wasted youth, the sudden passions, the bitter reactions, the agonies of farewells and the intolerable follies which await women cheated of youth and their mates.

There is nothing we can do, we say, and yet as this miserable year draws to a close, we should, perhaps, explore the cupboards of our memories and find such moth-eaten compensations as we can, the rusty courage, the dimmed sense of adventure, the forgotten cloak of good-fellowship which helped us through those years. Never again can we thank God for waking us from our sleeping by the horror of war. But we had never worked hard on a job before and there was a queer joy in doing a bit of real work. Never before or since have we had friends like those who raced down corridors of hospitals to save us from unpunctuality or forgetfulness, or shared our YWCA tent or showed us what was wrong with the magneto in the chilly dawn of Flanders.

We did not think of little homes and rent, of bathroom taps and saving for a car, in those days; we snatched each minute as it came. And when the Reveille sounded for the fallen we were not so miserably wise in our non-beliefs as those who mock at our outworn faiths today.

Such are the frail, beautiful robes of memory which we must shake out in tears if we have to watch another generation cheated in its turn. But with all our hearts we pray that we may lock that cupboard up once more, securely, and turn back to the fireside with our own old meaningless grudges once again.

CHILDREN LEAVE HOME (1939)

'T.T.'

The evacuation of children from Manchester was a sight which will remain with me all my life. Not that it was a dismal affair; far from it. I can assure Manchester mothers that their children went on their strange adventure in good spirits. The railway officials were obviously moved. 'Grit', said one to me. 'These kids are marvels.' Even allowing for the fact that the children were unaware of the full implication of their wholesale exodus it can be said that their discipline and cheerfulness were splendid.

The variety of bags they carried on their backs shows how different were the homes they came from. These bags were of all kinds of material and of all colours of the rainbow, some of them obviously home-made. Some of the children carried their belongings in paper carriers. There were some rum little customers. I asked one tough guy of about seven, 'Where are you going, sonny?' and he shrugged his shoulders and replied with a devil-may-care inflection 'You're asking me.' There was a sweet little maiden of about five nearby, and she did not like being left out of the picture. She pushed up a handbag for an inspection and chirped 'I've got pennies in my bag.' Heaven bless her.

I got in the midst of a family of six, with the youngest about four, and as a parent myself I could not help thinking of the awful gap in that home at bedtime. But by the looks of them they were children brought up to 'shape' for themselves, and they most certainly were not moping. One charming little girl was busy sorting out her favourites from a paper full of sweets.

'It's a job,' said one of the porters. 'It's a job, by gum.' Anyhow, from all sides it was a job well done. The precision of it all was marvellous, and showed what a free people can do about organising without any uniform nonsense or bully-ragging. The children marched onto the platform in line shouting and cheering, but immediately their headmaster blew his whistle, there was complete silence. The leaders, each in charge of the children, walked to the doors of the carriages and opened them, the children remaining still. Another signal

191

and the children filed quietly into the train. It was perfect.

Policemen, ambulance men, railway porters and officials all did their jobs with an occasional knuckling of eyes. 'Hurry up a bit there, love', and 'Keep your fingers away from the door, love' were repeatedly advised. There was no doubt about the sympathy from grown ups, most of them parents themselves. One of the press cameramen said the sight which got him down most was the evacuation from the children's hospitals. Most of the children were cripples, he said, but somebody had struck the bright idea of giving each child a lollipop, and they went away perfectly happy sucking them. Truly these are children to be proud of. They have been grand, but I don't want to see this happen again.

VOICE OF PEACE (1961-2)

Judith Cook

Judith Cook, then a young journalist with three young children and expecting a fourth, became nationally known through her 'Voice of Women' peace protest campaign and has continued to write books and articles from her Cornish home.

On 13 August 1961, the Soviet sector of Berlin was sealed off from West Berlin. The elevated railway was stopped entirely and a few days later a concrete barrier, topped with barbed wire, was erected at the Brandenberg Gate and other points along the border. On 31 August the Kremlin announced the resumption of nuclear weapon tests. The tension and near-terror which spread across western Europe and the United States was reflected in letters from *Manchester Guardian* readers to the Women's Page.

Talking later to *Guardian* reporter W.J. Weatherby, Mrs Judith Cook said 'One night in November we watched a programme that showed the Russian and American tanks facing each other in Berlin. The commentator interviewed an American colonel "who reckoned they'd be using nuclear weapons by next Tuesday". I sat down and wrote a letter to the *Guardian* from the viewpoint of an anxious mother. I didn't think it would be published, but it was. About 120 people wrote to me.' Mrs Daphne English had already had a great response to a letter (6 November 1961) inviting women to sign a peace petition.

Judith Cook's letter follows:

Although the cause may be partly physical – I am seven months pregnant – I find myself obsessed with the question of what is going to happen. I listen to the news bulletins like a drug addict and fall on the paper and read the crisis news. I have joined the Campaign for Nuclear Disarmament, though I cannot be a very active member. The questions I ask myself are 'Would any of us survive?' 'If so, for how long, and would we have to watch our children die of radiation sickness?' 'Given that we survived without serious radiation damage would we then starve to death through lack of help from outside, as all countries would be devastated?'

There must, of course, be countless others whose waking hours are haunted by such nightmares. If a government is prepared to use these weapons to settle national differences they should put the full consequences of a nuclear attack on this country plainly before us, not leave us to speculate.

'Standing firm', 'the values of the free world', 'our rights' are all meaningless slogans when balanced against children's lives.

What can one do to try to lead a normal life?

'Talkback'

That we have to learn to live with uncomfortable and dangerous knowledge is certain; it is also certain that more and more voices are being raised on behalf of humanity than ever before. I do not say that with complacency but with the conviction that in spite of the horror I share with other women, the voices will make themselves heard.

Mrs Hilary Sandle
London SE7

The first thing to acquire for peace of mind is some form of destruction for self and family, only to be used in extremity. Knowing that I could save my children needless suffering rids

193

me of my greatest fear. (I would sort this one out with God later, if need be.) Secondly, work out a plan for any warning we may have. Time yourself to collect your children, lock the house, get a supply of water etc. and balance your budget to stockpile enough tins to last at least a month. Now join your local church or any movement with peace at heart.

Then plant a tree, start to make a rug or tapestry that you know will take years to complete. Most important of all, bring up your babies as though they are to inherit the greatest new world that you and the philosophers can dream of. Teach them all the good you know. Show them all the things that you find beautiful. Be calm, for in you they will see the great wisdom and dignity of womankind. Nothing can offer more hope for their future than this.

Elspeth A. Walker
East Kilbride
Glasgow

Work and prayer are my answer. Send every spare penny, (and scheme to make more spare pennies) to organisations helping to ameliorate present distress; make each day for your own children a happy day (they may have few left); take an interest in every aspect of political life in case you can make your influence felt; and above all, pray.

P. Smart
Britwell
Slough

It may sound impossible for Mrs Cook and the many millions who feel as she feels about the threat of nuclear war to accept that those now in their forties and fifties felt just as desperate at one time during the last war. I am not comparing the last with any future war: I am comparing a state of mind that afflicts all young mothers before and during a modern war. It seems to me that only those of an older generation can, if they sincerely feel it, offer words of hope.

I pin my faith on the ideas expressed in Pierre Teilhard de Chardin's book *The Phenomenon of Man*. By all means let us form pressure groups to make world politicians recognise our fear. But is not fear the tinder wood waiting for the spark? Is

it not better to try to live on something else? This, for
instance: There is no such thing as 'the energy of despair' in
spite of what is sometimes said. What those words really mean
is a paroxysm of hope against hope. All conscious energy is,
like love (and because it is love) founded on hope.

Jane Penwood
North Wales

**By the end of December, Judith Cook had set up 'Voice of Women'
(despite the fact that her fourth baby was well overdue and her other
three children had German measles). Regional organisers were busy
recruiting in many parts of the country.**

**In April 1962, with four days' notice, Mrs Cook flew to New York
with her ten-week old son Nicholas, to take part in a women's
demonstration against the resumption of nuclear tests by the United
States.**

Judith Cook's report:
'Communists are you?' 'Peace mission eh? Well, we have
others like you over here too.' This remark from an
immigration officer at Idlewild – the first words spoken to us
by an American on American soil – was not calculated to make
me feel that a peace mission would meet with much success.
Followed immediately by the news that the first atmospheric test
had been made, it was a somewhat depressing start to our stay.

Next day, as I stood in the United Nations Plaza, waiting to
address the large crowd of women demonstrating against the
resumption of nuclear tests I felt an immense anger. The fact
that any nation, because of its size and technical skill can
disregard the voices of other nations and go ahead with a
programme which will cause death and disease in the name of
its 'national security' is a disgrace to our generation.

Later we were received by the US mission to hear their
arguments for the resumption of testing. Faced with questions
such as how they felt able to justify poisoning the six-sevenths
of the world not engaged in this political struggle their answers
could be divided into three categories. 'I don't know'. 'I'm
sure President Kennedy considered this before he ordered
testing to recommence' and 'These tests are necessary for the
defence of the free world'.

Just how free the world was we soon had an opportunity of seeing in Washington. In New York there was a feeling of hope and enthusiasm, but not in Washington. In fact, Washington came as a shock. The insolence of the police, the treatment received from the White House staff who passed us from hand to hand as if what they were doing had no need even of justification, the general air of apathy on the part of some and complete acceptance of the Government line on the part of others – all overlaid by an enervating heat – was an experience I shall never forget.

We joined a small line of pickets outside the White House, which included a Nobel Prize winner, and we became, I am told, the first British women to picket the White House since the Pankhursts.

On our return to New York, having failed to present our case to the President, the Russians invited us to their Embassy to meet Major Titov. At least the Russians ply their proposed fall-out victims with vodka, caviare and quite polite good wishes to soften the blow. After speaking to the most sympathetic reporter we had met during my stay in America I discovered he was from *Pravda*!

Eventually we handed our by now somewhat bedraggled petition to Adlai Stevenson in the knowledge that even though President Kennedy had not accepted it himself he had, in the popular idiom, got the message.

What did we achieve? Well, obviously, we did not persuade President Kennedy to stop testing, but we were another voice speaking for Britain during that week, speaking on behalf of the many people in this country who do not feel that being able to threaten mass incineration shows strength of character. More important than all this, I think was the meeting with the American and Canadian women and the discovery that on this issue we were completely at one.

I feel myself that the women of America, belonging to one of the two 'great' nuclear Powers could hold the key. They are a small, splendid, embattled minority, but if these women, these 'real' Americans, as they have been called, can successfully change the climate of opinion in their country they will be to a large extent responsible for the survival of man. We can only hope that they have the time in which to do it.

June 1, 1962: Mrs Patricia Godacre, one of the British women who picketed the White House with Judith Cook:

The attitude of many Americns we saw, especially the officials, was persecuted and defensive, and quite out of touch with reality. 'Why didn't you ask the Russians to stop their tests? Why do you put all the pressure on us?' These were questions we were asked over and over again and we could only repeat 'but we did protest just as strongly to the Russians, just as we are appealing to you. . . .'

Another 'picketer', Mrs Anne Kerr, writing from County Hall:

A letter has reached me from a Moscow lecturer and journalist which requested copies of reports of our 'inspiring efforts' and photographs of British women and children engaging in peace demonstrations. We are sending the pictures and asking the writer to help 'Mothers Against War' in our attempt to present our 'immediate cessation of tests, and total disarmament' petition to Khrushchev at the Kremlin and by inviting people in the USSR to march in protest at the present US nuclear tests and in protest if their own Government resumed testing.

On 1 August, Judith Cook reported on the visit to Moscow:

We are back. To me it has been an exhausting experience, physically and emotionally. But it was worth it. I went to the World Congress on General Disarmament and Peace to make my personal witness against nuclear war; to help in any way possible to prevent such tragedies as that of the mother who wrote to this newspaper about the death of her daughter from leukaemia: to see for myself what it was like.

As I was still feeding Nicholas morning and evening he had to accompany me once again and so he spent his days in a Moscow creche. It was in an old building which looked somewhat dilapidated, but the inside left nothing to be desired. The babies were spoilt, if anything, with cot rocking, cuddling and entertainment whenever they were awake. This love of babies seems to be a Russian characteristic and several times I stood rooted to the spot while a huge, stern Russian

197

looking far more fierce than Khrushchev bore down on me, only to find him burst into smiles and start talking baby talk to Nicholas.

I felt very much an amateur as I presented myself at the Congress Hall on the first day with an obviously new briefcase, clutching my pass. The plenary sessions did, of course, go much as was expected, the bulk of the speeches having been prepared beforehand. However a good deal that was said was valuable and I think all of us in the British delegation were proud of the speech by Sydney Silverman. I wonder how many of those who abuse us and call us fellow-travellers would have the courage to speak as he did.

On the Friday at a special women's meeting it was encouraging to realise how much we had in common with women of all nationalities present and how we shared each others' anxieties. In future we shall all be making a bigger effort to keep each other informed of what we are doing in the fight towards a saner world. The dangers of nuclear testing are really brought home when one speaks to a Japanese mother, a survivor of Hiroshima. (Every time my children clean their teeth I watch for the first sign of bleeding.)

The warmth of personal feeling towards us is well summed up for me in the note attached to a tiny suit of Russian clothes given me for my baby as I was leaving for the airport. It said – in Russian and in English, 'Dear Nick – from the Moscow Central Home of child care. From his friends who remained behind and will remember him for ever.'

Postscript: I would like to stress a point which I think has not been made sufficiently apparent. That is that after hours of discussion, argument and exchanges of views the final appeal contained these words: 'We are firmly opposed to *all* testing of nuclear bombs and similar devices, first because of their threat to the life and health of this and future generations, and secondly because they increase the tempo of the arms race.' This resolution was endorsed by 121 nations, and among the signatories were the USSR and Red China.

Judith Cook

13 Women in the Public Eye

It was not much before the 1960s that the long, in-depth interview or profile began to appear in newspapers, so the rather skimpy, flat interviews from the 1920s are included for their historic interest rather than their insights. From the wealth of later interviews it was almost impossible to make a selection. We meet Margaret Thatcher looked at when she was on her way up; Shirley Williams when it seems she might be the first woman Labour Prime Minister and a handful of others whose achievements or personalities were outstanding. Would that there were room for many more!

'BRIEF ENCOUNTER'

Vera Brittain

March, 1930: When Mr Baldwin unveils tomorrow the statue of Mrs Pankhurst he will be assisting in a process with which all historians are cynically familiar – the time-honoured performance of canonising the heretic. Throughout her life and even in her death, Mrs Pankhurst's instinct for the dramatic was unerring. She died at the height of the social and political London season; she was buried on the very day that the bill giving votes to all adult women passed its final reading in the House of Lords. Her memorial service was hastily arranged and took place in a comparatively obscure church, St John's, Smith Square. No decorations or academic robes were worn; there were only rows of women in black singing the hymns. Yet the atmosphere of the church was tense with individual emotion and the byways of Westminster were thronged with people of all ages and classes.

LADY ASTOR IN AMERICA (1922)

Anon

Lady Astor, the first woman to take her seat in the House of Commons, was elected as a Conservative member for Plymouth when her husband succeeded to his father's viscounty, in 1922.

Lady Astor's trip to America has been a most extraordinary success and she is evidently still surprised at the eagerness with which people came to listen to her. She had gone over under an engagement to speak at the Pan-American Convention of the League of Women Voters at Baltimore, and at one other meeting. It was not her intention to conduct what really turned into a campaign of propaganda. On arrival in New York she addressed a meeting of the League of Women Voters and on the following day attended a banquet given by the English-speaking Union. It was at these meetings that, in disregard of all the warnings given to her that the League of Nations was a most unpopular subject, she spoke out strongly in its support.

'You need not call it the League of Nations,' she said, 'you can call it anything you like. Give it a new name every week, but for God's sake give it a chance.' It was this message and her talk of brotherhood that stirred America to its depths and resulted in a flood of invitations for Lady Astor to address meetings all over the country.

'It was not me as a personality they cared about so much,' she said. 'It was what I said that appealed to them. I do not say that all the Americans are willing to come into the League of Nations but certainly all the people I saw wanted to come into a League of Peace. I do not believe that America is materialistic and I will guarantee that at the next election America is going to have some sort of a foreign policy.'

Lady Astor was not prepared to talk on the spur of the moment about prohibition, but she did say that she did not believe that America would go back to licence. People over there, she said, had no idea about what the English press is saying about the ineffectiveness of prohibition, and were quite horrified at some of the things she quoted.

When asked what American women are doing with their vote she answered promptly: 'They are breaking up the party machine. In Pennsylvania, where the Republican party machine was said to be stronger than anything in the world, the women broke it and through their efforts a very progressive man was chosen as Republican candidate for the State governorship.'

THE WORK OF THE MAYOR'S WIFE MRS NEVILLE CHAMBERLAIN (1925)

Anon

Mrs Neville Chamberlain was the wife of the Conservative leader who later negotiated with Hitler at Munich and announced the outbreak of war to the British people in September, 1939.

It was in 1915 that Mr Neville Chamberlain became Lord Mayor of Birmingham. As Lady Mayoress during the war Mrs Chamberlain did a great deal of personal work for the wives and children of soldiers, and secured the help of all women's societies and hundreds of volunteers all over the town to produce articles for a bazaar for the benefit of the Disabled Soldiers' Homes.

'In the war years everyone was eager to help,' said Mrs. Chamberlain. 'But I believe people are still anxious to work for the community, that the desire to serve is innate in human beings. If that strong desire was in abeyance for a time after the war it is now growing again. People generally seem to me to have more sense of responsibility. I used not to be in favour of the vote for women, but I am now. I think it has aroused women and increased their sense of personal responsibility. The work they do for political parties makes them realise the need of people who are less well off, and as they come more into contact with them they are more anxious to help them. To my mind social service and politics are so closely intermingled, you cannot separate them in your thoughts. The Mayoress who is interested in social service can

201

draw on a great number of people to help her and she has every opportunity for initiative.'

Her experience, Mrs Chamberlain said, had taught her that a Mayoress was a privileged person. She had access to every society, would be asked to attend their annual meetings and could study the special work they were doing. She feels very strongly on the housing question. Her work in Birmingham takes her into homes where people live in terrible conditions. These people are her friends and she realises the tragedies alike of birth and death where people live crowded into one room and no provision can be made for the most elementary decencies.

A Mayoress, she thinks 'has special opportunities for studying housing conditions. She can visit everywhere and do her part, then, to stir up public opinion and she will get every help in this from the medical officer of the borough. I feel that as Mayoress you see all the problems, the need for education, the need for recreation and the effect of recreation, the need for better health laws and better housing. The Mayor is necessarily occupied with administrative affairs and it is the Mayoress who can bring the personal touch. If she has been efficient during her term of office she will find that she is continually being called on for help in many directions and will be left with a much fuller life than when she entered into her Mayoral office.'

MRS DESPARD (1937)

'J.B.R.'

A militant suffragette twice imprisoned, Charlotte Despard broke away from the Pankhursts' WSPU in 1909 and formed the Women's Freedom League.

Yesterday Mrs Charlotte Despard celebrated her ninety-third birthday. I saw her a short time ago in her home in County Antrim, where she is recovering from an attack of influenza. She was bright, and looking forward to a trip to Spain, in the hope that by her presence and perhaps a speech, she might be able to help the Government forces in that country.

'I feel very strongly about Spain,' she said. 'I am in deep sympathy with the Spanish Government. The Spaniards are putting up a strong fight for democracy, and I feel that I might be able to encourage them.'

'People sometimes think that because of my age I ought to "take things easy" now. Why should I? I find life interesting even at 92 and beautiful. I love getting about, meeting people. Often I am asked to talk about the suffragette days, but I do not like talking of the past. It has gone, and only the present remains. It is the present we should live in. I am always being asked what I think of the modern girl. For the girl who works for her living and is independent I have the greatest admiration.'

Mrs Despard smiled as she recalled that when she was 25 and unmarried she used to be told she was 'on the shelf'. 'That sort of gibe would not worry the modern girl much,' she said. 'I did marry, but over forty years ago my husband died. We had an ideally happy life. I carried on with my work after marriage. I think it is a mistake for a woman to give up her career with marriage even when there are children. The very fact that there are children should make a woman more keen to do what she can to construct a better world for them to live in.'

I talked to Mrs Despard of her beliefs. 'I am a revolutionary thinker,' she admitted. 'I believe that everything must be changed. The terrible part of our social system is that it is so cruel. What we want is a reorientation. We must get away from the "I" in life, from dogmas and from creeds. They only tie us up. True development and true emancipation only come from being selfless.'

For a few seconds we touched on war and on Ireland. 'I hate war with every fibre of my being,' she said. 'Another war, of which everybody is talking, would be race suicide, but I think that Ireland would probably be neutral. I lived away from Ireland for a long time, but now I am back. I would like to see a United Ireland, an independent Ireland and I believe that some day it will come. At present the great thing is to try for the unification of Ireland.'

'Looking back on your life, Mrs Despard,' I asked, 'would you say it had been a successful one?'

She paused, then smiled. 'Well, I have seen a lot. Sometimes I think that I have lived more than one life. The feminist movement has not done all I had hoped, and there are many questions I think it ought to be tackling. For example, that of equal pay for equal work. I cannot say whether my life has been successful or not. What I can say, though, is that it has been a happy one and never a dull one.'

POLITICAL WOMAN (1962)

Taya Zinkin

Taya Zinkin was the Manchester Guardian *correspondent in India (Bombay) for several years. When she and her husband Maurice returned to London, after India became independent, Mrs Zinkin contributed frequently to the* Guardian *Women's Page. She has written many books, including two fascinating accounts of her childhood and adolescence.*

Four questions were uppermost in my mind when I went to see Mrs Margaret Thatcher, Joint Parliamentary Secretary to the Ministry of Pensions and National Insurance. Any memories that might have lingered in my mind evaporated as I listened to this smartly dressed, pretty woman whose shrewd common sense comes forth in the most mellifluous of voices.

In spite of her youth Margaret Thatcher is a veteran at the game of politics and her debut goes back to her Oxford days when she presided over the Conservative association. Her mind pigeonholes questions, answers and pitfalls with an ease which must make many a back-bench veteran's mouth water. With an eye on the clock, since she had been called to see her Minister, I unfolded my four questions: 'Is it more difficult for a woman to enter politics?' 'Are women discriminated against once they are in politics?' 'Why are there so few women in politics?' and finally, 'Would things be run differently if, for argument's sake, Britain was ruled by women instead of men.'

Margaret Thatcher was quite positive that women are discriminated against when it comes to entering politics, 'because of a lingering historical prejudice which makes it difficult for a woman to be selected as a candidate'. Many able women are thus kept out from the start and those who are chosen are given the more difficult constituencies because, after all, if they do not get in the party bosses think that nothing much has been lost. But once a woman has been selected she can be assured of a larger audience during her campaign simply because there are so few women standing that curiosity will draw people; this does not mean that they will vote for her, nor is there any evidence that women vote for a woman, although once they have a woman MP they will probably take to her personal problems they would never dream of taking to a man.

However, once a woman has got into Parliament the historical prejudice melts away because of a vague feeling that it is to the party's credit to give women their due, since this may please women voters. And there is no difference in attitude between Labour and Tory. If there are so few women in office this is not due to prejudice but to the fact that the number from which to draw is so restricted. 'After all there are only 13 women MP's on our side. To have given office to 3 is not bad.' But Mrs Thatcher would feel much happier if the number of women in Parliament were doubled so that there would be more choice.

Why do so few women go into politics? Mrs Thatcher unravelled a whole skein of reasons. To begin with, women who are admirably suited to committee work may not be good on the soap box or on the floor of the House where what is wanted besides ability is a 'voice' and the capacity to swing the audience to one's side. But far more important is the fact that many of the women who do such admirable work in their locality and devote all their spare time to committees do it on a part-time basis. Politics is a full-time job. Mrs Thatcher is fortunate in having a nannie to look after her children and a husband who believes in her calling and is both willing and able to foot the bill. There are other women who are not married or whose children are grown up, who have the same advantages but they are often not interested in politics and prefer to fulfil themselves through local or charitable activities. They are put off by the prospect of having to lead a double or even a treble life, divided between Westminster, their constituency and home.

'Here again, I am fortunate,' said Mrs Thatcher. 'Finchley, my constituency, is not far from Parliament and since I live in Kent I need not keep a flat in London and I can go home to my husband and children. Moreover I do not have to worry over money – as you know, we get no pension as of right; this can matter to those who have to support themselves. It is expensive to be in politics: one has to be mobile, one has to be well-groomed, and one has to entertain.'

However it is not in the end financial hurdles which keep women out of the political field but the fact that, due to their historical conditioning, women are usually more deeply concerned with their homes and their neighbourhood than with the wider political issues, particularly since their vote gives them some control over policy.

If Mrs Thatcher would like to see more women make use of their talents and participate in the national life, it is simply because she thinks it would be good for them and for the nation if those who have the talent used it, and it would act as an incentive for far more women to get more education – but it would not, she believes, mean that Britain would take some wildly different direction. 'There would be no difference if the Government were run by women,' Mrs Thatcher said. 'A Cabinet of women would have to consider men voters just as much as the Cabinet considers women voters.'

So in the last analysis, it is the suffragettes who have made it possible for women to cultivate their gardens in the peaceful confidence that their views cannot be ignored.

JUSTICE OF THE PEACE (1965)

Betty Vernon

Betty Vernon, long-time feminist and socialist, is the author of biographies of Ellen Wilkinson and Margaret Cole.

Although I am a comparatively new magistrate, I have found certain common factors in cases of violence. These cases concern mostly boys and men, not the female of the species. (There is some evidence that she prefers to incite her boy friends, rather than get directly involved herself.)

The juvenile court is confronted by bored, destructive, under-occupied small boys, many of whom are deprived of stable family life. Arson is their main offence, often an expression of hatred and anti-authoritarian frustration. But sometimes they seem to act from intellectual curiosity as well as devilment; as in the case of two highly intelligent boys who attempted to blow up a local town hall with some home-made explosives – after they had deliberately arranged their alibis. Drunkenness underlies many assault cases too – too often with the defendant using broken glass. One man recently had to have 33 stitches in his face, after such an attack at closing time. This is horrid, but I find it far less so than cases of calculated thuggery, such as robbery with violence – when three youths pushed a man into a field, held a knife at his throat and robbed him. Incidents of 'neighbourly' bad behaviour are common. Usually they involve disputes over fencing, trees and dogs; car obstruction seems to provoke the most intense aggression and the most vivid language. But bad temper, as a psychiatrist observed, 'is all right until it deteriorates into mental sickness'.

To me the most perturbing and most difficult problem of all is group hooliganism. This spreads into both juvenile and adult courts, and is exemplified by youngsters who smash 30 signal lamps and road repairing equipment, who toss park benches into lily ponds, uproot yards of fencing, trample on flower beds and tear up turf from bowling greens. This is a form of hooliganism which suggests aggression, hatred and bravado.

And to all this, intermittently – we only sit, on roster, two or three times a month – I ask why? The comment that 'human violence is a symptom of stress in human society', or that 'violence will out; it is a natural means of self-assertion', seems to me inadequate. So one makes one's own patchwork of deductions. A sociological patchwork built from background evidence of broken homes, inadequate parental guidance, starved affections, mothers at work, large school classes, extended leisure cocooning young people who often lack the wisdom and the training to use that leisure constructively. A psychological patchwork of people who seem bored, inarticulate, uncontrolled, who lack ability to anticipate the results of their actions, or the will to care, who, accepting violence in the pattern of their 'homes' are purposeless and unsure of the difference between right and wrong. Sucked into a highly competitive society which fosters a philosophy of 'I see, I want, I have', they accept in their world of eroded values a constant conditioning to the use of violence through every form of mass media.

Perhaps the largest question-mark hangs over the patent aimlessness of young people who move about in gangs. Group activity, as a probation officer reminded me, is both a normal part of adolescence and a source of security. And it is a sense of security above all that many exponents of violence and cruelty, old as well as young, seem to lack – views reinforced by an educational psychologist. The insecurity of adolescence he saw was often emphasised by the inadequacy of the 'father figure' in the home, and the 'non-cohesiveness of the family unit'. Young folk had an urge to seek a father-figure in the gang leader.

It has been suggested that adult society feels guilty about its offspring and their behaviour, and that we tend to push 'teenagers' into an unidentifiable mass. As a result they try to assert their individuality through the gangs, working out their feelings upon society, which they normally would express within their homes. Acts of violence grow out of a series of small incidents, until they become a cry of despair, often in the same way as an attempted suicide is often a cry for help.

It seems to me pertinent that magistrates should be alive to developments in the understanding of human behaviour, and should try to discuss them. Without being unduly critical, I do find that some of the experienced develop an inflexibility of mind and an aridity of feeling that circumscribes judgment. But in all fairness, there is a practical difficulty. Most lay magistrates, except the retired, are busy people with family, professional, business and public commitments, over and above their duties on the bench. We have, therefore, too little time for hard, consistent thinking about current problems arising from court; often we must rely upon the specialists and predigested information. So that all too often only one's native wit, one's prejudices and one's preconceived ideas remain to cement the cracks of one's ignorance.

One cannot, of course, evade the issues of punishment and penalties. My personal sympathies are towards seeking methods of retraining and help, rather than pursuing a punitive approach. But I am often told that: 'We on the bench are not a social service agency and we must protect property'. And some acts of violence are so deadly that it is only with difficulty that one refrains from demanding retributive justice. Yet even assuming that certain forms of violence have to be contained, on a long-term basis, can one not look further ahead? Do we do enough to anticipate violent situations before they arise? Could not parents, teachers, youth leaders, employers, who are apprehensive about certain behaviour patterns, or lack of activity, in young people, try tactfully to take preventive action? It is often forgotten that probation officers are there to advise and help *before*, as well as after, people who have got into difficulties. I have yet to meet a probation officer who, in spite of heavy case-loads will ever reject requests for help. Policewomen, too, will gladly help over anticipated family troubles.

Of one fact I am unshakeably convinced. There are depths of kindness, compassion and generosity in young people which can and ought to be plumbed in the interests of our community.

The alternative is that we all sit back, decrying the failure of modern youth, and ignoring our obligations. For I do find that from sitting on the bench, there is a real danger of losing one's humility and drifting into complacency. Yet I know, as firmly as I know anything at all, that to be an effective magistrate, one must try to face all the problems with curiosity and an open mind. One has to question everything, from the incontrovertibility of police evidence to the apparently hopeless brutality of human nature; and one must, too, challenge one's own attitudes. Curiosity as to motive, and compassion as to punishment, seem to me essential. These approaches may not resolve the issues concerned with violence, but they help one to face up to their complexity.

THE IRON BUTTERFLY: HELEN GURLEY BROWN (1968)

Catherine Stott

Catherine Stott was a feature writer in the Guardian *specialising in interviews for several years before she became Women's Editor of the* Sunday Telegraph.

'There are girls who read *Cosmopolitan* and enjoy it as voyeurs. They don't want to be that driven, to have that many affairs; they don't want more than one man or one dress at a time. They don't care about jewellery and they don't want a sable coat or Paris for the week-end. They don't want to work as hard as I do. But "my girl" wants it. She is on the make. Her nose is pressed to the glass and she does get my message. These girls are like my children all over the country. Oh, I have so much advice for them, and it's fun.'

Helen Gurley Brown was talking about readers of the magazine she edits with a stamp as personal as and not dissimilar from Hugh Hefner's on *Playboy*. It was Helen Gurley Brown who wrote the phenomenally successful *Sex and the Single Girl*, sold the title for $200,000 to a film company, and then began broadcasting its message for all it was worth through the columns of a moribund magazine which Hearst Publications asked her to edit, three years ago.

When she began, it was selling 650,000 copies. Now they are hitting the million mark and advertising has quadrupled; an unparalleled success with Madison Avenue. And all because this small, frail-looking woman they call 'the iron butterfly' has an uncanny eye for what women want, knows how to give it to them, edits every word herself, and spends ten hours a day and several hours a night working on it.

In a deceptively gentle voice she will explain to the listener that her success was motivated by fear not ambition. That she had a sad little childhood and a terrible growing-up. Although her simple little dress probably cost $100 a stitch and her jewellery may well come from Tiffany's, she looks as if she is afraid it may all be taken away, that she will be planted back in the Ozarks a fatherless girl with acute acne giving dancing lessons to the other kids at 25 cents an hour to help to make ends meet.

Her philosophy is one of self-betterment, extremely subjective, virtually autobiographical. She thinks of herself very much as 'a girl who had very little going for her. As far back as I can remember, I thought I was physically barely adequate . . . in the 1940s bosoms were the big things; legs didn't matter . . . if you were small-breasted it was bad luck. Then I didn't have money going for me . . . nor an outrageously wonderful personality and I didn't go to college. I was a terribly average girl who inherited enough of a brain to do a few things. Being stupid is the worst thing that can happen to a girl; much worse than being ugly.'

Talking to Helen Gurley Brown in her Manhattan office is very much like reading her magazine; she explains her life very much in terms of what other people could achieve in the same way. . . . 'I always say that anyone can do what I've done – not that it's all that much – but you can have a great career, make money and have some fabulous men in your life, and you don't have to be sensational to start with because I certainly wasn't.' She was the classic American dreamgirl who capitalised on what she had and finds it fun to watch others doing so.

It always charms her to see a girl who doesn't look like very much 'Coming on very sexy and maybe a little bitchy, but very attractive to men. My way would be to come on dynamic on the inside. To have something that gleams and burns inside you.'

What makes Helen burn? 'I think you get it because you feel deprived. You want to be more pretty, more of everything, more loved, perhaps. I wasn't ambitious when young, only frightened. I just got very scared during the Depression. Fear led me to do the best I could at everything. At school I was very competitive in a very quiet deadly way.

'I had to work the minute I got out of high school and all I could do was shorthand typing. I didn't think I should have been doing something better, only "if I get fired we'll all go down the drain". I was a secretary for 15 years, but always getting better until at 33 I was a whizz-bang executive secretary who got a whack at writing advertising copy.' She wrote sexy, girlish copy for seven years and was the highest paid woman in advertising in California. But the last agency she was with stopped giving her assignments, having stolen her from another agency for a vast sum so she asked her husband, David Brown, vice-president of Twentieth Century Fox, what she could write a book about. 'He said I could write for the single girl. He said "When I first met you, you were a kind of a swinger, but you were also a solid citizen. You were very respectable with lots of friends and dates and parties." So I wrote it, and it sold millions.'

She says it wasn't that good a book – a sweet nice book on an idea whose time had come, about single girls having a good life. 'Single girls had been sleeping with men for a long time, quietly and without being run out of town. But secretively. Well, along I came with my little book and said that single girls did have a great sex life and were often much happier in bed than they ever would be as married women because they had more choice and variety and didn't have to stay with a man they didn't like.

'Mostly the message was "don't worry and feel guilty if you are having an affair because so is everyone else . . .", a sisterly book by a girl who was doing it herself, who seemed to understand how it was for others. Like a nice letter from home. More than this, *Sex and the Single Girl* actually conferred a new respectability on spinsterhood, making it appear glamorous.'

She believes every girl has one thing she can do really well and must find it, if she wants to succeed, 'and I have made this one exquisite little talent for writing sincerely in short, sharp sentences into quite a thing.' She doesn't necessarily approve of waiting as long as she did to marry (she was 37), 'I would think anyone who doesn't marry until 37 is quite neurotic. My neurotic drive towards work and success is perhaps a healthy one. The other neurosis was a bad one, in that the men who wanted to marry me I didn't want to marry and vice versa.

'I talk a great deal about success and you'll notice the word "love" has scarcely entered this conversation. One is always criticised for that. Well, I adore my husband and I was in love with him when we married and there's not much point in going on about it! I don't say I wanted to marry a successful man –

212

just I never would have married anyone who wasn't successful, and that's not the nicest thing you ever heard, is it? But if I'm going to work like a bunny rabbit I don't want a passive man, but my kind.

'Suddenly, when I was 40, I fell into a glamorous life. . . . And I had earned it. And I've had some influence on other women. I work much too hard. I sound like a little girl from the Ozarks but I'm glad that at 46 things seem like fun and games to me. My forties have been my best years and I keep pounding the message home to my readers.'

BARBARA WOOTTON: THE DAUGHTER WHO BECAME DISTINGUISHED (1968)

Catherine Stott

Barbara Wootton, Baroness Wootton of Abinger, was once referred to by her mother as 'my daughter who might have been distinguished'. Less exacting critics regard Lady Wootton as one of the most distinguished women of our time, as a scholar, economist, senior magistrate of 43 years' experience, sometime governor of the BBC, member of various Royal Commissions, and one of the first women life peers.

Lady Wootton is the compleat committee woman, the ultimate organisation woman; a doer rather than a speech-maker. As a person she is both formidable and approachable: her conversation is decisive. She knew immediately when asked what had given her the most satisfaction in a long career. It was jointly being a governor of the BBC and being a magistrate. 'I liked the BBC so much because it was educative, my only chance to see how a big organisation works from the inside. Being a magistrate brings you in touch with real life at the circumference. In Whitehall you do not see the impact on ordinary people, so I cherish my contact with real life.

'I had to give up the children after 20 years and although I missed them I was quite pleased to go because I had come to the conclusion that young children of school age ought not to be brought in front of the criminal court. I became more and more embarrassed by having to conduct this procedure whilst

213

holding another belief. When I started the children began at 8 – I moved the amendment in the Lords to get it raised to ten, and was terribly glad when it took a million or so children out of reach of the criminal court.'

As a governor of the BBC, Lady Wootton recalls 'I don't think I actually did anything, but they were the nicest and most agreeable group of colleagues I have ever had.' She entered the Upper Chamber in 1958 and says, 'I would put the House of Lords quite high for company. What everybody says about it being a very nice club is indeed true. I don't give a great deal for their debates. I am well acquainted with the cliché that they are much better at debates than the Commons, which is, I usually feel, voiced by people who have not much experience of either. If you sat there day in, day out, you would not be very impressed by them.

'In fact I am not a good parliamentarian. I shall never get used to grown-up people making speeches for the sake of making speeches. . . . The art of debate is suitable for the Oxford Union but not for adults. I should prefer the Lords to be much less formal, with more of a committee pattern. Debates after all were invented during the days when people sat on the edge of their benches thinking which way to vote as they listened to the speeches. It has become farcical now, people know which way to vote before they ever start.'

Lady Wootton entirely agrees with Lord Brockway's proposal that the Lords should be a forum for ideas. 'Well, if you are going to keep it at all: and let it be peopled not with ex-politicians or MPs who are either defeated or too old to stand again, but with those who have something to contribute in a definite sphere – a House of specialists. I think I might be a tolerably good parliamentarian in revising legislation and if one's revision was effective I should be very interested.' She was charmed by 'the inactive peers who turned up rather sweetly to vote themselves out of a job'.

The Wootton Committee has been considering drugs for 18 months and will continue for another year. 'I see most of the stories leading off about drugs are most anxious to mention that I am 71 and I am sure that in this they are trying to convey the impression that this is a senile old woman trying to be with it, a "what does she know?" line. If you take a liberal attitude and say that the penalties are excessive, as I think they are, then it is just an old person trying to be young, as though one were wearing a mini-skirt. I'm disturbed about the leak of information regarding the drugs report because what this means is that until the report is published I cannot speak about it, and when it is published at the end of the year, it will no longer be news. One would like the opportunity of saying what the arguments behind it are. I only wish I knew how it happened, but I have formed theories.'

What Lady Wootton cares most about is the countryside. She lives in deepest, leafiest Surrey, which she loves. Consequently she finds disputes lost by the Countryside Commission, on which she sits, most disheartening. 'All my life I have fought battles – mostly losing battles – but one consoled oneself by thinking it was only a matter of time. If you lose over the countryside then you have lost for ever because the pieces of countryside have gone.

'The thing I like most in life is the countryside. I have had this house, High Barn, for 13 years. I think converting it from the original barn was brave to the point of foolhardy. When I get up in the morning I feel I want to stroke it. It is my chief stable anchor, now; I sleep here practically every night even if I am in London late . . . I think it is a sign of old age that you long to sleep in your own bed; to see one's own possessions, follow one's own routine. I always say to people "let me go home". One was more dashing when one was younger.'

Lady Wootton was widowed in 1964. she speaks of living alone calmly, sadly. 'No. I have not become accustomed to living alone . . . well, only in the sense that I do it, but I will never think it a suitable way to live. I prefer it to living with anyone who is not very close but I miss terribly not having anyone with whom to chew over the day's events. I think this is basic to proper human development; I have many friends but I am still very conscious of the loneliness.

'This house was not built to be lived in alone; neither was it built for close living with people who are not close to you. I have no thought of moving. Never. My friends said I should move back to London but I said I would commit suicide the first weekend. Here I work in the garden and have the donkeys for company. I have no help in the house; indeed, if I was to have a stroke it would be a long time before anyone knew about it.'

Her life is full and highly organised. When asked if she enjoys it she says 'Yes' very slowly. Then, 'No. Not really. I have enjoyed life.' And very quietly: 'I could really do without it now.' Smiling bleakly she said that the alternative would create rather a hoo-ha. 'I am prepared to go on on sufferance. But I would not if I had a serious illness. Quite a chunk of me has died since I have been alone, though one gets used to the day-to-day living but not the emotional loss.

'I have always regretted very much not having had children. It is the one great lack in my life but there were reasons against it. I would then have done something else, which I regard quite as worthwhile, namely being with one's children. But it would have disrupted my marriage at a fairly early stage, I think. . . . My husband couldn't cope with ties. . . . Yes, marriage is a tie, but he rode it very lightly.'

At the back of High Barn an early evening mist was rising on the meadow. Lady Wootton threw open the drawing-room window, saying that she would call the children . . . her friendly donkeys whom she says do no donkey work. But they didn't come, so she settled down in front of the log fire, a drink in her hand, saying softly: 'I regard this as my epilogue.'

TO HELL WITH THE ENGLISH (1970)

Catherine Stott

'The great sorrow and trouble of my life is that I was actually born in England.' But Wendy Wood says it quite cheerfully for one who has just, at the age of 77, written a forcefully anti-English autobiography, full of spleen against government and monarchy who, she considers, held her country in inhuman bondage. Nothing, she writes, puts her in better fettle than the sound of an English voice, and she describes the enmity as instinctive as between cat and dog. She also, in her book, accuses the Queen of accepting the Scottish Crown wearing 'a plain blue shopping dress like the produce of C & A at 35s. . . . a slap in the face for the nation.'

All this adds up, in prospect, to a very militant lady. In fact, face to face with a member of the English race Miss Wood is mellowness itself and shows no anglophobia to the individual. She lives in an elegant Georgian house in the Canonmills district of Edinburgh, which bears the nameplate of the Scottish Patriots on the door and is in fact the headquarters of their activities. Outwardly she seems a comfortable Scots grandmother figure.

Miss Wood was born in Kent and grew up in South Africa. She is by a profession an artist and writer. In 1928 she was in at the birth of the Scottish Nationalist Party and one of her best remembered exploits was when in 1932 she led a group of ardent nationalists to 'storm' the fortress of Stirling Castle to remove the Union Jack – 'the flag of our bondage' – and to replace it with the Lion Rampant. Although she was challenged by 50 soldiers with fixed bayonets she was allowed to leave unhindered. The Scottish Nationalist Party regarded this incident unfavourably and consequently Miss Wood parted company with them and went on to form, with the miners of Fife, the Democratic Scottish Self-Government Organisation – which had two enemies, the Communists and the SNP.

She was twice imprisoned as a result of her beliefs; once because she knew that the conditions were appalling in a Glasgow women's prison, and realised that the only way to make people believe the truth was to run a campaign based on personal experience. She served 60 days for non-payment of insurance contributions, found it as degrading as it was said to be, and started work on bullying the Prison Commissioners. Her efforts were finally rewarded when she received a letter saying the prison was to be demolished and a new one built. She was committed to Holloway after being arrested for trying to hold a meeting for Scots in Trafalgar Square on the night when the Stone of Destiny was 're-stolen' and put back in Westminster.

A full-time, full-blooded female patriot is a very rare animal indeed. Most nationalists keep it for their spare time. Miss Wood gave most of her adult life to it, holding meetings in the most outlying areas of Scotland, going on long walking tours, living on the collections of the meetings. Very few people prevented her from holding meetings. One was the town clerk of St Andrews who said that nationalism was a form of insanity in the family and as such should not be spoken of. Thousands followed her and she was known in Scotland simply as Wendy. What was it, in Scotland, one wanted to know, that inspired such devotion.

It was, she says, with a soft sadness in her voice, seeing everything so wrong in the country and feeling so personally helpless. 'Coming up here and seeing the land wasted. I felt immediately that here was a country that could feed itself and surely other people, given good management. I began to poke my nose in and went to the Glasgow slums and was, of course, absolutely horrified. We still have the worst housing in Europe, but then it was so incredibly awful that I wept to see it. There rose up in me this astonished determination of "Good heavens, we need to manage our own, what have we been doing for the last 250 years . . . just going down and down", and the feeling of intense injustice put the fighting spirit into me.'

Her yearning for home rule grew stronger with the years. 'After each war, when we had greater casualties than the English and had worse unemployment, I thought that we should be given home rule out of a sense of justice, and felt stupid when it didn't happen. I felt a deep bitterness that so much should go by without any recognition.

'We have tried for 250 years to live governed by another country and have honestly found it impossible. What rancours so much in me is that we are so heavily taxed and yet do not get the result of it used here. We want our own taxation. So few people understand our plight that I want to barge into England and hold meetings, but one is met with such confident scorn and accused of speaking nonsense.'

Speaking is the one gift she says she can give her country. Her great concern is that Scottish children know too little of their history and culture, and in 1931 she formed a youth movement called the Scottish Watch, to encourage interest in the past and to apply it to the present and the future. When the membership passed 3,000 the Church wanted to take it over and Baden-Powell protested that it was taking the place of the scouts and the guides. Miss Wood reminded him that in

South Africa she had been the first girl ever to become a boy scout.

'The Scottish Watch,' she says today, 'was the best thing I ever did and I was an utter idiot to let it go out of my hands. Had I kept it we should have bred a strong young race of patriots, but I had a foolish notion that women couldn't lead, which was strange because the whole Celtic tradition was for women to lead and to teach the arts of war.'

Miss Wood has been accused of many things, including witchcraft (she does have the Highland second sight) but it is the charge of fanaticism that has most often been levelled at her. With a broad grin she confesses that she doesn't mind that at all: 'Nothing in the world has been got without fanaticism. Christ was a fanatic and every great movement has had one somewhere. To me fanaticism means going beyond the consideration of self, and after all if one does not do that, one doesn't quite mean it.'

She would place first among her achievements her visits to so many places in Scotland. 'Although the lone walking tours seemed rather insignificant at the time, I now realise I was taking the word where it hadn't been heard before. I have felt myself to be some kind of a missionary in the true sense of the word.'

With confidence Wendy Wood predicts: 'I know home rule will come in the next few years, very suddenly too, as the result of a rush of exasperation. And when it comes, I will go back to painting and writing. I will be so deliriously happy, I shan't want any position, only to be a comforter and an encourager.'

SOCIALIST CLIMBER IN THE HOUSE (SHIRLEY WILLIAMS)

Linda Christmas

Shortly after contributing this interview with Shirley Williams, Linda Christmas succeeded Mary Stott on her retirement from the Women's Page.

'Tis a pity she's a politician. If Shirley Vivien Teresa Brittain

Williams were doing some other kind of job one would not think twice about cocooning her in compliments. She seems so nice; real Simon pure. But such is the nature of the protagonists in Buchan's 'Greatest and most honourable adventure' that it is necessary to tread warily. The more winsome they seem the more wily they are.

In Shirley Williams's case, surely, she hardly goes out of her way to make you like her. She's generally late for appointments, not a plot to produce sweet thoughts. She arrives, steaming along in a flurry, as the Commons attendant said she would, or gently whistling if she is in the more relaxing atmosphere of her home. Instead of apologising she announces that she has just 20 minutes to spare before the next appointment.

Our first appointment was curtailed in favour of the dentist and our second turned out to be a 'morning in the life of . . .' as I dogged her footsteps, darting in a question here and there while she showed a party of schoolchildren the wonders of Westminster and paid a much-needed visit to her hairdresser.

But this was to see Mrs Williams at her best: unpretentious, easy-going, relaxed and full of youthful energy. So youthful, in fact, that it was easy to lose her among a crowd of teenagers. It was only her euphonic voice which enabled me to keep track. 'Can anyone tell me why the Tudor rose is both red and white?' 'The chap in the mod cap is the leader of the Prussians.'

It is difficult to believe she is 41; she seems to belong to an all-purpose generation and with enviable agility can adapt to any age group, any situation. Depending on your vantage point, she could be the kind of girl mothers hope their sons will bring home, 'Labour's leading lady', or even Britain's first woman Prime Minister.

I am not very sure many mothers would take their ambitions any further if they could see her London pad: it is functional, drab and chaotic. Mrs Williams is aware of the mess, but resents time keeping it tidy. The same applies to her appearance, which everyone criticises in the same breath as they praise her abilities and achievements. 'I'm only prepared to spend ten minutes dressing, so what can you expect?'

But there is more to it than time. Shirley Williams wasn't

noted for sartorial elegance before politics made off with her life. At Oxford, *Isis* labelled her 'the Shetland pony' and described her at a union party 'wearing a loud yellow and blue striped dress, little tarty high-heeled shoes and the wrong sort of jewellery'. Freudians will feast on the fact that her mother, the pacifist author Vera Brittain, was elegant, tidy and punctual. 'So punctual that we had to catch every train with half an hour to spare. So now I do it with less than a minute.'

Oddly enough, Mrs Williams says her lack of interest in her appearance is symptomatic of her desire to be inconspicuous. 'I don't like to be recognised. I will go to a memorial service in an old hat and sit at the back. You might well ask why am I in public life at all. I just don't understand it myself. Perhaps it is because I have confidence in my mind but not in the way I look.' For all that, she is quite an extrovert.

And Shirley Williams is extremely able. This was apparent from early childhood, even though the war and her mother's desire for her daughter to experience a good social mix of schools meant that she had a chequered and interrupted education. Her eight schools varied from 'a crummy Dame school to a really tough LCC elementary school' and included a spell in America where she and her elder brother were sent to avoid the feared invasion. Both her parents were on the Gestapo blacklist for making anti-Hitler speeches.

At 16 she enrolled in the Labour League of Youth. At 17, from St Paul's School she got a scholarship to Oxford. 'My first wish was the London School of Economics but I got a place at Oxford and thought I would be daft not to take it, especially as it meant I didn't have to take A levels and leave school a year early. I didn't like school. I didn't go for the discipline. I also needed to get away from home; to go somewhere where no one knew my parents.'

The answer lay in milking cows on an Essex community farm and in being a waitress in Newcastle. Around this point, the unruly, inimitable Miss Catlin became a Catholic.

Oxford was a ball. She fell in love as often as possible, became an *Isis* idol, almost had her scholarship taken away and achieved her first 'first' when she became chairman of the University Labour Party. After a year in America studying trade unions, Shirley Catlin came back to London to try her hand at 'human interest' journalism, on the *Daily Mirror*, but 'when they discovered I was no Anona Winn they sacked me'.

It was now 1954 and time for her to make her first bid for Parliament in a by-election at Harwich. She was 24 and it took 10 years and three more fights to get there. Meanwhile she pursued her writing career with the *Financial Times*, married Bernard Williams whom she had known at Oxford and who was now a philosophy don, went to Ghana, became the first woman general secretary of the Fabian Society and had her daughter, 'Becky'.

Once inside Westminster the achievements continued to accumulate. Within a year she was PPS to the Minister of Health and within two years Parliamentary Secretary to the Ministry of Labour. Next step, Minister of State at the Department of Education and Science, followed by the same position at the Home Office. In October, 1970 she became Shadow Minister of Health and Social Security.

Wilsonian musical chairs did not make it easy for her to leave her mark on any of these departments. But it did give her the opportunity to learn to handle deputations skilfully, so skilfully that at times both sides came away thinking that they had her on their side – and to become known and generally liked by civil servants. They discovered that she was an 'ideas' person and one who is frustrated by practicalities. 'She is more concerned to create God's kingdom here on earth than whether or not it is possible' is one view. Others found her accessible, emotionally equable, challenging, compassionate, intelligent, and above all hard-working.

Such qualities in excess can bring problems. Mrs Williams allowed her compassion full rein at the Home Office. When she received a letter which appealed to her she would reach for the phone and ask the writer in for a chat. Such disregard for procedure may be endearing but it could clog the works. Her intellectual approach made her the scourge of many departments. She sniffed suspiciously at everything and asked question after question until she was satisfied. Such thoroughness, however, tended to lead to over-involvement. Each case and every problem received the same treatment, causing her to lose sight of priorities; decisions got delayed.

'No, I don't find decision-making difficult. Administrative decisions, decisions based on facts rather than opinions, are no problem at all. Although subjective decisions, decisions on political points where you have to gauge the reactions of others, are much more difficult.' She has in mind the Common Market. Although a supporter of it since the late 1950s, when she wrote a pamphlet 'The Common Market and its Fore-runners', the current issue has caused her a great deal of heartsearching.

On the principle that politicians should be able to get interested in any field, Mrs Williams has enjoyed her stay in all departments. She is now putting up a brave fight in the enormously complicated jungle of Social Services, but it is not the brilliant appointment everyone thought it to be. Her social idealism should have made this field her forte, but it isn't. Her mind is not the kind to master the technicalities of pensions at a stroke. Such detail depresses her. Her dearest wish may be to abolish poverty, but not by fiddling around with free school milk and family income supplements.

Shirley Williams loves economics, though few people seem to realise it (she read philosophy, politics and economics at Oxford). 'I wish I could have been in the Treasury in a learning situation – as Minister of State, for example. But it is too late now.' In an ideal world she would like to become a kind of female Geoffrey Rippon, not just because she is a pro-Marketeer but because it combines her twin loves – economics and foreign affairs. On a more realistic level she thinks she might make Minister of Education.

'No, not Prime Minister, or any of the four top jobs, because I am not sure I want them. I'm not sure I'm prepared to make the sacrifices necessary to get them.' The all-consuming nature of political life is undoubtedly a bother to her – 'I wish they would get this damn place organised to function from 10 a.m. to 8 p.m.' – but it is difficult to believe that a woman whose whole life has been geared to politics, a woman whose earliest recollection is not falling off a swing but listening to her parents talking about the burning of the Reichstag is not prepared to sacrifice a little more.

Her denial seems far more likely to stem from irritation at being labelled a possible future leader. 'Shirley Williams is one

223

of those very rare women who could become PM (and perhaps should) without losing a scrap of her good nature and charm and without thinking any better of herself for it,' said *The Times* a year ago. (The editor was at Oxford with her.) Without a crystal ball, political forecasting is hazardous especially for a woman who has hardly been put to the test as a front bencher.

In the House she is respected for her seriousness, which fortunately she manages to carry lightly. She has made few enemies and has an indefinable quality which makes one feel like trusting her or at least giving her the benefit of the doubt. Her rise so far has been steady and effortless and the fact that she has not had to struggle may account for the lack of aggression and ruthlessness which usually marks those destined for its top. Those not in the Williams camp think her rise has been solely due to fortuitous circumstances. She came to the fore when Labour's fortunes were seriously on the decline, because she was one of the few ministers who were able to put whole-hearted conviction behind the 'old-fashioned Labour message'. Members of this camp dismiss the idea of her becoming PM as 'ludicrous' but on the whole list weaknesses – lack of power-game decisiveness and authority on the floor of the House – which could be rectified with a few more years in office.

She has one 'hidden' political disadvantage: she is a Catholic. Ladbroke's quoted her odds on becoming Prime Minister four years ago as 500/1. Today they say they have risen to 33/1. But when I reminded their political expert that she is RC he doubled the odds to 66/1. Still pretty fair. But Shirley Williams is adamant about her ambitions: 'My career so far has been an endless series of lucky events. I was staggered to find myself in the Shadow Cabinet. This sort of luck runs out and the going gets tougher and tougher.'

And just to show how dispensable politics is she adds that she has already thought about alternatives: 'educational administration . . . I am a Fellow of Somerville and a visiting Fellow of Nuffield . . . if you get far enough in public life as a woman such appointments are not difficult to get.'

14   The Do-it-yourself Decade

People sometimes speak of 'The Swinging Sixties' and of hippies and flower people and student revolt. For many *Guardian* readers the 1960s were the 'Do-it-yourself Decade'. From their letters, or from articles by sympathetic contributors, at least ten groups and organisations grew which had a powerful influence in various ways. Here are reminders of some of the survivors . . . how they began and what they achieved.

THE HOUSEWIVES REGISTER (1961)

Betty Jerman

Letter from Mrs Maureen Nicol, 26 February, 1960

> Perhaps housebound housewives with liberal interests and a desire to remain individuals could form a national register, so that whenever one moves one can contact like-minded friends.
>
> Eastham, Cheshire

Betty Jerman, August 1962: Responding to this letter *Guardian* readers launched an avalanche of letters at the astonished Mrs Nicol, who swiftly fixed regional organisers and got the movement functioning. Now the number of members is unknown, since Mrs Nicol gave up counting and only guesses at four to five thousand. She had two young children under three, a three-bedroomed house and no help. She received 400 letters in one week and smaller onslaughts after any publicity. . . . She was often several pounds in debt for writing paper, envelopes and duplicating ink. In her two years as organiser she was anxious about money, overworked and, she admits, probably very irritable at times. But she still

225

does not regret writing that letter. Housewives working together, she feels, can tackle and in many cases partially solve their own particular troubles.

(*National Housewives Register, 245 Warwick Road, Solihull, West Midlands, BH2 7AH*)

PRE-SCHOOL PLAYGROUPS (1961)

Belle Tutaev

August 1961: Letter from Belle Tutaev – To the rescue of mothers desperate about lack of facilities for children under five comes a newly formed organisation with a do-it-yourself spirit, the Nursery School Campaign. One aim is to gather names for a large-scale national petition to the Minister of Education for more nursery schools and play facilities for children under five. The other is to encourage groups of mothers to start their own schools where they can find suitable premises, employing trained teachers.

VOLUNTARY MEANS (1962)

Belle Tutaev

The greatest problem for me was the suddenness of the growth of the interest, for which I was quite unprepared. Faced with all the housework, no help of any kind, two children, one at school, one at home, and a husband who works at home I had grown accustomed to busy days with relaxed evenings. What started off as a pleasant correspondence with 20 other mothers mushroomed into regular correspondence with over 150 women with letters at the rate of 10 to 20 a day.

Money is a great worry. Stamps, paper, envelopes, magazines, books, soon add up to an incredible sum. Helpers of the right sort are not easy to get hold of. For two months nearly every meeting we planned was wrecked by some family having measles, chickenpox, half-terms, moving or something similar. And bringing people into my home meant tidying up. As I picked up the dolls, the cars and all the bits and pieces the vision of an office, with all the papers filed neatly away seemed quite beautiful – but with our funds standing at £30 to cover all expenses up to next March, the only thing is to carry on – or else give up!

All my problems would be solved by money . . . but we have been told we can expect no financial aid from any Ministry as we are not within any form of legislation which allows for this.

But . . . within six years the DHSS was making the PPA a grant of £3000 a year and many local authorities were fostering the groups with grants, accommodation etc. The Pre-School Playgroups Association is now a large and influential national organisation.

(*The Pre-School Playgroups Association, 61 King's Cross Road, London WC1.*)

INVALIDS AT HOME

Even among the *Guardian*'s remarkable Do-it-yourselfers, Ann Armstrong is astonishing. Severely paralysed by poliomyelitis, and attached permanently to a respirator for more than 30 years, she has, apart from organising her own home, written books and a column in a local newspaper and edited a journal, *The Responaut*, to keep disabled people in touch. It was the response of readers to her first *Guardian* article, 'The Cost of Polio', which set her on her campaigning way . . . and also inspired Enid Hopper to form the Invalids-at-Home Trust, which helps disabled people to obtain the equipment and facilities which enable them to stay out of hospital.

(*Invalids at Home, 23 Farm Rd, London NW2*)

THE COST OF POLIO (1962)

Ann Armstrong

Assuming eight hours' sleep to be usual, there are 56 sleeping hours and 112 waking hours each week; as we have help for about 50 hours only that leaves 118 hours for which my husband is responsible. For the sleeping hours we cannot take

227

turns in looking after the children when they are awake. In order to avoid disturbing my husband I have a marvellous piece of equipment which I operate with my feet; it is a remote control panel for my book reading machine, bell, tape recorder, wireless, television and electric blanket. . . .

I have read that it costs anything from £33.16s. a week to keep a patient in a teaching hospital. Much of the home-help bill, and part of our electricity bill, all the nursing (physiotherapist – half-hour per week), are paid by the county. We are just managing to scrape through each month on my husband's salary plus help from various charitable organisations. I run a small mail order agency; my commission has varied from five shillings to a pound a week. . . .

Before my husband leaves for work each morning he does the usual chores of firelighting, shoe cleaning, etc., and then washes me, cleans my teeth and nose, brushes my hair, gives me a bed pan, changes me if I have a period, prepares breakfast for us all, gives the children theirs, has his own, and feeds me. However clever you are with time-and-motion study – and we have gone into this – these fiddling jobs take a couple of hours when there is only one pair of hands to do them all. We need at least an hour's help at this end of the day to cope with breakfast and feeding me – and another hour or two at the children's bathtime and bedtime.

MOTHERCARE FOR CHILDREN IN HOSPITAL (1961)

Len Chaloner

Len Chaloner only became a journalist after failing to achieve her ambition to become a concert pianist and, later, an engineer. She edited a number of journals and wrote for many others. Her books included Questions Children Ask, Feeling and Perception in Young Children *and* Helping Your Child to Get Well.

Sept 26th, 1962: Mothercare for Children in Hospital is the name adopted by a group of mothers in Battersea who have set out to try to help to bring about the Platt Committee's recommendations for the care of children in hospital. The Platt Committee, set up in 1958 strongly recommended the frequent visiting of parents to their children in hospital and favoured mothers being admitted with their children under five wherever possible.

To Len Chaloner's article a hospital paediatrician replied and a massive correspondence developed. Mothercare for Children in Hospital became the National Association for the Welfare of Children in Hospital (NAWCH) – still a very lively and energetic campaigning body.

(*National Association for the Welfare of Children in Hospital, Argyle House, Euston Rd, London NW1*)

HE ONLY WANTS HIS MUM (1970)

Shirley Lewis

On the way to the hospital I had decided that if our fifteen-month-old baby had to stay in, I should prefer to remain with him. His fears in the X-ray room confirmed these feelings. So I asked if I could remain with him. The doctor saw no objection. Eventually I approached staff nurse and put the question.

This enquiry clearly threw her. At this point all the campaigning of the National Association for the Welfare of Children in Hospital became totally understandable. We all know that the Department of Health's official policy is that mothers should be allowed to stay with their children if they wish. But just as NAWCH maintains, the whole policy falls down at ward level. . . . The staff nurse spent several minutes trying to convince me that it really wasn't necessary for me to remain. 'In the end all the children settle down.' At this point I almost gave up but the doctor reappeared and assured us that it was the hospital's policy to permit mothers to stay.

At last, about 11 p.m., night sister came. By now I was ready to atomise her with my spray gun if she showed the least signs of resistance. With little appearance of joy she offered the choice of a bed downstairs or one at the end of the baby's ward. I chose the latter as I wanted to be with the infant when in the shadows of the night strangers picked him out of his sleep to hurt him with injections. Some time after midnight I stretched out on my bed. Endlessly the nurses' rubber soles squished-squashed up and down the wooden floors. Infants were mewing and bleating, the sounds of very sick babies. Above all this was another noise, incessant and pitiful, of a Persian boy, aged about six, crying for his mother. It went on all through the night and day, as it had done, apparently, the day before. This child had been in England a week and his mother was thousands of miles away.

Over the rice crispies next morning a little Cockney boy who had spent an unsettled night next to the grieving Persian child said to me, 'Miss, his Dad come here last night. But it's no good. He only wants his Mum.'

SINGLE AND SILENT (1963)

May Abbott

January, 1963: May Abbott outlined the plans of the Rev. Mary Webster, a Congregational Minister, for setting up a National Council for the Single Woman and her Dependants. The article drew wide support, in letters and donations, and the Council was formed two years later. Miss Webster did not live to see its full success for she died at the early age of 45 in 1969. Later the Council enlarged its scope and became the National Council for Carers and their Elderly Dependants.

Among our most put-upon fellow-citizens is the single woman who struggles, stoically and alone, in caring for one or more dependants. Most of us know her personally – the last unmarried daughter in the family, finding herself left to care for ageing and ailing parents or handicapped relatives.

Her lot is unenviable. Often she has to take on the duties normally shared by husband, wife and nurse, organising the housework, perhaps earning its main income and working in the sickroom. Even though she may qualify for a dependent relative's allowance for income tax purposes she cannot, as can the widower or divorcee with a child or children, claim an allowance for a resident housekeeper.

The single woman in this position has little leisure outside the home, little companionship within it. Unlike the widowed or unmarried mother who can look forward to the time when her dependants will not only be able to fend for themselves but perhaps will become her support, she can expect only that her burden of responsibility will increase as she gets older. When it is finally lifted her own youth, even her middle age, may have vanished. She is unmarriageable, and even more alone.

(*National Council for Carers and their Elderly Dependants, 29 Chilworth Street, London W1*)

THE DISABLEMENT INCOMES GROUP (1965)

Megan du Boisson

March, 1965: In reply to an article on the Women's Page, Megan du Boisson and Berit Moore wrote: 'We suggst the foundation of a group – it could be called the Disablement Incomes Group – or DIG. It would exist to correlate the work of other groups concerned with long-term diseases in regard solely to the *right* of disabled persons, irrespective of the reason for their disablement, to pensions from the state to enable them to live in a reasonable degree of independence and dignity in their own homes.'

DIG got off the ground very quickly and over the years achieved much. Its present general secretary estimates that at least a million people receive basic benefits which were not available when Megan started her campaign. Megan, an incomparable publicist and lobbyist, died tragically in a car accident in 1967. Her work and her inspiration will survive.

My friend, Berit Moore, who is 27, and I both have one of the degenerative and incurable diseases called multiple sclerosis. Because we have husbands with well-above average incomes – although neither of us is rich – our children have a reasonable expectation of life going on roughly as before. Our husbands can afford to pay for the domestic help we need and so we can go on as best we can being mothers and home-makers.

But what about all the other families of disabled persons, where the family income is so much less than ours – in fact the great majority of families? We have discovered that, although a mother can be cared for in hospital, at a cost to the state of anything from £12 to £50 a week, and her children taken into kindly care by the local authority at a cost of not less than £8 per week (more for a baby) – not one penny could the mother get from the state if she decided to stay at home and manage as best she can, looking after her family: indeed, if the shortage of hospital beds took the decision from her and she had to stay at home, the same is true. Not a penny.

There is this fiction that a housewife and mother does not 'work'. 'Does your wife work?' 'Oh, no, she just looks after the home and the children.' So it follows that it does not concern society if a housewife falls chronically ill with a degenerative disease, or becomes disabled through accident. It is more than likely that she has not contributed 156 contributions to the National Insurance within the past two years, either, so she has no money – no money to help to compensate for the vital work which is her service to her family and to society. . . .

No woman living with her husband is entitled to apply for National Assistance if he is in work, no matter how lowly paid, no matter how sadly her health and home circumstances decline; she is not considered as a *person*, but as an extension of her husband. She is, I learned, 'covered by her husband's insurance'. This being so, I thought perhaps if she should fall chronically ill she would be covered by her husband's sick benefit in some way, but no; here we are told that she is not 'gainfully employed'. So her work is not to be valued and when she cannot do it, she cannot do it and that is that. No matter how long the illness, how serious the disablement – in Ann Armstrong's case not only her work but her very breath may be at the courtesy of another.

DIG exists solely to work for a rational approach to the money spent on the chronic sick. DIG proposes a modest basic income, say equivalent to the old age pension and pegged to the cost of living, with supplementary allowances according to the number and situation of dependants, and the degree of disability, after rehabilitation. This basic income would be called the National Disability Income. It would be taxable, and so would the supplementary allowance, so that it would be of greater benefit to the poor.

The Disablement Incomes Group asks not only for compassion but for commonsense in the national approach to disablement.

(*Disablement Incomes Group, 28 Commercial Road, London E1*)

15   Children's Corner

Guardian women take their family responsibilities seriously, of course – but not all the articles in this section are excessively serious. It was odd to discover that Evelyn Sharp, notable feminist, suffragist and commentator on the political aspect of women's life, started her long spell as a *Manchester Guardian* Women's Page regular contributor writing about children – and about fashion occasionally, too.

HOLIDAY FROCKS FOR A LITTLE GIRL (1922)

Evelyn Sharp

When I remember the kind of clothes that little girls of my generation had to wear, I cannot think how we ever managed to play games at all. I remember one dreadful fashion which compelled one to wear a broad sash tied tightly round the skirt just above the knees, so that one ran with the action of the hobbled donkey. I remember a thing called a collarette, a square expanse of stiff white pique, fastened at the back of the neck with a button which always caught one's pigtail and held it firmly and painfully. I remember layer upon layer of cumbrous underclothing, stiff buckram waistbands, starched frills that scrubbed one's neck and arms – these were only a few of the torments that made little girls in the Victorian era long miserably to be little boys.

But today the little girl is no more tormented by her clothes than her brother is. Indeed, I am not sure that she does not actually score over him in hot weather, for no form of boy's suit is so cool as what the shops call a girl's 'tub frock' or sometimes 'wash frock'. This is made sometimes with and sometimes without a waistband of the same material; personally I think it is much better without, because a belt is a trap for protruding nails and for the handle of racket or scooter or other plaything. A tub frock made with short, loose sleeves in zephyr or any pretty washing material is a perfect frock for the little girl to play in but the home dressmaker should be warned that it may turn into a caricature if the fullness of the skirt piece is increased so that it stands out all round in a bunch, or if the whole frock is made quite absurdly short. It would be better, I think, to let the child play in blouse and knickers, like her little brother.

Under the ordinary tub frock knickers of the same material are usually worn. Indoors the latter can usually be dispensed with where 'playfrocks' or 'rompers' take the place of the tidier sort of frock. These are not beautiful and it is a question whether sacrifice of appearance is ever justified. It should be possible to combine absolute freedom of action with beauty of line. It would be far-fetched, though, to expect the busy mother who has a small income and a large family to condemn rompers on the ground of ugliness, though she would probably agree with me that beauty of line in children's clothes is of real importance educationally.

MY KINGDOM FOR A FATHER FIGURE (1959)

Catherine Storr

'And what is Jemima going to do when she leaves school?' the headmistress asked, and my heart sank; because Jemima was there in person, and it seemed hard that the child should have to condemn herself right at the beginning of an academic career. If I'd been alone with Miss Smith I'd have been able to hedge or to get out of answering the question somehow. But no; this was one of those parent-pupil-teacher interviews which the head of Jemima's future school found so helpful and enlightening.

'Well,' Jemima said, 'I used to think I might be a ballet dancer but I shall probably be too tall for that, so I shall be a show jumper and teach riding in my spare time.'

Jemima is eleven and already weighs 8½ stone. For some

time it has been clear that she is not going to be the sort of size that a male ballet dancer tosses negligently from hand to hand. In the recent past it had been a relief to me that Jemima had apparently resigned herself painlessly to this fact. What I had not bargained for was the immediate ascendancy of the horse.

The horse crept into our family life unobtrusively, like many another pest. When Jemima first announced that she wanted riding lessons I was mildly sorry that we lived in London, where riding is a rich man's amusement. But I didn't take it any more seriously than I had the demands, six months earlier, for a white satin tutu, a ciné camera and a typewriter apiece for each literate member of the family. I coped equally light-heartedly with requests for a pony which was presumably to be kept in our third-floor flat, as stabling for a push bicycle in our part of the town costs over 10s. a week.

I suppose I first realised the horse had come to stay when I found Jemima, reading a book called *Iron Shoes and Steel Bits*. For one horrified second I imagined it was a treatise on mediaeval tortures; but when I looked over her shoulder I was disappointed to find it was not in the least grisly, only excessively boring. Jemima, however, found it absolutely thrilling, and said it told one all sorts of vital things one ought to know about the horse.

'For instance,' she said, fixing me with an accusing eye, 'I bet you didn't know how to snaffle a short curb' (that's what it sounded like) 'when you were my age?'

'You'd win your bet. I haven't the remotest idea how to do it now.'

'But it's all about it. All that page you were looking at while I was reading.'

'Well, to be honest, Jemima, I didn't find it terribly interesting, so I probably didn't really quite take it in.'

Jemima groaned. 'If you only knew how often you've told me that it takes a bit of an effort to get into a really good book, and that I must keep on trying with some dreary old thing like *David Copperfield* and then you don't even stick to a single page of *Iron Shoes*.

It was a just reproach and I had no defence. I could bear the books. After all, I didn't have to read them. I could bear the monotonous discussions between my daughters on equestrian problems; I didn't have to listen. I was embarrassed, but not unbearably, by the ecstatic screams which greeted any equine quadruped, from the police horse which patrols our street to the rag and bone man's pony. I even conceded riding lessons of a sort – on a farm in the country where we take our summer holidays; dungarees and sweaters instead of jodhpurs and hacking jackets as in London, and a considerable difference in price.

But what puzzles me is that the horse saga seems to be entirely divorced from reality. What actually happens when girl meets horse has no effect at all on what girl imagines about horses. Jemima remains in her saddle with caution and some dexterity, but with no confidence at all. Matilda, three years younger, looks like one of those stuffed clowns you see tied to the back of a kicking mule in a circus. She doesn't come off very much, but there isn't that innate sympathy between horse and rider that my reading has taught me to expect from one who is, she says, going to be the show jumper of the century.

It was some slight comfort when I discovered that mine was not an isolated case and that obsession with the horse wasn't a symptom of feeble-mindedness or perversity on the part of my two daughters; it is one of those mysterious, pervasive fashions which you can't escape. It's like shocking pink, or the names you choose for your children. You believe you have thought of it quite independently. Although you know you might set a fashion, it never occurs to you that you are only following it, as usual, until little Jemima comes home from her very first nursery school with the news that there are three other Jemimas in her class. 'Isn't that funny, Mummy?' And so my horse-enthralled girls are surprised and delighted to find that 70 per cent of their contemporaries are potty about ponies too; and their bewildered mammas can make what they like out of that.

But it doesn't explain the phenomenon. One mother I know took the problem to a psychoanalyst and I and all the rest of her acquaintances waited on tenterhooks for her report. But oracles traditionally speak in riddles, and this was no exception. The horse, we were told, is a father figure; he also represents the Id. The resolution of the adolescent girl's subconscious ambivalence to authority is therefore supremely symbolised by her fantasised relationship with the horse; through which she can work out repressed aggression following early traumata inflicted by the parents, and at the same time express her infantile dependence. This leaves me as much in the dark as ever.

Yet occasionally a pinpoint of hope for tomorrow pierces the dark sky of today. Yesterday Jemima, who has the largest appetite of anyone I know, came in to tea after an arduous day at school and looked witheringly at the fairly well-stocked table.

'Is that all there is?' she asked. 'I'm so hungry I could eat a –'

She didn't finish her sentence. She looked at me and I looked at her. I laughed, and she very nearly did. But I have an uneasy feeling that the psychoanalyst would say she could both eat her horse and have it.

LAUNDERING THE LOVE TOKEN (1959)

Betty Jerman

In the early days of expecting our son my husband and I discovered a new kind of reading matter: magazines for parents. We read them from cover to cover and were particularly fascinated by the letters. Of these one letter stuck in my mind. It was from a woman who related how her young son sent himself to sleep by chewing a green blanket. It fell to pieces, each piece deteriorated to smaller bits. Since he screamed himself silly without his bit of blanket she faced the prospect of the last scrap with horror. But, inspiration, she bought a new green blanket and sewed the old scrap to it. All was well. Apparently he grew out of the habit before well started on the destruction of the second blanket.

With the assurance of utter ignorance I classed that mother as an easy target for old wives' tales.

Now my son's layette included three yellow, satin-bound blankets. Soon after his arrival a friend in America sent him a blanket, blue, satin-bound, with a pattern of rabbits woven into the wool. And somewhere about one year we noticed that our son had developed a passion not for the easily washed and interchangeable handkerchief, napkin or even sheet (some of the other 'Love objects' I see other children have), not even for one of the yellow blankets which are indistinguishable from one another, but for this one blue blanket.

In no time the delicate blue satin and soft wool began to lose their brightness as the blanket was trailed round, dropped on the floor and collected again. Our baby never chewed it but just 'breathed in' its closeness, which spelt comfort and sleep for him. That blanket is now as important in our lives as a passport when travelling abroad, or a purse when going shopping. For a visit during which he would sleep we could forget napkins and change of clothing, but never the blanket.

But useful as it is to have an object which induces sleep, it has its problem – not of chewing but of washing. We do not mind that the ribbon, continually pulled undone and re-sewn till it looked like string, finally fell off nor that the wool is grey and matted. But there comes a time when the blanket is ripe (and that is the right word) for washing. But when do we do it? It is needed for the midday nap and again for the night's sleep. That leaves under four hours, morning or afternoon, for washing, drying and airing. It will not dry naturally in that time.

When we lived in a flat we used to dry it on newspapers spread on the plate rack over the gas jets. The odour of steaming wool, the disregard for every rule for laundering wool meant nothing. Would it dry in time? In our new house the blanket is hung to dry in the garden and finished wrapped round the hot water tank. Our new gas cooker has an eye-level grill instead of a plate-rack. On blanket-washing day I regret the exchange.

I cannot help feeling that even the neighbour who has a two-and-a-half-year-old son and for whom she keeps a constant supply of baby bootees drying over the gas stove, has a more reasonable article to deal with.

But now I face a new possibility. Any day I expect to hear the rip of much-abused blanket. A child-nurse tells me her son took his 'comforter', an eiderdown, to boarding school with him, though he allowed her to re-cover it. Maybe I should write to my friend in America to find out if an identical blanket can be bought, or maybe a supply of them.

BORED MUM (1959)

'*J.B.H.*'

I love both my sons devotedly, but I suffer the most excruciating boredom in their company. I have no problem of wanting to go out to work. I shall be perfectly happy when they are both at school. Then I shall work like a maniac all morning (but at least I can think while I do so) and then each afternoon I shall have two heavenly, rounded, free, peaceful hours for myself, to do what I like in.

But oh! my sense of guilt. Do you think that some kind soul whose older children still love her would care to comfort me by confessing that she too felt like this?

'Talkback'

Once a woman confesses boredom with any aspect of her God-given role of wife and mother it is a very short step to finding the whole thing intolerable, and to do so J.B.H. must have forgotten the millions of weary, bored women, on whom civilisation was built and depends for its continuance, and whom she has to thank for her position.

My two boys are nearly grown up now, we can talk together as friends and my years of bondage and boredom are finished. I have tried to make them love life and look forward to its enlargement and their own increase. But do they love me? I have not the vaguest idea: I have never thought to ask them.

Aileen M. Brandt
London W2

Congratulations to the young mother for fearlessly confessing that her children bore her. Many of us are temperamentally unsuited to young children, and I think an alert and inquiring mind feels the gulf more than the serene and placid type. Consolations are that the children grow older and change constantly as they do so and that the best of us are still adaptable to difficulties.

As a mother of four whose ages range from 18 to 4 I can assure her that I was very bored but the results have been well worth the suffering.

Olive Foyle
Coulsdon
Surrey

I have five children and I found those baby years about which my child-loving friends wax lyrical, full of the most appalling boredom and weariness. It did not get better. It got worse with each one and is just as bad with my grandchildren.

But I will point out to J.B.H. that the women who tell you that the years when the children are small are the happiest in your life are the ones whose children are well past that stage. They convenietnly forget the everlasting mess and noise, the continual aimless questions (how loathsome that word 'Why?' can become!), the habit of the toddler, just when things are comparatively peaceful, of falling down and emitting ear-piercing shrieks for a non-existent injury, and because they believe that all really nice women enjoy their children all the time they build a rosy haze about those years and pretend to themselves and others that they enjoyed them. J.B.H. and I are only being honest and admitting what most mothers will not admit.

My children are all grown-up and appear quite fond of their mother.

S.L. Suckling
London NW1

I have two young teenage boys and throughout the long summer holiday I have had to pay attention (while endeavouring to cook and clean) to explanations of technical details of little cars, watch target practice, spot camouflaged military vehicles in a small garden etc. until I have nearly gone

241

mad: but I can still remember the thrill and pleasure when my mother took an interest in my own silly little games.

Evora N. Snook
Hereford

WATCH DOG (1963)

M. Mountfield

On Thursday morning I felt apprehensive. Three days had passed without undue disturbance. None of the children had been sick. No one had caught measles. We had not had a medical examination, a fire drill or the windows cleaned, to distract us. I had been teaching long enough to realise something must happen soon. Admittedly there had been several fights and John had threatened to bring his father to beat me up, but he did this daily, and anyway I knew his father, a charming coloured gentleman who spoke no English. He came to collect his son when he was out of work, which was often. We communicated by smiling broadly at one another and waving. Once when John was away he burst into the classroom rolling his eyes and beating his chest. He shouted 'cough' and retired smiling. This, I felt, was progress.

This particular morning we had the story of the Good Samaritan and then arithmetic. Playtime came and went. I sat at my desk watching the children come in. The Robinson twins, one so much bigger and brighter than the other. Charles, Ian, John, another John. Amwar, black and beaming. Afaral, the colour of milk chocolate, David, very pale and thin. The line went on. Then the girls: Mary, Zara, Patricia, Evelyn, always so neat, always clean. The Chinese children were all clean. One saw me looking and smiled, her eyes shining. Jane. Alice, the other Mary, Tal, fat as butter, black as coal, and the rest of them. The desks filled up. The air was full of chatter. Angela came at the end of the line. She walked across to me, tossing dirty ringlets. Rightly named, I thought, blonde, angelic beauty under the grime. At my desk she looked at me with clear blue eyes. 'Billy's turned into a dog,' she said. I sighed. The children were watching me.

The door opened a little and a head looked round it, about 6 inches from the floor. It was Billy on his hands and knees. His red hair fell in straight locks over his forehead and into his eyes. Two pink ears stuck out astonishingly far on either side. His face was completely covered in big freckles and dirt. I have never seen anything looking more like a mongrel puppy in all my life. Not even a real mongrel puppy. He barked, or rather yapped, and wriggled round the door and across the room to me, where he sat up on his hind legs, begging. I settled the children into their reading groups and selected the first child to read to me. Billy was pottering around the room now, sniffing at the children and barking quietly from time to time. Occasionally a child would pause to pat him but in general they took no notice. Finally he crept under his desk and, putting his head between his paws gazed at me soulfully. I worked steadily down the list of children until I reached his name.

'Come and read to me, Billy,' I said, and waited, wondering why it was that my training college had never mentioned the possibility of a situation like this. Billy sat up, opened his desk and took out his book with his teeth. On hands and knees he trotted over to me and laid the book on my desk. I opened it at the place. Billy shut his mouth tightly and looked at the page. Then followed 10 minutes during which I tried everything I knew to make the child speak. I worked systematically from kind coaxing to anger. Billy smiled, wagged his behind, shook his ears, but not a word came from his lips. In desperation I sent him away. I had other children to think of. He spent the rest of the morning wandering about or under his desk.

The afternoon was the same except that I discovered he must have spoken to someone during the lunch hour because when the children came in they were calling him Fido; and Ian said Billy had chosen the name himself. I felt sure the afternoon would bring a change of heart in the boy and I continued in this hope even when he answered the register with a bark. We had painting and clay modelling. The sand and water were in use. There was dressing up and puppets; all the things the children liked best. Forty-five children busy and happy, working and talking and enjoying themselves – 45 children and one dog. Billy remained on his hands and knees the whole time except for one brief moment when the headmistress came in. Then he begged prettily, his head on one side. She did not see him, and as I prefer to keep my battles to myself I said nothing. Even during the story at the end of the afternoon Billy sat under his desk on his haunches.

That evening I went to a lecture. The lecturer was a wise woman and generations of children had passed through her hands. A teacher, she said, was like a mother. A mother had only to raise her eyebrows at her child for him to know that he had hurt her. A teacher needs only to do the same. I went home and practised raising my eyebrows. The next morning, going to school, I walked past the house of one of my pupils. His elder brother was wandering down the street and his mother stood on the doorstep. 'Dennis,' she called. Dennis went on walking. 'Dennis,' she yelled. Dennis went on walking The mother took a deep breath. 'Dennis!' Her voice rang through the street. 'Come here, you . . . ,' and she followed this with a description of her son which genuinely made me raise my eyebrows – in admiration. Every epithet in the English language, and not one repeated. Dennis turned and ran for home.

In the playground I met Billy on all fours. He barked. 'Billy,' I said, 'snap out of that or I'll beat the living daylights out of you.' He looked at me.

'O.K., Miss,' he said and skipped off. I raised my eyebrows.

A DAY IN THE PARK (1964)

Janie Preger (aged 15)

It is half past nine on a Tuesday morning. The old red bus is rumbling on to the edge of a rotting stretch of waste ground. Little boys and girls are rushing as fast as their legs can carry them towards the bus. Some of them carry Woolworth's fishing rods in their arms; others cram ice lollies of hideous hues into their mouths. One catches a tiny girl with the net of his rod and drags her to the bus shouting 'Elaine Baker's Mum is daft in 'er 'ead,' at the top of his voice. No one apparently takes any notice of this minor incident. They are all too busy watching Angela Boothby being banged on the pavement by Keven McHugh and Stewart Jones.

At last they are all in the bus, screaming, yelling, spitting, sweating, crying, eating and laughing grotesquely at the misfortunes of poor Ann Levy who is rather fat and as a consequence has fallen off the seat and on to the floor. 'Just look at her, too fat to gerrup, aintcha?' This from a tiny boy with two front teeth missing, and a blue balaclava which makes him look like a reject from the Round Table Knights of King Arthur. He pokes a grubby index finger up his right nostril and pulls down the prize which he sucks with obvious enjoyment.

'Yer bleeding' swine, gerrof me net. Ah miss, tell 'im to gerroff me net. I'll tell me Mam of you.' This from a spotty-faced child on the back seat with a turquoise lolly in his hand trying desperately to retrieve his net from a horse-faced girl. She bashes him on the head with a fist like a joint of beef and proceeds to view with enjoyment the tears of woe that pour down the individual's spotty face. 'Yer great soft nit. Ay, Marleen, yer Graham's crying. Come and look.' Marleen steps gracefully from her seat then gallops down the aisle as if at Newmarket and shares the tearful sight with a glee that could hardly be described as maternal concern.

So the journey progresses. And with a certain amount of relief we reach the iron gateway of that demi-paradise, Heaton Park, Manchester, where the children are being taken for a day out.

A cheer goes up, and with childhood's carefree charm the little creatures jump from the bus and hop excitedly up and down the health-giving gravel path with rustic green seats along its flower-filled way. Some children have never been so far into the country as this. After all, what can you expect? This is only 1964.

The sound of young laughter is borne in the gas-laden breeze and the quick scampering of feet echoes on the air. We are now by the fishing pond and small eager bodies fling themselves at the dubious depths and proceed to fish with zeal if not with dexterity. Various water creatures of all shapes and sizes blink fishily at the plastic-sandalled humans around them.

Small dirty fingers trail languidly through the slime, in the hope of finding a splindley-legged water beetle that can be dissected by means of Doris Eadie's mum's hatpin. Some hum in a half undertone to themselves. One cannot really tell precisely what they are humming, though it reminds one vaguely of drunken bumble bees and off-beat sewing-machines. A few words can be caught in between breaths and more hums each such as 'Come 'ere fish, Fishy, Fishy. Hum hummmmmmmmm.' 'Gerroff.' 'Gotcha.' 'Hum, hummmmmmmm. Gerroff', or 'I'll tell our Moira'.

Not every child hums. Others are too intent on pushing their playmates into the water, or nicking off with the paddlers' abandoned sandals and net dresses. Regretfully, and loath to leave the silver waters, the children straggle along the paths towards the huge dinner tents blowing in the wind.

Dinners have been given out and egg lingers on button mouths and crumbs trickle like sand down the feasters' chins and clothes. Orange juice is gulped in chesty gurgles and the sausage roll traces are trodden into the ground. Apple cores are hurled in gay abandon and a small greedy boy sidles a grubby orange into his pocket. Hands are wiped on anything available across the luncheon ground.

A voice booms through a megaphone so loudly that at first one fears Judgement Day has arrived. It is only announcing the end of lunch and asking the children to form into lines. Reluctantly and haphazardly the children obey, and trail off to another afternoon of joyous activity. Small ones lag behind dragging their plastic-covered deformed feet along the dusty paths and say plaintively 'I want me Mam'. In fact they are overwhelmingly affectionate and will attach themselves to any outstretched arm that is friendly enough not to mind sticky hands and dirty mouths.

So we go on and on and on. The day alternately drags and then flies. Children fall into things, out of things, and over things, and often there is a wail of anguished tears. These children seem strangely ready to accept the fact that you are from a completely different walk of life and 'Sir' and 'Miss' spring readily to their lips. They are both naive and knowing and sometimes reveal an almost uncanny insight into life. Many are possessive and jealous of each other's triumphs and small pleasures, yet they manage to stumble along. All too soon the day draws to an unwanted close. Tired legs droop back to the world of HP, bingo, chips and the emptiness of their small lives . . . so empty that a day in a municipal park is a day to anticipate and to remember with joy.

We recall that in 1934 the White Heather Fund, organised by the *Manchester Evening News*, took deprived children by tram for a day in Heaton Park. We are still doing the same in 1964, only this time by bus. Roll on 1994 when we will be able to take them by aeroplane.

SLEEPLESS NIGHTS (1965)

Margaret Drabble

Margaret Drabble is one of the outstanding novelists of our times. Her sister A.S. Byatt is also a leading novelist. Their mother, Marie Drabble was a loyal member of the National Council of Women's executive committee for some years.

I know I shall get little sympathy, writing about sleepless nights. People just don't believe it when one says that one hasn't slept more than an hour at a time for days, just as they don't believe that babies are really heavy; they think that mothers are endowed with a special extra maternal strength, and that a 14 lb.-baby is somehow not nearly as heavy as a 14 lb.-sack of potatoes. I used to watch people carrying children without giving a thought to the question of weight: now, when I see a mother standing at a bus stop with a huge year-old child slung sleeping across one shoulder my arms ache in sympathy. I took my 'measly' teething youngest, now happily nearly two, into town with me the other day for the first time for ages – indeed for the first time ever alone – and the effort of lugging him on and off buses and carrying him when he got tired of walking was enough to stop me trying it ever again, except when driven by necessity. I should have taken the push chair, but the push chair is too heavy, too, and getting it on and off buses is no joke.

The problem of sleeplessness is one that I remember with a

peculiar horror. I'd always been a very sound sleeper, needing a good eight hours a night and when the first month's excitement of having a baby to feed wore off, I couldn't think what had hit me. My first baby didn't need nearly as much sleep as a baby should, and he started teething at a ridiculously early age, so I spent many hours of many nights trying every device and subterfuge to get him off to sleep. Oh those songs, those endless repetitions of 'Ten Green Bottles', those sessions in the rocking chair, those jogglings of the cot, those pattings of the back. Oh those dreadful moments when the small head would rear itself up again just as I was about to creep away, made bold by two minutes of stillness and silence. Sometimes he would start to scream if I so much as shifted my position, so suspicious was he that I was about to escape back into my bed. It's easy enough to say that one ought to let them cry: it takes a brave woman to sleep through the yells of a baby. I've had some really humiliating moments, at which I confess I now look back on with a certain nostalgia! At one point I worked out a marvellous system for getting the baby to sleep by rocking the cot while crouched upon the floor between it and the door below eye level, so that when silence had set in I could creep out backwards on hands and knees, unobserved, without letting my shadow fall on the wall as I retreated. I was also an expert in the art of arranging the door so that I could get through it without either making it creak or letting the hall light fall on the child. On such details can a precious hour's sleep rest.

Once, in an unfamiliar bedroom, I got the child to sleep, and found that I myself was wedged more or less under the cot on the floor with no possibility of getting out without causing a disturbance: and like a coward I stayed where I was. It's a good thing the babies can't see what fools they make of us.

I tried to make use of some of this subject matter in one of my novels, where the principal character is the mother of two small children, the smaller of which is a bad sleeper. I thought I'd conveyed the sense of crushing fatigue and despair lest the fatigue should never end, but looking at it now I realise I didn't state it strongly enough, and those who don't know about it don't even notice that aspect of the heroine's predicament. Perhaps it's a state that can't be imaginatively conveyed. Childbirth is always treated by men and by childless women with a kind of respectful awe, but the subsequent states of maternity are rarely regarded. And they do pass quickly. I can say that now, but it seemed an eternity at the time. Some of those nights seemed as if they would never end. And I shall always retain a sense that sleep is one of the greatest pleasures of life. I remember the luxury of a night when my mother had the baby and I had sleeping pills with such gratitude that it wipes out many of those chilly hours of vigil.

'Talkback'

Margaret Drabble's article on sleepless nights seems to have evoked memories in many mothers' minds. It certainly has in mine – her mother's. Margaret may say that she needs eight hours sleep a night now – she probably does – but in the first few months of her life she made sure that her mother did not have them. She is my second child and I must be one of the first rebels against Truby King.

If my children cried, and it was not 'tummy, temper or pins', I comforted them. I felt that a need for Mama's presence should be satisfied as much as any other needs. My other children accepted this, and once they realised they would not be left to cry, slept peacefully. But not Margaret. Hundreds of green bottles crashed to the ground, hundreds of nigger boys met their diverse fates, and she was still awake. Not even an endless saga with original words and drawling tune had any effect. Once she had summoned me with a wail she ceased to cry but became brightly conversational.

However, everything passes and finally she slept through the night – I had learned to snatch cat-naps during the day. The next phase was that of dreams, when she would scream for me in her sleep. Her reply when asked what she wanted was invariably, 'Nothing,' said very angrily. One night on receiving this reply on my fourth visit, I gave her a sharp smack and said 'There is something now' – and we both went back to sleep.

Perhaps I warped her personality permanently, but it seems

to have been productive and my grandchildren now find their grandmother a comfort in the night and in the early morning.

Marie Drabble

PRIMARY SCHOOL PROFANITY (1967)

Agnes Madden

Agnes Madden began her working life as an assistant in a public library, and qualified as a primary school teacher and then a teacher of the deaf. Now retired, she is completing a book on the hearing-impaired child.

Five-year-olds take the business of profanity very seriously. Whenever anyone is denounced for swearing, the situation has all the trappings of high drama. At the words: 'Miss, Billy swore . . .' everything stops. The children playing in the sand tray freeze, while the sand trickles to the floor; the painters halt; even the absorbed brick-builders abandon their towers. Everyone waits for justice to be done.

The denouncer is almost always a little girl. Eyes cast down modestly, bridling a little, she makes her accusation. 'Ian swore'. The accused, already bright pink, makes an impassioned, automatic denial: 'Miss, I never.'

'He did,' his dearest friend hastens to get on the side of the angels. 'I heard him, Miss. He swore all right.'

The class waits. With luck the accused may be put in the corner. He might even cry. I urge them to get on with their work and murmur to the accuser, 'Can you tell me what he said, or is it too rude?'

She hesitates. Clearly it is too rude to say, but she intends to say it just the same. She looks censoriously at the class, who are all open-mouthed, straining for every word, bats her eyelashes at me a few times to show that she's just doing this out of a sense of duty, then leans forward: 'He said "*underpants*!" '

There is a shocked silence. Ian is undoubtedly one of the boys, but this is going too far. . . . Underpants!

On another occasion Jane approached me wearing the

250

dedicated air of a denouncer. 'David and Peter are saying rude things.' I looked across at the accused who were building an impressive fort and they returned my scrutiny unconcerned. There was no denial and no heightened colour: clearly they were innocent. I said as much to Jane, but she was convinced of their wickedness. 'Honest, Miss, they did say rude things: they said "kidneys" and "adenoids".'

Once I was betrayed myself into saying a rude word. Stephanie whispered in my ear that Sean had said something very rude. 'Like on the board but ruder,' she alleged. I look blankly at my innocuous 'I can jump' in large script.

'That isn't rude,' I protested.

'Yes, it is rude, if you said jump with a puh', she insisted.

Still baffled, I murmured 'Juh, uh, mm, puh' – jump.'

'No, not with a juh at the front, a *puh* at the front.'

'Puh, uh, mm, puh – pump.'

The brighter children were appalled. They drew in their breath with a sharp hiss. Their own teacher saying rude things! A nice state of affairs. . . .

The real swear words are occasionally quoted, but they are outweighed by the home-made offerings. 'Shut up', 'dirty pig' and 'knickers' have all been offered more than once, and one pretty five-year-old could not be persuaded that 'Give us a kiss' (a proposition from a susceptible boy sitting near her) was not a 'rude thing' of the deepest dye.

On one of the rare occasions when the denouncer was masculine I lost a great deal of face. When Peter rushed over to denounce, there was no reticence displayed at all.

'Janet swore – she said "basket". It's a swear word,' he gabbled, triumphant at the blameless Janet's disgrace.

'That isn't swearing,' I said firmly.

'Course it is,' he said. 'Basket is a swear word.'

'Don't be silly,' I blustered. 'It's in our reading books.' Short of Holy Writ, nothing carries more weight than our reading books. He was thrown for a minute but rallied.

Looking at me shrewdly, he countered. 'There's two words. One means "basket" and the other means "basket" but swear word basket.'

'I don't think so.'

He looked at me pityingly. Just his luck to be in the class of a woman who didn't even know the difference between *basket* and basket.

I've come to the conclusion that swear words are what you make them. If they shock and disgust they *are* profanity. Perhaps next time you feel like a good round curse you could try the new swear words; after all the old ones are wearing rather thin. If you want a string of oaths, try: 'Kidneys and adenoids! Underpants and knickers! Give us a kiss! Dirty pig! *Basket* and basket!' Remember to keep the dreadful one for a desperate situation and spit it out with venom: 'Puh; uh; mm: puh.'

'Talkback'

My small son, now himself a father, paraded the house one day using a string of incredible swear words faithfully learned from a neighbour, whose gardening language is vividly adjectival. Something had to be done. In the bathroom I pretended to have scalded my hand and yelled 'Chookey'. On being asked the meaning I covered my mouth and replied 'Oh dear . . . you must never, never say that terrible swear word.'

His triumphant use of the word 'chookey' (as a means of embarrassing his parents) was a joy to behold for a long time.

Harriette Lewis
St Margarets
Middlesex

Agnes Madden's primary schoolchildren clearly live a sheltered life. In this comfortably-heeled district one nursery school has never quite recovered from the son of a successful left-wing playwright who called his teacher a '– old cow' at the age of three.

Margaret Till
Highgate
London N6

THE HIGH RISE KIDS (1970)

Elisabeth Dunn

Elisabeth Dunn joined the staff of The Guardian *in 1971 to establish 'Checkout', the paper's first column on consumer affairs. Since then, she has written a range of feature articles for many leading newspapers.*

The high rise block of flats has become a recurrent theme not only of architecture but also of social study. Concerned researchers climb up and down stairs soaked with the neuroses of tower-block life, analysing the anguish of the isolated housewife and the rootlessness of the old-age pensioner. But it is a world where whole families are at risk and the conflict inevitably rebounds on the children.

In one family on the Pepys Estate in Deptford, the father threatened to jump out of a tenth-storey window in defiance of police, ambulance and the fire brigade services. His wife, walking to the shops, tried to edge both herself and her three-year-old daughter under a bus. Both attempts failed but the only solution anyone has come up with is to put the family on the transfer list. Other families, living on a tower level of suffering are left to make out on their own.

And in spite of the attention focused on the problems, high density housing projects still sprout. With them comes a generation that will never know what it is like to live on the ground with the nosey, accessible life of the terrace streets; children who live in units, like fledglings nesting on the face of a cliff.

The most recent survey was done by the NSPCC – 'Children in Flats: A Family Study' – and it concluded: 'The housing in flats of families with young children is restrictive, undesirable and productive of a good deal of human discomfort if not suffering'. The NSPCC interviewers spoke to 281 flat-dwellers but unhappily only talked 'incidentally' to the children.

The cliff children of the Pepys Estate, a dockyard redevelopment scheme, are sharply divided in their attitude towards the flats: the boys are happy to be sent out in the morning to play football and amuse themselves without adult supervision. The girls, living a more restrictive life, reflect the views of their mothers with astonishing fidelity. Perhaps the saddest are the young children whose mothers are scared of dirty old men in the park across the road, dare not send them out and who consequently are kept in the flat. There is nowhere else to go since the landing is a banned area and the flats were built without verandas.

The headmistress at the local infants school, Deptford Park, on the fringe of the estate, says that Monday mornings are full of stored up energy which needs a couple of hours vigorous, therapeutic PE before the children can settle down. The girls and the younger boys face much the same loneliness as their mothers: 'I don't have many friends,' said Lisa who is 7 and lives on the fourteenth floor of one of the three high blocks on the estate. 'I only know the people on our landing. That's where we play. We're not supposed to, but we do.' She giggled; 'Toni did toilet on the stairs yesterday. Only because she couldn't get up to her flat on time. She's on the twentieth. She's not really a friend. I just see her at school sometimes.'

Karen, also 7 and her brother Howard, 5, live next door to Lisa. 'What I hate about these flats is there is only two parks to play in,' said Karen. 'We're not allowed to go to the big one because you have to cross the main road and we're not allowed to go to the river park because of the strangers there . . . old men, you know . . . we just have to play in our bedroom and I have to share a room with my brother which I don't like very much.'

'You should have heard them last night,' said Lisa. 'The noise next door . . . laugh, laugh, laugh. I couldn't get to sleep.' She looked stern. 'If they do it again tonight I'm going to bang on the wall.'

'My brother torments me,' said Karen. Howard widened his eyes as if the thought had never occurred to him. 'If I'm talking to the baby,' she said, 'he gets one of his toys and then comes up and starts playing with it. He upsets me. Mostly we just stay in our room and play games like Ludo.'

All the children like the view, whether for aesthetic reasons or because they can see to each other's flats. The boys like the blocks for the sense of bravado they induce ('I like them because if you had a parachute you could jump off the top,' said a five-year-old) and their opportunities for localised illegality. There are few limitations on your activities if you can put 20 storeys between you and adult authority: 'See, the porter lives on the ground floor, doesn't he, so he can't get you if you're up on the top, can he?', reasoned one twelve-year-old. Since he had just had his tea and was watching television with his parents he was reluctant to go into details of the cliff games.

On the twentieth floor Deborah, aged 11, said that gangs of boys came up to their floor and threw bangers along the access corridor. 'Another time they were going up and down the landing banging all the letter boxes. My Dad caught one of them and gave him a clip over the ear.' On this floor the boys use the communal drying room as an operations centre.

The erratic lifts provide more sport in the way of yo-yoing through 22 floors and obstructing anyone who actually wants to go up or down. None of the games is organised out of any feeling of serious malevolence; it is simply that there is little to be got out of playing football in the rain, and according to the children there is positively nowhere to go when the weather is bad. In the past year two playschools have opened for pre-school children; there is a youth centre for adolescents but very little for those in between.

The boys, in general, seem happy to spend the rest of their lives in tower blocks accepting as part of life's pre-ordained pattern the thin walls, unpredictable heating and broken lifts that seem inalienable from mass council housing. The girls want to get out: 'When I grow up,' said Lisa, 'I want to live in a big house in the country with lots of fields all round it and a lot of animals. I don't want to stay here.'

16   Mainly for Pleasure

Guardian Women's Page articles are sometimes just for enjoyment.
Here are a few of the articles that gave the editor of this book especial
pleasure. Some are funny, some are quirky, some are quiet and
serene, like Dame Margery Corbett Ashby's account of her holiday in
Norway, at the age of 82.

It is important to remember, perhaps, that earnest-minded
Guardian readers can laugh at themselves, as the last piece in this book
by the distinguished columnist Jill Tweedie, makes clear.

YOU SAY 'TOMAHTO', WE SAY 'SNEAKERS' (1959)

Joan Dash

Before our family left for England it was pointed out to me by
a kindly Englishwoman who makes a hobby of explaining her
country to Americans that in Oxford there is a college named
Magdalen and pronounced 'Maudlin'; that there is a college in
Cambridge called Magdalene, pronounced 'Maudlin', a street
named Magdalene, pronounced 'Maudlin'. And in the town of
Oxford there is a street named Magdalene pronounced
'Magdalene'.

No sooner had we set up housekeeping in Cambridge than
the full impact of this inconsistency hit me firmly between the
eyes. I set off on my first shopping expedition with disposable
diapers at the head of my list; the British for 'diaper' being
'napkin'. I entered the nearest chemist's shop with a request
for a packet of disposable napkins. The clerk (clark) favoured
me with an empty stare.

'Paper ones,' I elaborated, 'the kind you flush away when
they're soiled.'

Now a gleam of understanding crossed his face. 'You mean serviettes,' he told me, placing on the counter a package of paper dinner napkins.

'These are serviettes?' I marvelled.

'Yes, madam, two and sixpence the packet. I believe you Americans call them napkins.'

'Aha. No let's start all over again. I want some disposable diapers to put on a baby. They cover the lower portion of the body. . . ,' I described them at length, concluding humbly, 'You see, I thought you called them napkins.'

He fingered his chin, smiling. 'Well we do – but no one ever says anything but nappies. Paper nappies, that's what you want.'

Paper nappies they were, and the chemist was out of them.

I took the serviettes anyway, and turned the corner to enter the nearest grocer's. Cornflakes were the next on my list; now what in the world would be British for cornflakes? Maize flakes, perhaps. Then I spied a familiar package on the shelf. 'One of those, please,' I pointed, turning the package round to discover its name. Cornflakes. I relaxed a bit. I read off the rest of my list with gathering confidence. My request for oatmeal was immediately met with a box of Scotch porridge; oleomargarine turned out to be oleomargarine, chummily known as 'marj'. Instant coffee was Nescafé, pronounced 'ness-caf'. Chocolate pudding? This called for consultation among the clerks, while I rummaged on the shelves for a box with a familiar picture. There it was – chocolate blancmange powder, pronounced blum-monj.

My last request was for a sponge. I was given a smallish box labelled 'sponge' and displaying a handsome picture of a large golden cake.

'What's this?' I asked.

'Sponge, madam. In a box. You simply add water and bake and you have a lovely sponge just like the one in the picture.'

'Oh nuts,' I muttered to myself in American. 'I mean the kind of sponge you use to clean up the kitchen.'

'That would be a washing-up sponge,' the clerk pointed out. 'You might try the hardware shop.'

At this point madam gathered up her purchases, pocketing her change with a vow to learn all about English coins any day now, and inquired if it were possible to place a grocery order by phone.

'Certainly,' said the clerk. 'We're listed in the directory, Merton's of Northampton Street.' Only she pronounced it 'Murton's'.

'Not Marton's?' I gasped.

'Murton's,' she replied firmly. 'M-U-R-T-O-N-S, Murton's.'

I turned away, baffled. 'But you are a clark, aren't you: C-L-E-R-K, clark?'

Smothered laughter from the other side of the counter and I left the shop wondering what other amazements were lurking, or perhaps, larking, to wait for me.

British bathrooms and attendant paraphernalia are a complete subject in themselves, but I will diverge for just a moment to point out that washing-up is what one does to the dishes after dinner; before dining, one 'has a wash'. And in the evening, if one is hardy, one baths. Only Americans bathe. To ask a Britisher the location of the bathroom only leads to confusion; in public places such as at theatres, the cloakroom is what one wants. And on city streets – well I asked a London bobby for the nearest public bathroom and I clutched two squirming children and a baby while he told me to take a number 83 bus, get off at Terrapin Street and walk straight on for three minutes, you can't miss it (which latter is British for you'll end up right back here at the end of an hour). I repeated his directions, readjusted the baby and the camera and was about to start off when he blurted out 'But are you sure you want to take a bath?'

'A bath? No; I – we –' and the eldest tightened his legs in a fashion that bridges all linguistic gaps.

'Oh,' breathed the bobby, at last, 'you want a public convenience!'

Not all difficulties were as graphically resolved; when I asked the milkman for skim milk, he told me that the law did not permit it. 'All our milk has to be pasteurised, dearie, that's the law,' said he, and I left it at that. I discovered that skim milk cannot be bought anywhere. The British frown upon it and proceed to pour the cream off the top of their unhomogenised milk and into their cornflakes, leaving the skim for the children who don't care for milk anyway unless half of it is tea. Potato chips masquerade as potato crisps, the salt wrapped up separately in a twist of blue paper. Pie is something you find at the butcher's, filled with sausage meat and eaten cold; fruit pies are called tarts. Bacon comes in eight different varieties and what Americans mean is 'lean and streaky'.

From grocery shopping I graduated to the purchase of clothing. When our five-year-old came home from school with the announcement that 'teacher says I've got to bring some plimsolls to school' she pondered the message for a moment and added 'I guess she really said pencils'. We sent the child to school with a good supply of pencils, and she came back with a request for a pair of soft shoes for indoor wear.

Soft shoes? Sneakers, perhaps? Yes, said the child, everyone else has sneakers and they leave them in school. By now an experienced shopper, I head for Marks and Spencer's, the British equivalent of Sears without catalogues and asked for sneakers.

This brought an expression of impotence to the salesgirl's face. What sort of object was a sneaker, she wanted to know.

'A soft shoe for playing tennis.'

'Try the sporting goods shop,' she suggested, reasonably enough.

'But the school said I could get them here.'

'Well, kindly look around and if you see what you want, point to it.'

Around I looked, past underpants marked 'knickers', and undershirts called 'vests', and there they were, on the counter, serried rows of child-size sneakers, all black. 'Those things,' I said triumphantly, 'those black sneakers.'

'Plimsolls,' said the salesgirl.

THE POLICE OF MY AUNT (1961)

Alice Bragg

*Lady Bragg was the wife of Sir Laurence Bragg,
internationally famous physicist who was awarded the
Nobel Prize for Physics in 1915 for his work on x-rays*

and crystal structure. She herself took an active role in
many public service fields.

Police were my aunt's hobby, or to put it accurately, her life's
work. It would not have been so remarkable today, but a
hundred years ago it was a curious form of welfare work for a
young woman to adopt. However, my aunt, Mary Hopkinson,
was a strong and even masculine character, and in her early
twenties she started her activities by holding a Sunday school
for young policemen in Manchester, where her family had
made a name for itself in public service. She then organised a
police orphanage, a benevolent society for police, and
embarked on an endless round of visiting members of the
force either in hospital, or wherever her help was needed.

Her conversation had to be interpreted in terms of police.
Reference to a station, a superintendent, a sergeant, headquarters, when made by my aunt, could only mean police. All
of her relatives knew of this obsession. My aunt, it was often
said, was 'wedded to the police'; in fact she never married. We
were proud of her and I remember as a child, my father telling
us at breakfast one day that my aunt had been co-opted on to
the Watch Committee, and that she was the only woman to
serve on it. Everyone seemed so impressed that we children
did not like to ask what my aunt would watch, but we felt sure
that it could only be the police. From then on it was fun to go
about with her occasionally and be saluted by policemen, and
handed across the road, my aunt holding up her long braided
skirt.

Towards Christmas she would start on one of her major
tasks for the police, the sending out of about three thousand
personal cards. I can see her now, settled in her sitting room,
which was all sage green and dark red, the table with its velvet
cloth fringe with bobbles, covered with those cards, the texts,
and her own specially printed Christmas 'message'. All these
items had to go into each envelope. She was assisted by her
cook, who in cap and apron sat sorting and folding, but
forbidden to address the envelopes. This cook was with my
aunt for over fifty years, and was allowed certain liberties,
such as an occasional joke about police, which my aunt would
not have tolerated from any other quarter. When my aunt

went off to the railway station to carry out her various missions the cook would hold her bicycle while she mounted, and with a gentle push-off send her on her way.

A short time after my marriage I most mistakenly decided to take advantage of my aunt's unique position with the police. One Sunday morning when we were away the wall of our front garden was breached, apparently by some heavy vehicle. I wrote to the Chief Constable (casually mentioning whose niece I was) and asked his help in the matter. Within twenty-four hours the act had been pinned to the driver of an ice-cream van. Armed with his address, we confronted him in his shop, with the result that he and his mate came over and mended the wall. Delighted, I made a good story of this to my aunt, but she was not amused, and indeed very angry. I was only restored to favour by giving a select tea party in our garden to a selected group of sergeants and wives who arrived, headed by my aunt, in two busloads. Smoking was not permitted in her presence, but I think she knew quite well that my husband escorted some of the guests to the bottom of the garden for a quiet smoke behind the bushes.

There was no question that the police respected, admired, and I think loved my aunt. In later years she became rather deaf, and once when crossing the road was knocked down by a tram. It was difficult to persuade the police that this accident was in no way the fault of the driver. The force was shocked. I was driving my father to the hospital to visit her when I was stopped by the policeman on point duty. I had this instant feeling of guilt that grips one on these occasions. Slowly the man walked to the car window, his face grave. 'How's your auntie?' he asked anxiously.

After 50 years of devoted service the police decided to mark the occasion by giving my aunt a party and presentation. This, it was generally understood, would be the moment for her retirement. A watch bracelet and a radio, suitably inscribed, were given to her, and there was an air of farewell about the occasion. But for once, the police reckoned without my aunt. She rose, and in thanking them all heartily, said that this tribute had put new life into her and she now felt ready for another ten years' work with them.

Time passed, and my aunt was rising 90 when she confessed

to us that she wished she might witness her own funeral. There would undoubtedly be a police band, police singing her favourite hymns, the Chief Constable reading the lesson. Since her active participation was out of the question, she went over the ceremony in detail with the Chief Constable, and derived much pleasure from discussing arrangements which were, in due course, carried out according to plan.

HOLIDAY AT 82 (1966)

Margery Corbett Ashby

Dame Margery Corbett Ashby was one of the most remarkable 'public women' of this century. She was appointed secretary of the National Union of Societies for Equal Citizenship in 1904 and in that year went with her mother, Marie Corbett to the meeting in Berlin which set up the International Alliance of Women. She remained a life-long internationalist (she was substitute British delegate to the Disarmament Conference at Geneva in 1932). She helped to set up the National Union of Townswomen's Guilds in 1928, and made her last public speech at Women's Action Day, organised jointly by the Fawcett Society and Women in Media in November 1980 when she was within sight of her hundredth year.

'Kill or cure,' said my husband gloomily as I urged a last fishing trip to Norway, where my family had fished for more than 60 years. 'Uncle caught his thousandth salmon when he was 80; we can beat him in age, if not in catches.' Off we went. We had a great welcome from the village and our party of four soon set to work. We were three octogenarians and one energetic young friend with a car. It proved one of our best seasons since the war.

Sitting in a boat in a steady drizzle (20 days wet out of 21) I thought I would let my husband play any fish I hooked. Luckily, he had caught several, including one of 29 lbs., before my chance came, for all unselfish thoughts vanished as I felt a pull on my fly. For 30 minutes I was using every ounce of strength as a heavy fish shot like a torpedo towards the mouth of the pool. Slowly the boat rowed upstream and I could reel in. Twice more the fish took out a great length of line. At last we could reach the bank and I got out to try to bring the fish to the gaff. Great was the joy as a 30 lb. salmon lay before me.

Days went by and I had to be content catching trout for breakfast or sea trout caught in the evening. Then luck came my way. Again I had a heavy pull. For 20 minutes I hauled and held with all my strength. This fish fought gamely; at one moment all my line and a large part of the backing was off my reel. Then as I reeled slowly in and the boat moved slowly upstream the fish did a fearful boil at the surface about 50 or 60 yards away and my line went slack.

My husband and I cried 'he's off' but instantly the line tightened. The fish had headed for the boat and swerved away. Now I could bring him slowly to the bank. As I suffer from giddiness if I get up suddenly I warned my husband to hold on to me as I landed. He held on as I walked backwards up the bank where the choice seemed to be between standing on his feet or on a slippery tussock. In a few minutes a beauty of 31½ lb. lay on the bank, the biggest of the season.

It was another thrill to find I could still walk. After some preliminary practice I decided to try a climb to the upper farms. Past the lower farm on the grassy road to the small hay fields I found the path had almost disappeared. It is an age-old pony track across Norway from the fjord. High up, at 1,000 feet there are vast stones laid as steps up and down where we used to meet ponies and men taking milk and cheese down from the saeters and taking up the bacon and coffee for the women and children who spent the summer there. Now with a new motor road to the high farms the path is not used. I struggled up 500 feet pushing through bracken and bushes and high wet grass before taking breath. Then up to 700 feet where the road reaches the first farm. Then came a four-mile swinging walk up and down easy gradients back to the village past two more farms. Glorious views I had feared never to see again met me, views of snowy mountains, dark forests, swift river and broad lake.

On a Sunday morning (when there is no fishing) our young friend drove us 1,700 feet up the new road, being built for a new power station to bring water from one valley through a mountain ridge into our valley. We drove on until the road became impassable and ended abruptly. I gazed wistfully at the cairn high above us. 'Why don't you go to the top?' I asked our young friend.

'Come too,' he said.

'I can't,' I replied, 'but I will go as far as I can.'

Up we went beyond the tree line as hand in hand I was hauled up the steeper places. Then came the long walk over rocks and springy reindeer moss with superb views opening out. The great icefields were hardly visible but the snowy sides of Grausiden, the lake and the fjord beyond, the steep valley below us held all their own magic. I had never hoped to reach the top but at 3,025 feet I proudly added my stone to the cairn. Hot and triumphant we rejoined the others for a large picnic lunch at 3 p.m.

Another Sunday in rain we drove up a side valley to the end of the road and then walked on, and as we came to the last farm of the small settlement the farmer called to us from the balcony. It was 25 years since, exhausted, wet and muddy from a twelve-mile walk and a climb of 3,000 feet my husband and I had been called in to rest and given cakes and coffee. Now we were treated to a wonderful spread of sandwiches, cakes and coffee while the three generations stood round smiling and we exchanged news of family and fishing.

As we sailed from Bergen for the last time we could look back on a land of wonderful memories, of friendly people, and many adventures on land and river.

THE SWISS FAMILY SCHARNSCHIFF-SCHNAYBARGER (1966)

Pippa Phemister

Pippa Phemister has written for a wide variety of newspapers and magazines, including New Society, Punch, *and* The Guardian. *She now lives on the shores of Galway Bay, where she is engaged in one of her favourite activities, converting an ancient house to modern use.*

After writing a long, scholarly thesis on the problems of de-
racinated people I went and added to them: in my late
twenties I married an immigrant German-Swiss. Now if he had
only been a Muslim or a Japanese, I really do believe all might
have been well. We would at least have expected the chasms
of difference that daily yawned between us. As things were,
we fell headlong into them; because we believed at the outset,
and through 13 baffled years that being Swiss or being English,
is really much the same thing.

He, I sometimes feel, had his apprehensions. For he does
wait until the dice is finally thrown, until I am irrevocably
pregnant, before he takes me to his country to face up to my
Swiss in-laws. I am very ready to take them to my heart, but
one look at them tells me that this is not going to be easy. For
they live in a grandiose schloss off the Canonengasse, outside
Basle Town. It is very like a lugubrious prep school in Kent.
Except that inset into most window-panes is a stained glass
talisman shaped like a three-legged biscuit. This is the
cantonal emblem: three rods tied together. 'Yes,' scowls my
Swieger-Papi punitively, 'it's really a kind of flail. . . .'

And then there are six enormous military cousins: handsome,
but jackbooted up to the armpits. And a ponderous wolfhound
called Yauni. And everyone, including my erstwhile public
school husband, speaks nothing but Borzelditch. This dialect
sounds very like a clutch of Welsh miners up for the cup final;
but without the joy. Only Yauni can't speak it either. Like me
she responds anxiously to hand signals. In her I find a crony. I
lure her to my room with noxious sweetmeats called darvelis.
'Ah zo', says my senior aunt, in her fluent Mayfairditch, 'It is
the English. Good only with dogs. But her claws are bad for
my parquet. They must be worn down. Zo – you vill tek her
for long, long walks. . . .' The fifteen years of attrition have
begun.

I seek solitude on a mountain top. I have yet to learn that
there are very few Swiss mountain tops whose solitude is not
ruined by the rush of an electric train. And Yauni remains
immovable, like the good gun-dog she is, deaf to vocal
entreaty, her medieval paws planted firmly in the middle of
the railway track. I run through a whole semaphore of hand
signals. She remains where she is, immobile and fascinated,

265

unseduced by my inappropriate gestures. When I do step on to the track only my palpable pregnancy stops the train.

'Ah zo,' my aunt explains to the furious stationmaster, 'it is the education. She is not consequent. . . .' Then she throws down the gauntlet: 'Tonight,' she threatens coldly, 'you will iron his shirt!' I have a vivid picture of her streamlined kitchen entirely filled with incomprehensible electric gadgets. Besides, there is something about folding and I have never ironed anybody's shirt anyhow. My husband is distraught, but loyal. No one, he explains carefully, has as yet found the time to teach me how to iron clothes. What then, have I been doing? Everyone in that drawing room is stunned. But not into silence. 'Ah,' gloats the wife of a military cousin openly, 'it is the pants she will find impossible, all those pleats. . . .' And she smiles with that plump satisfaction at a fellow-female's demise that I have learned to expect, uniquely, from Swiss women as a whole. Never mind; the food is good; the cellar is even better; they throw lavish dinner parties to show me off to the mystified citizens of Basle. Zo, I have been to the university. In England that is often zo for women. What, then, do I think of the Wote? I admit that so far I have never really thought about the Vote. Just like, I venture brightly, I have never ironed pants. This, evidently, is blasphemy. But not slanted quite the way I think.

'Ah, zo,' breathes my aunt in acute shock, 'for the woman, domestik is all. The Wote, nothing.'

'My father,' I venture mildly (but I am already hauling in male authority to give strength to something I can think very well for myself), 'my father doesn't think that. And my suffragette aunt burnt down two barns.'

'Zo it is – when the woman has the Wote. No consequent!'

'And,' hisses a younger Swiss matron, 'Ve Swiss wives are too busy to wote!'

'What at?' I ask her rashly, for Johannisberger has falsely enfranchised me, 'Ironing pants?'

That evening our bedroom is visited by the aunt. My young husband courteously bows out, for that, it seems, is the drill. What is more, he has seen the gleam of battle in her blue codfish eyes. And her very diamonds glitter cruelly in the moonlight. 'Zo,' she gasps with passion, 'I vill not hev you upsetting my girls.' This can only be the military wives. 'Vot I tell you, once and for all, without a man a woman is a very poor fish!' And then with a train of thought that to this day eludes me, 'And that nightgown is too frivolous for a married woman.'

But I am already learning Borzelditch, fast. Compiling, in the secrecy of my room, philological gems of the first order. For it bristles with words that English cannot echo; like a man who waits for legacies – he is an earthcrawler, an *ertshleerer*; or a parsimonious husband – a collar creaker, a *geetskrager*; and gossips like me – we're *klutchbarzers*, or jaw-waggers. The basic brand of the dialect, of course, is to attach the diminutive 'li' to everything, even bulldozers. On top of all this Baslers like prefixing proper names with the definite article, with overtones. Thus my husband was 'der Ruedi', said like prince. And I was 'die Pippili', said like freak.

Of course once I begin to grasp the dialect I feel sure I will understand my relatives better. And I am riven with curiosity. Who is it that my aunt telephones every morning called Frank? My husband denies his existence. My aunt is a 'korrekt' widow. And no Scharnschiff-Schnaybarger could ever answer quite simply to the one name, Frank. Goaded by curiosity, we eavesdrop. Sure enough, someone has brought a note of passion to my aunt's chill voice. But alas, Frank is no human lover. It is the welfare of the Swiss franc that enchants her. For Basle is a mercantile city; its superb banks still cluster round the ghost of its long-vanished Basilica. And its people burn with love for money just as we burn for love, for horses or for land. So when a young, beautiful military wife goes off every Wednesday morning beperfumed, furred and in a new hat, I harbour no suspicions about her honour. She does, in fact, meet a man. She remains closeted with him in his chambers for two hours. Together, in the closest privacy they speak of the things that are nearest her heart; capital, investment and interest. He is Gusteli Berger, her broker; a wealthy and deeply *korrekt* man; he alone can fire her soul with the unlimited possibilities of the Swiss Bourse; and she comes home glowing, like a bride.

Only one uncle, a worldly German one at that, does his best to rescue me. 'Ah zo, die Pippa,' he breathes through his cigar

267

(but he says it like woman, not freak), 'keep all that dictionary secret . . . and the writing, secret. Bek in England perhaps you vill do it. Ven it is over, *then* you will do it. But for the Schnaybargers, vile it lasts – it is not the style.'

LETTERS (1967)

Questions inspired by John and Elizabeth Newson, who claim that in many societies the problem of sleepless babies does not exist 'because the baby sleeps snugly against his mother's body and so allows her to sleep too'.

Poem

Give praise to the primitive mother
Whose instincts are always so right,
Though the books say small children will smother
If they sleep in our beds through the night

No doubt the strong child of the peasant
Can be rolled on and still stay alive.
But what interests me is the question
Just how does the mother survive?

Do these placid and bucolic infants
Never push, never kick, never scratch?
Do they never let draughts through the bedclothes
As gales howl through the primitive thatch?

Do they never sit up feeling chatty
And at 3 a.m. start a discourse
(To make perfectly sure of attention
Prising open Mum's eyelids by force)?

I sit yawning, O Newsoms, and ponder
Is the simple life really such bliss?
Or is it they're merely resigned to
Children making life hellish like this?

(Mrs) Pamela M. Nixon

Life Among the Liberal-Minded . . .

I have never been very sympathetic to the sleepless nights
suffered by many young mothers. It was with great interest
that I read the letter from John and Elizabeth Newson
(28 February) as my five young sons have all slept in
'companionable peace' – indeed, they still do.

At 41 I am now pregnant again and will bring up the new
baby on the system which has worked so well for the others.
The cot is in my room, next to my bed. When the child
awakens he is hauled into my bed and there offered my breast.
He and I fall asleep as he suckles, and so he continues to feed
and sleep all night. His presence doesn't disturb me in the
least. Indeed, to be honest, I gain a certain, doubtless
primitive, satisfaction from the whole performance. What is
perhaps more important, my husband, a hard-worked doctor,
sleeps on undisturbed.

We have an enormous bed. This was a very good buy at an
auction sale when we were newly married and childless. A
good buy because, at times, the whole family are in it. All
seven of us – all eight of us soon. A professional family too.
Just think of it. In a ten-bedroomed house as well. So it's not
just lack of space.

Sometimes we do sleep alone – as the size of our family
indicates – but the children know that the solace of our bed
and the animal comfort of our bodies is there to assuage any
griefs. At eight, the eldest went off to his prep school and
settled down splendidly. I like to think the early security found
in our bed helped. We certainly sleep all right, whatever your
readers may think. – Yours etc.

Ursula Warren

Home-making

I have been surprised to read in your columns that some
women find the making of a beautiful home, with all the tasks
that this entails, an irksome chore, and that they feel
unfulfilled. I have never felt this, and take a positive pleasure

in my daily round. I make everything for our simple needs, from moccasins to mutton fat candles. Contrary to popular belief, these latter do not smell unduly, and their light is conducive to harmony in the home.

I do not see the necessity for new clothes and am still wearing the homespun goat's hair cardigan and hand-woven skirt in which I was married. My husband's duffle coat has been turned six times; the muffler he had when first we met is a tea-cosy, and I hope soon to find a use for his balaclava. Khaki is a very versatile colour. We never disturb, nor are disturbed by, members of the opposite sex.

My children are perhaps my greatest triumph. At school my son had to bear the slings and arrows from less fortunate children, but this only served to strengthen his character. Witness the fact that he is now running a home for fallen women in Greek Street, Soho. Many times I have said I would like to go and see him in his wonderful work, but out of consideration for me he implores me not to. My daughter, alone in a one-room flat, against a hostile world, is researching in alcoholism. This necessitates her close participation in this dreadful thing, but she does not shirk her duty.

Yes, I am more than satisfied with my life, and I know that the heaven on earth I have created for my family is my just reward. How I wish the discontented women of your columns could know some of my joy.

– Yours faithfully,
Christine Dinsdale

THE FEMININE MISTAKE: A MORALITY PLAY (1971)

Jill Tweedie

CAST: a psychiatrist, his client, peasants, satyrs, fetishists, sexologists, television personalities, jet setters, etc.

CLIENT: God knows I tried, doctor. One thousand and one ways, I tried. But to what end? A week last Monday he left me to take up residence with another.

PSYCHIATRIST: *Nicht Rauchen?*

C: No, no, there was none of that. Nothing wrong with our marriage. We'd jogged along together for what, 15 years, and never a cross word. Very cosy we were really, Fred and me.

P: *Gesundheit?*

C: Ah, because of this book I bought, you see. *The Sensuous Woman* by courageous outspoken anonymous 'J', an all-female female or possibly male (W.H. Allen, £1.75). It caught me on the hop, thinking everything in the marital garden was lovely and then reading about how I was actually driving Fred into the arms of a mistress because of my negative sexual and concomitant emotional patterns.

P: *Ich liebe Dich!*

C: I knew you'd say that. Of course I was forced to ask myself was I the lithe siren of Fred's early dreams or your average run-of-the-mill mono-orgasmic housewife? Had I ever problem-analysed my gluteals, abdominals or levators in the light of the act of love? Had I pondered the priority concerns of boudoir attire even once since my knickers fell down at the Haberdashers' Ball? Obviously there was a communications gap, waiting to be filled by a female with a higher response threshold than mine, so I started.

P: *Ach so!*

C: 'J's' sensuality programme of course. Daily exercises to increase the tactile sensations of erogenous zones. In the privacy of my bedroom I primed my sensual release mechanisms by saying coarse and candid words aloud, in preparation for saying them into Fred's ear as a revitalising factor. Can you believe, doctor, that all I'd ever said until then was 'I love you'?

P: *Gott sei mitt uns!*

C: You're very kind but I do blame myself. When, in 15 years, had I ever scotch-taped to Fred's bathroom towel a note saying 'You have the most exciting body I have ever seen'? Had I ever spent a whole weekend offering up, lustfully, every square inch of my body for Fred to feast upon? Is it surprising that he never exposed the plethora of sensuality lying fallow within?

P: *Verdämmter Englander.*

C: Don't mention it. When I think how I worked my gluteals to the bone for that man. . . .

P: *Weltschmerz?*

C: It's nothing doctor, I'll be all right. Well, after my body had become an unparalleled erotic vessel, I set about transforming the outer packaging. What man wants to come home to the same woman each day? What man desires the same old body night after night? Every husband, as 'J' points out, is a polygamist at heart, a lurking savage intent on grabbing every female in sight.

P: *Bei mir bist du schön.*

C: Ah, you hit the nail on the head, doctor. Fred's polygamy was so repressed, so profoundly inhibited that I never glimpsed any signs of it at all during our marriage – I had to draw it out of him with all the wiles of my richly feminine nature. It is, after all, the woman's responsibility to give her husband the sexual variety and adventure in the home that he could find so easily elsewhere. Right?

P: *Sieg Heil.*

C: My feelings exactly. My first venture was when Fred visited his mother up North. I worked like a fiend. By the time he came home I had dyed my hair Reckitt's Blue, and transformed our dull suburban bedroom into an exotic wigwam complete with machine-washable 98 per cent acetate bear rug upon which I stretched my aroused limbs clad only in fringes of buckskin, burning joss sticks all the while.

P: *Sauerbraten mit Kartoffeln?*

C: You may well ask. He looked at me more carefully than he had done for years, I will say that. Unfortunately, momentarily blinded by joss fumes, he tripped over the bear rug and did himself an injury. But there was a moment, as his manly body crashed upon mine, when I distinctly felt tremors of passion. So I persevered.

P: *Ach du lieber Augustin.*

C: You're right, I was literally haunted by the fear of Fred lingering late at the office, ripe to fall into the bed of a modern Aphrodite. Over the next fortnight I became a Lolita (my old gym slip), a Folies Bergere show girl (a two-way-stretch with tulle), a gipsy fortune teller (the quilt from

272

the spare bedroom), a Roman slave girl (copydex up the legs) and a geisha girl (my flocked nightie with a cushion up the rear) in that order. It was no picnic but where there's a will, there's a way.

P: *Wie eins Lili Marlene . . .*

C: You can say that again. Fred began lingering late at work, clearly overcome with the new chameleon me, but I had faith. I knew that, once in bed, I could drive him mad with my ecstasy-prolonging techniques. Oh, we'd had our fun before but I had never really made his chemistry blossom. I had never broken down the doors of perception and swept him into piercingly beautiful experiences. Then, at last, I got my chance.

P: *Donner und Blitzen?*

C: I'm glad you asked me that. I groaned and moaned with passion. I fanned him with tasteless French photographs ('J' says men's temperatures rise more quickly with basic literary stimuli); I circled upon the bed moving my abdominals clockwise and counter-clockwise, making figure eights and squares.

P: *Deutschland, Deutschland uber alles.*

C: Not so's you'd notice. Fred said, Minnie, I worry about that asthma. He said, Minnie, you're not a well person. He said not tonight I've got one of my headaches. But it was my duty to bring him to full sexual bloom and I kept right on trying.

P: *Oh Tannenbaum?*

C: I doubt it. 'J' says men crave unexpected lovemaking locations, so next I devoted myself to this enterprise. I turned up, naked under my Crimplene, at Fred's office, covered his face in Cooper's Dundee Marmalade and hoovered it off again with my insatiable lips. I dragged him under the piano at the local and ran my wanton hands across his braces. I did liberated things to him behind a bush on Wandsworth Common and I interfered with him on top of a No. 12 bus. What more can a woman do?

P: *Östpolitik?*

C: On the contrary, it seemed to make no difference. And then I faced the terrible truth – already another woman was draining off his energies in some squalid hotel room. I gave

The Sensuous Woman one last try ('Swapping and Orgies', p. 158). On the Friday I arranged a body-painting party with two broadminded friends. There I lay in the altogether on the uncut moquette while Ernest and Ethel Gapp painted my secondary sexual characteristics in a rainbow of primary colours. Then Fred walked in. He said good evening, Ethel and Ernest, goodbye forever Minnie, and walked out of my life.